AWKWARD

TORN CURTAIN PUBLISHING
Auckland, New Zealand
www.torncurtainpublishing.com

ISBN Softcover 978-1-991299-83-3
ISBN EPub 978-1-991299-84-0

A combination of American and Canadian spelling has been used throughout this book.

Unless otherwise noted, all scripture is taken from the New American Standard Bible®, Copyright © 1960, 1971, 1977, 1995 by The Lockman Foundation. Used by permission. All rights reserved. www.lockman.org

Scripture quotations marked ESV are from the ESV® Bible (The Holy Bible, English Standard Version®), copyright © 2001 by Crossway, a publishing ministry of Good News Publishers. Used by permission. All rights reserved.

Scripture quotations marked NIV are taken from the New International Version®, NIV®. Copyright © 1973, 1978, 1984, 2011 by Biblica, Inc.™ Used by permission of Zondervan. All rights reserved worldwide.

Scripture quotations marked AMP are taken from the Amplified® Bible (AMPC), Copyright © 1954, 1958, 1962, 1964, 1965, 1987 by The Lockman Foundation. Used by permission. www.lockman.org.

Scripture quotations marked NLT are taken from the Holy Bible, New Living Translation, copyright © 1996, 2004, 2015 by Tyndale House Foundation. Used by permission of Tyndale House Publishers, Inc., Carol Stream, Illinois 60188. All rights reserved.

Cover design by Daniel Giesbrecht
Typeset in Minion, Myriad, and Raleway

Cataloguing in Publishing Data

Title: Awkward: Gospel-centred conversations about sex and culture
Author: Bonnie Pue
Subjects: Christian living, Family & relationships, Sexuality; Faith and culture; Gender issues; Pastoral resources; Christian parenting; theological frameworks; marriage and sex; history of sexuality; redemptive conversations; sex and culture; biblical sexuality; teenage issues.

A copy of this title is held at the National Library of New Zealand.

Bonnie Pue has written an intensely practical book that is grounded in hard-earned experience and careful biblical application. Every Christian parent will find help and hope in this book as they navigate the increasingly complex world of raising children in our current culture. I wish I had Bonnie's book to help me have important and sometimes awkward conversations with my own kids, but the good news is that my adult children will benefit from her wisdom as they parent my grandchildren!

Rev. Len DenBraber
Focus on the Family, Canada

Bonnie Pue couldn't be a better author to write about teaching our kids about sex—a very awkward topic for most parents. In leading *The Union* with her husband, Bryan, they have extensive experience on the topic as they have ministered in numerous settings over the years. As they have taught God's truths surrounding sexuality, they have also successfully used them in raising their six sons. This book is an excellent resource for parents who don't know how to broach the issue, an issue that needs to be discussed with our children since they live in this very broken sex-filled world.

Jim and Lisa Anderson
Founders and Directors of *Sexuality Unmasked*

With compelling storytelling and sharp insight, Bonnie tackles today's sexual confusion with clarity, empathy, and boldness. This book is a timely guide that will equip and encourage families.

Andy Steiger
Founder and President of *Apologetics Canada*

Awkward is the rare intersection of the right book at the right time. A constant theme we see in our ministry is that parents feel lost in the cultural current and uncertain how to navigate difficult subjects with their kids. Bonnie uses purposeful theology and earned wisdom to unpack the most thorny topics of parenthood, making hard conversations feel not just approachable, but also empowering. This book should be in the hands of every parent, as well as anyone who wants to feel equipped to answer the big questions facing Christians today.

Layton Boeve
Liberator Podcast

This book is a gift to every Christian parent navigating conversations about sexuality in today's culture. Bonnie, a brilliant and wise woman, offers profound insight with unmatched grace, gentleness, and truth. Her voice is calm, clear, and deeply grounded in Scripture, bringing both courage and clarity to a topic many find overwhelming. In a culture of confusion, she speaks with compassion, conviction and a sense of humour, helping parents lead their children with confidence and faith. A must-read for anyone longing to approach this vital conversation with love and Biblical truth. You will come back to this resource again and again as your children grow through various stages of development.

Heather Thiessen
Cornerstone Christian School
Vice Principal/Inclusive Education Coordinator
Mother of two teens

In a world that is ever-shifting in mindset towards gender and sexuality, Bonnie Pue provides readers with tried, tested, and timeless truths to help navigate conversations with young people around God-centered, biblically grounded sexuality. Being a mother of six boys, she humbly shares practical, everyday wisdom, which has been refined through many years of experience. This book is sure to be an invaluable resource for parents, guardians, and ministry leaders for years to come!

Allen de Jong
Veteran Youth Worker
District Ministry Leader for PAOC

We love this book! As pastors, we love the Biblical and philosophical foundation laid out in the first 5 chapters. As marriage and family educators, we love how the next 14 chapters look honestly at the significant issues parents want and need to talk about with their children. Bonnie Pue has identified the right topics and taken the right approach, mixing compassion and conviction. Far from a "just-do-this" approach, each chapter provides questions for helpful, honest dialogue between parents and kids. We will be giving this book to our children for their own parenting journey and to our staff around the globe.

Neil & Sharol Josephson
FamilyLife Global Resourcing

Awkward is a timely and necessary contribution to the cultural landscape we are all working to navigate. Bonnie Pue offers both biblical clarity and genuine, heartfelt wisdom to a subject often clouded by confusion and uncertainty. While parents will certainly find her insights invaluable, this book really is a fantastic resource for every believer searching for a grounded, faith-filled perspective on the many questions surrounding human sexuality, marriage and relationships. I am so deeply grateful for the ministry of the Union Movement and their courage in addressing such an important issue in our day.

Bryan Davis
Lead Pastor of LifeSpring Church, Abbotsford, BC
Chairman of MFI Canada

Awkward delivers exactly what parents need: practical wisdom for navigating essential conversations about identity and intimacy with their children. Bonnie masterfully combines biblical truth with compelling scientific research, showing how God's design for relationships remains relevant and necessary today. This comprehensive guide addresses the "why" behind biblical boundaries around sexuality and holy living. Bonnie's thoughtful approach demonstrates how scriptural principles align with modern research, giving parents both a theological foundation and practical confidence for these "awkward" conversations. If you've ever felt unprepared to discuss these topics or wondered how to explain God's heart behind His guidelines, *Awkward* will equip you with scripture-based answers and inspire you to guide your children toward healthy, God-honouring relationships with wisdom and grace. As I read this book, I kept asking the same question: Where was this book when my kids were little?

Krista Penner
Team Lead of *Immerse Program* and *Fellowship Pacific*

Awkward is biblically rich, relatable, and full of gospel-centered wisdom. Bonnie writes with both conviction and compassion, equipping readers to stand firm in truth while walking in love. A must-read for parents, pastors, and anyone navigating today's cultural confusion.

Kyla Gillespie
Founder of *Renewed and Transformed Ministries*

AWKWARD

GOSPEL-CENTRED CONVERSATIONS
ABOUT SEX AND CULTURE
(a book for brave parents)

BONNIE PUE

For my mom and dad, who prayerfully made unconventional choices that changed the trajectory of our family line. Thank you, Mom, for serving our family in a selfless way, teaching my sisters and I countless lessons, and ensuring we had family dinners every night. Thank you, Dad, for welcoming my thoughts and opinions on random topics, and for filling the house with the sounds of worship as you played the guitar and made pancakes for the family on Saturday mornings.

CONTENTS

INTRODUCTION

Welcome to one of the most awkward conversations of all . . .

I get it. I really do.

My husband and I have six sons, ranging from four to sixteen years of age, and whenever we prepare to sit down for the 'official' conversation about how babies are made, I still get a little awkward. My mind races. *What if they look at me differently? What if they are too young to understand this?* Or perhaps even worse, *What if they've already heard about it—from another source?!* Over the years, I have figured out how to play it cool, and I'm grateful when I see that our confidence in God's design for human sexuality is being transferred to their hearts.

In reality, my husband and I have been talking to our boys about matters of sexuality in subtle, foundational ways for years, long before they hit puberty. We have been slowly and steadily painting the big picture about God-honouring, healthy sexuality and relationships ever since they were infants and toddlers.

These are tricky topics, not often easily articulated even among us as adults, let alone with our children. Thankfully, the scriptures provide foundational concepts that can help us get the conversation started long before they ask, "But how does the baby get *inside* the mommy's tummy?" and definitely before they grow armpit hair or head out on their first date.

In this first part of the book, we are going to spread some biblical road maps out on the table and have a look at God's heart on the important themes around sexuality. We'll find insights from the early chapters of Genesis and explore how these pertain to human identity, gender, and marriage. We'll explore the context for sexuality, and how sin and shame try to destroy us but how Jesus is a great Redeemer. The goal in part one is to ensure that you, as a parent or caregiver, have your feet firmly planted in the traditionally orthodox Christian worldview and understand how that worldview influences one's sexual ethic.

In the second part of the book, we'll zoom in on the map, landmarking specific issues and offering corresponding recommendations on how to have valuable conversations with your child. We'll spend time looking at topics such as pornography, the LGBTQ+ community, mental health, puberty, dating relationships, and more. You won't find scripts to follow or charts of how many months old a kid should be when they hear certain terms and definitions. My heart is that your conversations with your kids will flow uniquely and naturally as you lean into these topics and grow in your reliance on the Spirit of God.

Now, if you're anything like me, you have a pile of half-finished books on your nightstand. They are evidence of curiosity, good intentions, and a fast-paced life. I wrote this book with busy parents in mind. I hope that this book will be a resource that can be revisited over the years as your children grow, new topics come up, and you find yourself searching for new levels of support or practical advice.

Because of the complex nature of these topics, I feel it necessary to acknowledge that every chapter in this book could easily be expanded upon. For this reason, I have included in the appendix a list of recommended resources so you can glean from other voices that I've learned from over the years. In the meantime, as you turn the pages of this book, I pray that you will find wisdom and grace in equal measure as you lead your own unique family.

I realize that, for many parents, these conversations won't come easily. Maybe no one ever had these kinds of vulnerable discussions with you. Maybe you gained all your insights from the locker room, from biology class, from movies or music videos, or even from porn culture. For many adults, the lack of guidance has led to relational fumbling, confusion, and pain. I pray that the truths in this book will be a source of healing for anyone who has experienced that kind of pain or neglect. I am confident that when you bravely face the past, with all of its awkwardness, healing can and will occur. And when *that* happens, you will have created an invaluable inheritance for your kids. A treasury of soul that can be passed down to coming generations.

In the years since my husband and I founded *The Union Movement*, a ministry dedicated to helping people find wholeness in the areas of sexuality, identity and relationships, I have seen a dramatic change in the cultural landscape. I know I'm not the only one who has noticed.

Whenever we speak at events, we are met by concerned parents, grandparents, and educators. The cultural pressure is mounting. There aren't just outlandish ideologies in far distant places anymore. The narrative is reaching into our homes. Parents and guardians often feel outnumbered and overwhelmed as they try and get a word in.

It reminds me of the biblical story of Esther. At her time in history, the people of Israel were in exile in Persia. Esther was a young Jewish woman who had been taken into the harem of King Xerxes. The Israelites had retained their identity as God's people for many years, despite being surrounded by a foreign culture. During Esther's time, however, they were targeted for their religious beliefs. It all came to a head when a man named Haman came to power. He had great influence over the king and manipulated him into declaring an empire-wide genocide against the Jewish people. But neither Haman nor Xerxes realized that the newly-crowned queen, Esther, was also a Jew. In the face of an existential threat to her people, God gave Esther the courage and wisdom to expose the threat and enable the Israelites to defend themselves. Seeing the Jews were prepared for the fight, the enemy backed down, and on the day which could have been a most bloody one, there was instead peace. Not one life was lost.

We live in an era of overt sexualization. The digital world is no longer only a land of imagination and wonder. Sexual images, algorithms and predators target our children, trying to lead them down dark alleys. These awkward conversations about sex and identity and relationships that you're going to have with your kids are not just a nice idea. They are an essential way that we are protecting our children—but more than that, we are preparing them to thrive.

I suspect that you will find some aspects of this book to be lighthearted and fairly straightforward. Maybe some of the stories from our family will bring you relief and make you laugh as you realize how *awkwardly normal* we all are. How delightfully human we all are.

You may also find some portions emotionally heavy to deal with. Some of what I write may trigger difficult memories for you. I may unknowingly confront some of your belief systems. On the occasion that I step on your toes, I merely ask that you take the time to consider these topics and trust the Lord for His wisdom and guidance in all things. May you find peace and courage as you journey through this book. Parenting is a wild ride, but you are your child's best bet. You've got this.

THE FOUNDATIONS

1

THE BIG PICTURE

It's all connected. Our bodies. Our relationships. What we desire. What we have done. What others have done to us.

But we feel like we can't talk about it. So many of these conversations are layered with regret and longing, often tinged with sorrow and shame.

We fear that to speak of it will only make things worse. We feel that to speak of it is to risk rejection.

But can you hear the Spirit of God? He is confident—and comforting. He whispers wisdom and invites our honest admissions. He does not blush in the midst of the most awkward of conversations, but rather leans in.

I was standing with my mom at the busy intersection of Marshall and McCallum Road in Abbotsford, British Columbia. It was a warm day, and I must have been around seven years old because I can remember roughly how tall I was, there beside my mom's left leg, waiting for the signal to change so that we could step onto the crosswalk.

As the light changed, my mom instinctively reached for my hand. For the first time ever, and without thinking, I pulled my hand out of hers. Mom looked down at me with surprise in her eyes but she didn't say anything. We stepped out together, my little legs hurrying to match her pace, and we made it across safely.

That day, my mom wordlessly allowed me to transition to a new stage of childhood and I have never forgotten it. Now that I am a parent, I realize how much intuition it takes to know when to hold a child back and when to let them venture out and make their own decisions.

We had walked across roads together for years. Mom and my dad had guided me consistently, always reminding me, "Look both ways", "Don't run out", "Don't stand too close to the edge". The time eventually came, years later, when my older sister and I would head out, walking down to the 7-11 for some slurpees and sour candies. We were now on our own, but our parents' voices were there to guide us even when they weren't physically with us.

There is a phenomenon of human relational attachment—that if children are convinced of our care, they will more readily receive our instructions and values. This takes an investment in the relationship. It is not a formula, where we put in x number of hours of quality time plus y number of instructions in the hopes that we will get a perfected outcome with no heartache. That is not the case at all. Yet there are principles at work, and we cannot deny the power of a healthy relationship with our kids and the impact of biblical wisdom to shape their worldview.

The Bible gives language to this phenomenon in Proverbs 6:20-22:

> *"My child, observe the commandment of your father and do not forsake the teaching of your mother; Bind them continually on your heart; tie them around your neck. When you walk about, they will guide you; when you sleep they will watch over you; and when you awake, they will talk to you."*

In our culture today, we stand at the edge of a busy highway, holding the hands of our children wondering how they will ever navigate through matters of sexuality, identity, and relationships. There are so many issues to think about and the last thing we want is for our kids to run out into the traffic and be hit by negative sexual encounters or harmful ideologies that could rob them of their potential and destiny.

The Bible describes a way through the chaos, a crosswalk from the naivety of childhood into the maturity of adulthood. We get to hold our child's hand for a season, but the time will come when they will need to walk confidently without us by their side.

Our job is to teach them to look both ways.

Looking To The Past

Every generation has the benefit of learning from history if they are wise enough to do so. The Bible gives us insight into the trends and cultures throughout the centuries. We can also look at more recent trends to get our bearings on where we are now as a society. Even our personal history can be useful in instructing our children about the pathway to life.

As we consider these different points, remember that our goal is to be able to understand God's intention for our design and learn to break that wisdom down in age-appropriate ways that we can bring to our children. Let's begin with the biblical narrative. I trust you will see that these conversations about sexuality are ones that God has been initiating with humanity for centuries.

1. Biblical History

When we read through the Old Testament, it can seem like the God of heaven, the deity of the Israelites, was the strictest parent in the neighbourhood, giving such firm boundaries for His people. He says it clearly and repeatedly throughout scripture: *"Sexual relationship only with your covenant partner. Husband and wife only. And your children are treasures, not to be abandoned or destroyed."*

This was incredibly counter-cultural at the time. Israel was surrounded by nations with an entrenched system of idol worship, much of which involved orgies, genital mutilation, gender fluidity, and pedophilia. Perhaps even more gruesome was the practice of child sacrifice—bronze altars where babies were burned alive as the beating of drums drowned out their cries. These sacrifices were believed to secure a season of fertility in herds, protection from enemy armies, and an abundance of crops. They were designed to appease the gods.

No wonder God didn't dodge the topic but rather gave clear instructions: *"Don't mess around with the customs and worship patterns of the neighbouring people groups. Don't make excuses or allow those patterns to infiltrate your families."*

God's intentions are not those of a harsh dictator but of a loving father who knows what will lead to human prosperity and relational flourishing.

He knew the potential for legacy that His people carried if the family unit was honoured and valued. He wanted them to understand the blessing that children can be to an entire nation. The giving of the law was an expression of His heart and desire for their good.

For the people of God, this was a big mind shift. For many generations, they struggled to yield to His instructions.

Psalm 106:34-39 tells us that the Israelites,

> *"... mingled with the nations and learned their practices, and served*
> *their idols, which became a snare to them. They even sacrificed their sons*
> *and their daughters to the demons and shed innocent blood, the blood*
> *of their sons and their daughters, whom they sacrificed to the idols of*
> *Canaan; and the land was polluted with the blood. Thus they became*
> *unclean in their practices, and played the harlot in their deeds."*

Why was it so difficult for God's people to resist these pagan practices? Psalm 106 gives us a hint: "They even sacrificed their sons and their daughters *to the demons.*" These worship practices were not just cultural ideas—they were demonically-inspired directives that played on human weaknesses and tendencies.

The early church that was birthed after Jesus' ministry on earth was surrounded by a similar culture. Corinth, Ephesus and Rome were epicentres of polytheistic ritual. Temples were dedicated to a myriad of gods and goddesses, and not surprisingly, sexual encounters were again elevated as a form of worship. Once more, the resulting babies were often the ones to pay the ultimate price, facing abandonment and death. For the people of God, it was a repeat of all the same elements, just with different geographical locations and different names attached to the idols.

Throughout history, the fall of every empire has been characterized by two key factors: the devaluing of human life, and an increase in sexual perversion. There is clearly a cosmic battle at play. God hasn't shied away from the conversation about healthy sexual expression. While the enemy's goal is to deceive and lead people into a lifestyle that will cripple individuals, families, and ultimately entire nations, God is giving His people the keys that will sustain the foundations of civilization.

That's often why these conversations about sexuality are so complex. This is not just about culture or human propensity. There is a spiritual component that the people of God need to be aware of. The preservation of civilization starts in our homes.

2. Human History

As a twenty-one-year-old, I was preparing for an upcoming mission trip to Peru and decided to study their history and religion. I was astonished to find that sexual immorality and the sacrifice of children were hidden in plain view—right there in the centre of the Incan Empire. I was haunted by the fact that the most beautiful of the little girls and boys were selected as temple prostitutes, taken from their families, and ultimately, sacrificed on the heights of Machu Picchu. I have found this pattern repeated over and over again in nations around the world whenever I've scratched the surface of their history.

We may shake our heads in bewilderment at what past generations have done, or find ways to justify the fact that these were real children and real men and women engaged in those heart-wrenching practices. But do we have eyes to see what is going on in communities and society? Can we honestly say that our culture today is much different? Recent events and studies show that the number of children who are enslaved in sex trafficking and child pornography is greater than ever. The reality is, children in our society are undervalued and even from the point of conception, are as vulnerable as ever to exploitation, abandonment, and even death.

Obviously, there is darkness in our era of history too. But there is also a lavish amount of grace. God is still looking all over the earth and sees those whose hearts are fixed on Him. He is as committed as ever to show Himself strong on our behalf and on behalf of our children.

3. Personal History

When it comes to sexuality, you may find that looking into the ancient past is not nearly as challenging as looking into the rear-view mirror of your own life. For many people, their personal sexual history comes with deep pain and regret.

The first thing I'd like to tell you is that you are absolutely not alone. Before we go any further, you need to know that there is hope. You can find freedom from the pain of your past. It is possible for those memories to no longer have a grip on you.

Jesus truly is the Great Physician. Isaiah 61 tells us that He is the one who brings good news to the afflicted, who binds up the broken-hearted, who proclaims liberty for captives, who comforts all who mourn, who gives gladness instead of mourning. No one is excluded! The incredible thing is that the prophet Isaiah goes on to promise that the very people who were once addicted, tormented, trapped and broken-hearted will become the builders and repairers of what had been devastated within their culture. As you continue in these pages, I believe that the Lord will begin and continue that healing work in your life. Through Jesus, your past does not have to disqualify or limit your future.

I am confident that you are the courageous parents who are willing to look at your own past and say, "For the sake of the next generation, I will go through what I have to go through and become who I need to become." And in doing this, your personal history will become a testimony of redemption. Your freedom will change the story for future generations.

Looking To The Future

As parents, it's easy to look to the future and feel fearful, even panicky at times. The pervasive pressure makes many people want to isolate themselves, shut the blinds, and keep their kids away from it all. Some couples are even choosing not to have children at all because they can't imagine raising them in such a conflicted world.

But this kind of fear is never from God, and for parents, it is a terrible motivator. You can't build a life-giving future for your children on a foundation of fear or dread. We want to be wise parents who see the bigger picture and make loving decisions with hope for our children and families in mind. The tendency for all of us when we're feeling afraid is to micro-manage our children's choices. When we entrust them into the hands of the Lord, however, it will bring a level of freedom and joy to our parenting journey.

In the face of difficult circumstances, we decide to trust and declare in prayer that the safest place for our child is in the hands of the Lord. We must cement ourselves in the belief that He loves them more than we do, and that He is eager to extend the resources of heaven into their lives. When we hear the whisperings of darkness that threaten the demise of our children, we must shout back the promises of God for them.

We have been assigned a position of guardianship of the next generation. This isn't just about food, clothing, and getting them a good education. This is about their destiny as men and women. It's time to rise up, parents. We must not start conversations with our children because we are afraid, but because we have a vision for the future and recognize that our young ones are looking to us for guidance.

One of my favourite passages of Scripture is found in Isaiah 54:13-14:

"All your children will be taught of the Lord, and great will be the peace of your children. In righteousness you will be established. You will be far from oppression, for you will not fear, and from terror for it will not come near you."

Here's a spoiler alert in case you aren't familiar with early church history: unlike past generations, the early church did not succumb to the sexual immorality of the Greek and Roman culture of their day. Empowered by the Holy Spirit, the early believers were empowered to follow in the ways of Jesus. Rather than false god worship systems upending the church's culture, the church's culture prevailed, multiplied, and spread. Temple prostitutes were redeemed and given the chance for a new life. The infants abandoned outside the city walls were rescued and adopted. People were forgiven and healed from their sexual deviances and found a place in the family of God. Women were treated with respect. The idea of a fresh start became a possibility.

When the time comes for our kids to make life-shaping decisions for themselves, moralistic deism or religious traditions will not suffice. I am convinced that one of the greatest lessons we can teach our children is to rely on the Holy Spirit and on the truth of Scripture. The Holy Spirit is the promised gift from heaven who will come be with us, counsel us when we don't know what to do, and empower us to make hard choices.

That way, when it is time for our children to 'cross the road' without us, they will know that they are not alone, and they will be empowered to make a difference in the world around them.

2

THE FOUNDATIONS OF FAMILY

The stage was set; the backdrops were painted. The land was formed, the seasons were set into motion. Then, onto the scene, emerging from the very heart of God was one unlike any other. But it was not right that the one should dwell alone. So the Creator formed another. Now there were two. Mysteriously those two would become one again. And from that union, new life could miraculously multiply. Life begetting life. Love begetting love. It was not good that anyone should be alone. From the heart of God came the remedy. A remedy in the shape of family.

From the very beginning, it was in the heart of God to create family. I realize the word 'family' carries a lot of emotion. For some, family is the safest place on earth, the place where they are seen, heard, celebrated, and cultivated. For others, the word family brings up thoughts of rejection, abuse, or neglect. However, for most, our experience with family lies somewhere on the spectrum between these extremes: a little bit of good, a little bit of bad, with some quirky traditions and silly memories mixed in. And most of us spend our parenting years working to take all the good that we received in our childhood, with the hope of passing on something even better to our own kids.

To find some clues to help us cultivate a healthy sense of family in our homes, we can look to the early pages of the Bible. I believe that it is a worthwhile endeavour to search out God's original intention for family.

In Genesis chapters 1 and 2, we read that God masterfully designed an entire universe, speaking it all into existence by the force of His words. He filled it to the brim with mountains to climb, animals to encounter, and colourful fruits and flowers to enjoy. Then we discover the pinnacle of His creation:

> *Then God said, "Let Us make man in Our image, according to*
> *Our likeness; and let them rule over the fish of the sea and over*
> *the birds of the sky and over the cattle and over all the earth,*
> *and over every creeping thing that creeps on the earth."*
> *God created man in His own image, in the image of God He*
> *created him; male and female He created them. God blessed them;*
> *and God said to them, "Be fruitful and multiply, and fill the earth,*
> *and subdue it; and rule over the fish of the seas and over the birds*
> *of the sky and over every living thing that moves on the earth."*
> **Genesis 1:26-28**

It is important to note that before humanity was brought onto the scene, God was already complete and lacked nothing. God didn't create us because He was bored or in need of something from us. We were not made in order to fill some missing parts in a heavenly worship choir or to prop up God's self-esteem and give Him earthly minions to boss around.

Rather, we were given life because of the perfect love within the heart of God. God is love, and as the universe is somehow all-encompassing yet still expanding at an incredible rate, it seems to me that His perfect love continues to expand as well. Love does not seek its own way, but seeks to pour itself out to others. God made us in order to pour His love into us. He is our heavenly Father, our divine origin. He made us in His image—to be like Him—and He made us to be in loving relationship with Himself and with one another.

MADE IN HIS IMAGE

Let's note again what it says:

> *Then God said, "Let Us make man in Our*
> *image, according to Our likeness."*
> **Genesis 1:26**

How interesting! It sounds like God has called for something like a conference meeting with Himself! While it is true that God is One, we now see that He is more integrated and complex than this. He is triune in nature. Traditional Christian doctrine uses the word "trinity" to describe this "three-part" nature of God, and throughout the Bible, we discover that these three parts are essentially one God in three persons: Father, Son, and Holy Spirit. They were all present and collaborating together at the glorious event of Creation.

As humans, we too are complex beings. God has made us in His image, in His likeness. This means that regardless of our age, our socio-economic background, our appearance or intellect, or our ability to make a meaningful contribution to society, each of us has innate worth. In the kaleidoscope of humanity, we see the wonder, the beauty, the creativity, the wisdom, and the intellect of the triune God. We were created to reflect our heavenly Father.

One way that we demonstrate the image of God is that every one of us has also been given a triune nature. We all have a body, soul and spirit, yet as individuals, we are holistic beings. The body is the material part of who we are. The soul refers to the mind, will and emotions, and contains aspects of our unique personality. Finally, the spirit is the part of us that most often interacts with the Spirit of God and the unseen, immaterial realm. Together, the body, soul and spirit, make up who we are.

These days, my preschooler has been enjoying getting his hands on watercolour paints. Once he's mixed multiple colours together, it's impossible to pull them apart. Blue and red together make purple. Red and yellow make orange. They no longer exist separately from each other. In the same way that our body, soul and spirit make us who we are, what we do with one part will inevitably affect our entire being.

Now remember, in the garden that God created back at the very beginning, humankind was unmarred by sin, death, or decay, and they enjoyed daily communion with God. It is hard to imagine, but their bodies were free from disease or fatigue. Their minds and emotions were at ease and perfect capacity, and their spirits were alive and well. The material and the immaterial could walk together in unhindered relationship. This was paradise.

MADE FOR EACH OTHER

There in the garden, God saw all that He had made and declared emphatically that it was *good*. Except for one thing.

> *The Lord God said, "It is not good for the man to be alone."*
> **Genesis 2:18** NIV

Here was the one thing in all of creation that was not yet good. Something was incomplete; both God and Adam knew it. Just as it had been in the heart of God to pour out his love on the human race, so also Adam needed someone to pour his love onto. As a carrier of the very nature of God, the newly created man longed to have a companion, someone who was of the same essential nature as him.

God already had the solution in mind. Genesis 2:20-24 says,

> *"So the Lord God caused the man to fall into a deep sleep; and while*
> *he was sleeping, he took one of the man's ribs and then closed up the*
> *place with flesh. Then the Lord God made a woman from the rib he*
> *had taken out of the man, and he brought her to the man.*
> *The man said, 'This is now bone of my bones and flesh of my flesh; she*
> *shall be called 'woman,' for she was taken out of man.' That is why a man*
> *leaves his father and mother and is united to his wife, and they become*
> *one flesh. Adam and his wife were both naked, and they felt no shame."*

The earth's first problem—that of aloneness—had been solved with the introduction of the female! Adam had at first been one within himself, then God reached within him to make another.

In his book, *The Divine Romance*, Gene Edwards gives a poetic account of this creation story:

> "Now if one thrusts his hand into water, he shall surely bring forth water. And, perchance, if one thrusts his hand into the earth, he shall surely bring forth earth. It follows, then, that should the Living God thrust his hand into the side of man, he would surely bring forth humanity. And this very thing he did, drawing forth from within man a portion of that man. A part of the man's own being was now separated from man, yet that portion was still of man . . ."

He imagines God speaking:

"Man . . . shall now have one beside him. One of his very substance, his being . . . extended. I shall now build flesh from his flesh. Bone from his bone. Thus shall he gain a counterpart. A counterpart who is oneness. A counterpart upon whom he may pour out . . . his love."[1]

How could this be? What a grand mystery this is!

Thousands of years after Creation, a leader of the early church, the apostle Paul, wrote to some believers in the ancient city of Ephesus, reflecting on the topic of marriage. He said:

> "In this same way, husbands ought to love their wives as their own
> bodies. He who loves his wife loves himself. After all, no one ever hated
> their own body, but they feed and care for their body, just as Christ does
> the church— for we are members of his body. For this reason a man will
> leave his father and mother and be united to his wife, and the two will
> become one flesh. This is a profound mystery—but I am talking about
> Christ and the church. However, each one of you also must love his
> wife as he loves himself, and the wife must respect her husband."
>
> **Ephesians 5:28-33 NIV**

What Paul is saying is that love and marriage are not just earthly dynamics that can be separated from spiritual realities. There is a glorious, heavenly aspect to our marriages and the establishment of our families that is representative of God's eternal family. The thrill and beauty of the bride and groom on their wedding day reflect the glory of a deeper, even more firmly established truth—that of the love of God towards humanity.

So, when we talk about the relationship of a husband to his wife, we are speaking of the heavenly reality of Christ and His church. Just as God reached inside of Adam to build Eve, so also He reached within Himself to fashion for Himself a bride—His church. Just as God calls husbands and wives to be fruitful and multiply, so also He calls His people to multiply and make disciples, expanding the family of God for the flourishing of humanity and to the glory of the Father.

---

1 Gene Edwards, *The Divine Romance*, Tyndale House, Publishers 1993.

No wonder marriage and family feel so difficult. We are constantly tempted to promote individual identity and interests when God has made us *for each other*. And if we are to fully embrace this type of love, we need to understand God's original design for family.

1. Created Male and Female

While there is no denying that, as humans, we all equally represent the image of God and have so much in common, we are also created distinctly male and female. Those masculine and feminine differences are evident on a cellular level, but also on a sociological level. (More about that in a future chapter.) What we need to hold onto is that both the masculine and the feminine demonstrate powerful aspects of the nature of our Creator. The Lord is a defender, an initiator, a cultivator of covenant . . . *and* He is a life-giver, a comforter, and a nurturer. When working together at full strength and purity, the male and the female natures create beautiful rhythms in family, community, and nations.

From the moment that we were conceived, male or female was marked in our chromosomes and replicated in our bodies through our DNA. Because of the body-soul-spirit integration of humanity, our 'male- or female-ness' extends beyond anatomy. At a soul level, we are either male or female. And at a spiritual level, we are either male or female. And God's proclamation over the man and the woman at creation still holds true today: "This is *very* good!"

2. Naked And Unashamed

As those made in God's image, we are also relational beings who naturally seek to belong and to love. In Genesis 2:24, we read about how in that original garden setting before sin had scarred the landscape, Adam and Eve were "naked and unashamed". Because of their covenant under God and because of their innocence towards sin, they could be completely bare before one another and feel no shame. They did not fear rejection or ridicule; they did not fear pain.

In his book, *Our Bodies Tell God's Story,* author Christopher West writes,

"Only a person who is free from the compulsion of lust is capable of being a true 'gift' to another. The 'freedom of the gift' then, is the freedom of the heart to bless, which is the freedom from the compulsion to grasp and to possess. It is this freedom that allowed the first couple to be 'naked without shame'."

This was the ideal scenario and context for sexual expression. The first man and woman were able to offer their bodies to one another with abandon. In that place of sexual intimacy, the two became one. In the deliberation of their wills and by the passion of their desire, they were made one flesh once again.

The Bible gives us a clue about the aspect of intimacy within marriage. You'll see throughout the historical narratives of the Old Testament that whenever a husband and wife came together sexually, the writer says that they *knew* each other. For instance, Genesis 4:1 says, "Adam knew Eve his wife, and she conceived." In the original language, the word 'knew' is the Hebrew word *'yada'*, which means to have an experiential knowing of someone or something. It means to consider, be acquainted with, to make known and become known, to reveal oneself. Interestingly, whenever we read of a man and woman who were not in covenant, the wording is different. The Bible describes them as having merely 'laid together' with the Hebrew word *'sakab'*, as in the case of King David's adulterous sexual experience with Bathsheba (2 Samuel 11:4).

Timothy Keller, a pastor and teacher from New York, once said, "To be loved but not known is comforting but superficial. To be known and not loved is our greatest fear. But to be fully known and truly loved is, well, a lot like being loved by God. It is what we need more than anything."[2]

To know and be fully known—this is the intimacy that we were made for.

---

2 Timothy Keller, *The Meaning of Marriage: Facing the Complexities of Commitment with the Wisdom of God*, Penguin Books, 2013.

3. God Of Generations

In the first chapter of Genesis, we hear God's instructions to Adam and Eve:

> *God blessed them; and God said to them, "Be fruitful and multiply, and fill the earth, and subdue it; and rule over the fish of the sea and over the birds of the sky and over every living thing that moves on the earth."*
> **Genesis 1:28**

The desire to find meaning and discover purpose in life is woven into our inner fabric. Wrapped inside this Genesis mandate is God's call to both a familial assignment and a vocational purpose:

> **Be fruitful and multiply.** Even as every other living thing has a seed within it and would multiply according to their own kind, so also the seed of humanity was to be multiplied so that the whole earth could be filled with the good image of God.
>
> **Fill the earth and subdue it.** Within this statement we find God's direction for us to establish culture, to steward resources, to develop infrastructure, and to cultivate healthy governance throughout the nations for the good of all.

It is a glorious thing to see the dynamic nature of God represented in so much variety through the individuals and cultures of this earth. Some people are masters of the arts, thinking and communicating in an abstract, poetic way. Others develop and administer systems of order that allow for ease and peace in society. Some influence and lead with purpose and vision, communicating clearly about changes that should be made. Some entertain and bring laughter, while others nurture and heal. None of us depicts the entirety of God on the earth, but we all have unique abilities and personalities that carry the signature of heaven.

HAVING A VISION FOR FAMILY

As we've previously emphasized, God is a relational, personal God, with more than enough love in His heart for all of us. In the Gospel accounts, we find that Jesus most frequently referred to God as 'Father' and then invited his disciples to view him as their Father too.

Scripture tells us that our heavenly Father knows the number of hairs on our head and that He knows each one of our days before even one has come to be (Luke 12:7, Psalm 139:16). He is close. He is intimately acquainted with all of our ways.

However, He is also an eternal God who thinks beyond just our lifespan and into the realm of generations. Thousands of years after Adam and Eve were created, God approached a man named Abram and offered to make a covenant with him. And in that first recorded encounter, God spoke to Abram not just about the impact this covenant would have on his individual life, but about the ripple effect that his choices would have for future generations. Genesis 12:1-3 records the invitation and promise that God made:

> The Lord had said to Abram, "Go from your country, your people and your father's household to the land I will show you. I will make you into a great nation, and I will bless you; I will make your name great, and you will be a blessing. I will bless those who bless you, and whoever curses you I will curse; and all peoples on earth will be blessed through you." (NIV)

At the time, Abram and his wife Sarai were living in the land of Ur, surrounded by people who were worshipping and serving idols. That was their normal—it was all they had ever known. Sarai was also barren and they had spent years wondering if their dream of having children would ever happen. When Abram heard God's voice, they took a risk and left all they had known to head west. They didn't know it then, but they were sojourning into the land that would one day be the inheritance of his descendants. God preemptively changed his name to Abraham, which means 'father of multitudes', even though it wouldn't be until many years later that they would see God's promise come to pass. A son was miraculously born and they named him Isaac. When Isaac had grown up, he married a woman named Rebekah, and they gave birth to two sons, Jacob and Esau.

In the coming years, when God would introduce Himself to those heirs of Abraham, He would call Himself, "the God of your fathers, Abraham, Isaac, and Jacob." He was reminding them, "Though I see you as an individual, I also see you as a part of something much bigger. My faithfulness extends beyond just you to the generations coming after you."

Abraham's family started out as small and insignificant, but over time, that one son became a great nation. Just as God promised, all peoples on earth were blessed through Abram's faith legacy in the greatest way possible, because the Redeemer Himself, Jesus Christ, came through that lineage.

The significance of the family still exists for us today. We are not just individuals, fighting for our personal place in this world, to be self-made and self-contained. It was through a *family* that all nations on earth were blessed. As we serve our children, we are investing our strength and love beyond this present day and into future generations.

When my husband and I were both twenty-two years old, we stood at the wedding altar and exchanged marriage vows. We laugh a little now when we look at pictures from that day. Our starry-eyed, unwrinkled, baby faces stood there determined to honour God in our relationship. Yet we were also undeniably infatuated with what we thought that would look like in the coming years. We really could not have understood what we were getting ourselves into. In time, we would discover that there is a significant, continual cost that must be paid in order for "the two to become one".

I want to share with you now some words from Dietrich Bonhoeffer, a German pastor and philosopher from the mid-1900s. On our wedding day, we had this passage printed out for our guests to read in the hope that they would also be encouraged about the significance of their marriage relationship. That is my hope for you as well:

"God is guiding your marriage. Marriage is more than your love for each other. It has a higher dignity and power, for it is God's holy ordinance, through which He wills to perpetuate the human race till the end of time. In your love you see only your two selves in the world, but in marriage you are a link in the chain of the generations, which God causes to come and to pass away to His glory, and calls into His kingdom. In your love you see only the heaven of your own happiness, but in marriage you are placed at a post of responsibility towards the world and mankind. Your love is your own private possession, but marriage is more than something personal—it is a status, an office. Just as it is the crown, and not merely the will to rule, that makes the king, so it is marriage, and not merely your love for each other, that joins you together in the sight of God and man.

As you first gave the ring to one another and have now received it a second time from the hand of the pastor, so love comes from you, but marriage from above, from God. As high as God is above man, so high are the sanctity, the rights, and the promise of marriage above the sanctity, the rights, and the promise of love. It is not your love that sustains the marriage, but from now on, the marriage that sustains your love."[3]

Now, nearly eighteen years into our marriage, we can speak of the sweetness of intimacy that is reserved for those who are willing to pay the price. Oh, how our joy has been multiplied, and the weight of our grief has been made more bearable! We have learned to trust each other more and more, allowing one another into the deeper places of our hearts. Though we will never experience the unhindered intimacy that Adam and Eve briefly enjoyed in the Garden, we can attest that the joy of companionship and partnership in building a family together is well worth the cost.

---

3 Bonhoeffer, Dietrich. *Letters and Papers from Prison*, edited by Eberhard Bethge. Simon and Schuster Touchstone: New York, 1997.

3

THE TREASURE AND THE SERPENT

All treasures are worth protecting. Not all that glitters is gold. All dangers warrant a boundary. Not all whispers can be trusted.

In Eden's garden paradise, humanity walked with God. Their bodies were whole, their souls were unclouded, and their spirits were vibrant. The eternal Creator and the everlasting Created experienced the joyful comfort of fellowship. Remember that God never intended man and woman to live as minions to do His bidding, or as programmed robots who execute His orders. We were made for love, and all true love is an offering freely given.

So, the Lord God did not cage the man and the woman as animals but rather gave free will to these spiritual, physical beings. There was only one prohibition in the entire created space:

> *Now the Lord God had planted a garden in the east, in Eden; and there he put the man he had formed. The Lord God made all kinds of trees grow out of the ground—trees that were pleasing to the eye and good for food. In the middle of the garden were the tree of life and the tree of the knowledge of good and evil ... The Lord God took the man and put him in the Garden of Eden to work it and take care of it. And the Lord God commanded the man, "You are free to eat from any tree in the garden; but **you must not eat from the tree of the knowledge of good and evil,** for when you eat from it you will certainly die."*
> **Genesis 2:8-9, 15-17 NIV**

God said they may eat from all trees, except for one. Which one? The tree of the knowledge of good and evil.

God was telling them that in order to protect and enjoy the treasure of the life they possessed, they were not to seek their understanding or identity from an outside source. If they wanted God's design for them to keep functioning as intended, they had to keep seeking the One who knew them best—their Designer, their heavenly Father. Even as the sun sustains physical life here on earth, God was their Source of spiritual life. God had already spoken blessing over their identity. He wanted them to see themselves only as He saw them—bearers of His image and perfect in His sight.

God knew that eating from the tree of the knowledge of good and evil would distort the way they saw themselves, and ultimately, jeopardize their relationship with Him. But more than that, God also knew that eating from the tree of the knowledge of good and evil would leave Adam and Eve second-guessing themselves, unsure of their belovedness and their place and purpose in the world.

And into that context, a serpent enters.

Seeds of Doubt

Genesis 3:1-5 lets us in on the conversation that upended life as they knew it.

> Now the serpent was more crafty than any of the wild animals
> the Lord God had made. He said to the woman, **"Did God really
> say,** You must not eat from any tree in the garden?"
> The woman said to the serpent, "We may eat fruit from the trees in the
> garden, but God did say, 'You must not eat fruit from the tree that is in
> the middle of the garden, and you must not touch it, or you will die.'"
> "You will not certainly die," the serpent said to the woman, "for
> God knows that when you eat from it your eyes will be opened,
> and you will be like God, knowing good and evil."

"Did God really say . . .?"

The whispered doubts fell like seeds into the woman's heart. At first, the woman responded confidently, repeating what God had instructed. "Yes, I'm sure we cannot eat of it."

The serpent countered with a direct accusation against her heavenly Father's intentions: "*He is only prohibiting these things because He is keeping something from you. Because He doesn't want you to be like Him. He lied to you, Eve. He can't be trusted. It won't kill you.*"

The woman looked a little more closely at the tree of the knowledge of good and evil. The fruit *did* look good, and she was kind of curious about what this new wisdom might be. The Bible says,

> "*. . . she took some and ate it. She also gave some to her husband, who was with her, and he ate it. Then the eyes of both of them were opened, and they knew that they were naked; and they sewed fig leaves together and made themselves loin coverings.*"
>
> **Genesis 3:6 NIV**

The temptation all began with a defamation of the nature and character of God. Before that day, the woman had seen no reason to distrust her Creator. But as soon as they had eaten, their perception of Him changed. They no longer ran towards Him as they would a father who could help them repair the damage they had done. Instead, they ran away from Him, afraid of judgment.

When Adam and Eve ate from the tree, they did not instantly fall down dead. But something within them certainly died. By following the deception of the enemy, they forfeited the glory that had been given to them. The force of death began to creep in, causing the light of their spirits to be eliminated, their bodies to age and break down, and their souls to be tentative, self-focused, and shame-filled.

THE TARGET ON OUR BACKS

What did the serpent have against the woman? Why did he come after the children of God? It was because he had his own plans for ruling over the earth, but God had intended for humanity to have dominion over the earth, including over "every creeping thing". When the enemy targeted this first son and daughter, it was a part of his scheme to get them out of the way—or bring them under his control. He knew that if humankind filled the earth with their God-given glory, he would forever be on the back foot. He hated the image of God in Adam and Eve—just as he hates the image of God in us.

Today, the evil one continues to come at us with temptations and doubts similar to the ones our ancient parents faced under the shadow of the tree of the knowledge of good and evil. These temptations include, but are not limited to, all matters surrounding sexuality and identity. Because these matters are foundational to our personhood and to our ability to flourish as humans, we find that the enemy of our soul targets sexuality and identity with a vengeance, seeking to distort who we think we are in an effort to keep us at odds with our heavenly Father and with ourselves. We hear the underlying question, "Did God really say?" and the thought comes, *Maybe God is not trying to protect us. Maybe He really is trying to control and repress us.* An invitation to self-actualization and independence soon follows: "This is your life. You do you. You know what's best for you."

No wonder we wrestle with matters of morality. We know we have a sinful nature on the inside of us, we struggle under the pressure of external systems that resist God, and we often feel cornered by a cruel enemy who continues to oppress us. The enemy and his demonic forces have the same mode of operation today that they did back then—to lie, to kill, and to destroy.

HALF THE BATTLE

Living in a post-Enlightenment era, many people have been taught that the material realm is all there is. They believe that unless you can scientifically analyze a thing, it cannot be real. But the Scriptures remind us of the immaterial—there is more to life than what meets the eye. There is an invisible realm, ruled by our Creator, our heavenly Father, and there are angelic and demonic forces exerting influence on humanity and our world systems.

Ephesians 6:12 tells us:

> *"We wrestle not against flesh and blood, but against principalities,*
> *against powers, against the rulers of the darkness of this world,*
> *against spiritual wickedness in high places." (KJV)*

In the hustle of modern society, we can easily lose track of the larger storyline that is playing out around us. We feel like we're just normal people, living normal lives. We are trying to get what we need from the grocery store, trying to save enough money for a family holiday next summer, trying to renovate the kitchen. We so often forget that we were born into a battle and that there is no neutral territory. We must be alert.

In 2 Corinthians 2:9-11, the apostle Paul, an early church leader exhorts the local church in Corinth:

> *"Another reason I wrote you was to see if you would stand the*
> *test and be obedient in everything . . . in order that Satan might*
> *not outwit us. For we are not unaware of his schemes." (NIV)*

I have seen two primary schemes of the enemy pertaining to sexuality and the family:

Scheme #1 To disintegrate an individual, convincing them that the most important part of who they are is either their physical, material self or their inner perception of self.
Scheme #2 To disintegrate the family, dividing and isolating generations from one another.

Knowing God's design for humanity, we can more fully understand why these strategies would bring so much destruction, not only to individuals and families, but also to nations. Almost every distorted idea about sexuality can be traced back to these two deceptions.

My prayer is that you will have eyes to see the way these schemes impact your daily life, because as you grow to recognize the enemy's evil strategies you can teach your kids to do the same.

Remember, though, that understanding the strategies of darkness is really only half the battle. On our own, we have no strength to overcome the devil's schemes. No amount of behavioural modification can bring us back to the glory that was once ours in the beginning. Religious systems or political legislation cannot do it. All of us, our children included, are in need of the Redeemer named Jesus Christ to restore all that was lost. And we need His promised Holy Spirit to give us the strength to resist the enemy's schemes, the cultural shifts around us, and our own personal tendency towards sin.

4

——

THE REDEMPTIVE PLAN OF GOD

"What have I done?"

"I should have known better."

"I'll fix this myself. No one has to know."

Shame soon follows sin. At first, it is a few grains of sand—an irritant in our eyes that distorts how we see. Unconfronted, it grows into mountainous secrets that alter the landscape, blocking us from the life we dreamed of and the people we want to be close to. Shame says it is all over, that our course is fixed. It leaves us with no hope.

But then we hear rumours of mercy. Good news floats in on the wind. A voice calls to us by name. We are not forgotten. We are not forsaken.

Succumbing to temptation is a common experience for us as humans. I have plenty of memories from my early childhood of doing the exact thing that I knew I wasn't supposed to. I remember one incident. I couldn't have been more than four years old. Practically a baby! But I vividly recall sneaking into my sister's school supplies and rubbing her liquid glue all over my hands so that I could enjoy the sensation of peeling it off when it dried. I knew I should not do it. When she caught me, I blushed and squirmed. I probably offered a shy apology.

When our son Charlie was still a little guy, just learning to write his name, I found dreaded Sharpie marks on the walls in the downstairs bathroom. "C-H-A-R..."

He had stopped halfway through the exercise, likely gripped by sudden awareness of what he was doing. Either that or he had heard me coming and ran to hide the incriminating instrument.

Though these examples are quite harmless, they demonstrate the fact that temptation is common to all of us, and the resulting shame is equally familiar. We see these elements in Adam and Eve's story. Remember the account in Genesis:

> *"...she (Eve) took some and ate it. She also gave some to her husband, who was with her, and he ate it. Then the eyes of both of them were opened, and they knew that they were naked; and they sewed fig leaves together and made themselves loin coverings."*
> **Genesis 3:7 NIV**

The fruit Adam and Eve hoped would improve their lives quickly soured in their mouths. They didn't feel wiser or more like God at all; they felt afraid and ashamed of what they had done. Whereas they had previously been gloriously naked and unashamed, now they were painfully aware and self-conscious of their nakedness.

Genesis 3:8-13 explains,

> *Then the man and his wife heard the sound of the Lord God*
> *as he was walking in the garden in the cool of the day, and*
> *they hid from the Lord God among the trees of the garden. But*
> *the Lord God called to the man, "Where are you?"*
> *He answered, "I heard you in the garden, and I was*
> *afraid because I was naked; so I hid."*
> *And he said, "Who told you that you were naked? Have you eaten*
> *from the tree that I commanded you not to eat from?"*
> *The man said, "The woman you put here with me—she*
> *gave me some fruit from the tree, and I ate it."*
> *Then the Lord God said to the woman, "What is this you have done?"*
> *The woman said, "The serpent deceived me, and I ate."*

Here we see that the all-knowing God asked questions, not because He was lacking information but because He was inviting the man and his wife into conversation, tenderly drawing a confession from them. *"Where are you? What have you done?"*

Though both man and woman attempted to make an excuse and pass the blame, in time they admitted, "We ate what we should not have."

Every generation since Adam and Eve has wrestled with the shame of sin. When we violate a God-given boundary, shame shows up like a 'check engine' light on the dashboard of our soul. If we have ignored or resisted God's instruction, shame will often push us into hiding. Fearing rejection or punishment, we stay away from the very place where shame can be broken.

Just as Adam and Eve made loin coverings out of fig leaves, the temptation for us today is still to fashion coverings for ourselves out of temporary, fragile materials. We put on a good face, hide under our accomplishments, and try to be likable, flying under the radar so that no one will look past our facade. Maybe somewhere deep within us, we know that we were made to be clothed with the glory of God, but now we just feel vulnerable and ashamed. God didn't want to leave Adam and Eve in that condition, nor does He want that for us. By His Spirit and because of His great love for us, God continues to invite us to be honest about our sin. Because honesty is the first step in the re-establishment of a relationship free of shame.

A Curse On The Serpent

God is never eager to pronounce judgment on his children. When Adam and Eve acknowledged what they had done, God's response was to address the serpent. While the man and woman were held responsible for their decisions, judgment was first given to the deceiver:

"Because you have done this, cursed are you above all livestock and all wild animals! You will crawl on your belly and you will eat dust all the days of your life. And I will put enmity between you and the woman, and between your offspring and hers; he will crush your head, and you will strike his heel."
Genesis 3:14-15 NIV

The statement that there would be enmity between the woman and the serpent is far more of a problem for the enemy than for us. God was acknowledging that the serpent would view the woman and her offspring as his ultimate foe, and would live forevermore with the awareness that the seed of the woman would one day crush his head.

On the very day that sin deformed creation, God made a declaration that darkness would not reign forever but would ultimately be overcome. There in the Garden of Eden, the Father foresaw a time when the 'seed of the woman', Jesus, would bow his knee in the Garden called Gethsemane and offer a prayer of surrender, "Not my will but Yours be done" (Luke 22:42), thus undoing humanity's rebellion.

Jesus came to earth to destroy the works of the evil one and set captives free. Though Jesus was struck and crucified by the religious and political leaders of His day, after three days, He rose again, ultimately crushing sin, Satan, death, and the grave (Romans 5:18)!

Jesus had overcome the evil one. At his ascension, he gave the church the 'Garden Commissioning' once again. We are to go into all the world, preach the gospel, and make disciples, thus expanding the family of God once again. Our job is to partner with God for the restoration of the earth and everything in it. We do this by liberating the demonized, healing the sick, and ministering wholeness to the broken.

No wonder the serpent has enmity towards the woman and her offspring! It was the offspring who would be his ultimate ruin.

THE CONSEQUENCES WE FACE

Even though Adam and Eve were given this promise of future victory, God also spoke to them about the consequences that they would face in a world that was now under the influence of sin,

> *"To the woman he said, 'I will make your pains in childbearing*
> *very severe; with painful labor you will give birth to children. Your*
> *desire will be for your husband, and he will rule over you."*
> *To Adam he said, "Because you listened to your wife and ate fruit from the*
> *tree about which I commanded you, 'You must not eat from it,'*
> *"Cursed is the ground because of you; through painful toil you will eat*
> *food from it all the days of your life. It will produce thorns and thistles for*
> *you, and you will eat the plants of the field. By the sweat of your brow*

you will eat your food until you return to the ground, since from it you were taken; for dust you are and to dust you will return."

Genesis 3:16-19 NIV

Everything Adam and Eve had been created to accomplish and enjoy had now become a whole lot harder. Bearing children would be painful. Living in the covenant of marriage would feel complicated. The land itself would resist being cultivated. Ultimately, they would taste physical death. From dust they had come; to dust they would return.

A GOD OF REDEMPTION

But a short, powerful verse is tucked into this complex story.

"The Lord God made garments of skin for Adam and his wife and clothed them."

Genesis 3:21

Where did the Lord God find these garments of skin? They weren't made of celestial fabric hiding in heaven's hallway closets. No, these garments came from the skins of a sacrificed animal! If their shame was to be covered in a more enduring way, it would require the shedding of blood.

God removed their fig leaves and exchanged them for animal skins.

And today, because of the shed blood of Jesus, the Lamb of God, He provides robes of righteousness to cover our shame. He still calls us to come out of hiding, confess our sin, and receive his forgiveness. He still longs for us to be restored to our full relationship with Him.

THE STIGMA OF SEXUAL SIN

Ever since Adam and Eve rejected the instruction of God in the Garden of Eden, sin has been present on the earth and in our lives. God had warned them that on the day that they disobeyed, they would experience death for the first time. Romans 3:23 tells us,

"For all have sinned and fall short of the glory of God."

Sin leaves a mark on our soul, distorts our understanding of God, and can cause shame. After years of communicating about God's design for sexuality and preaching about the redemption available through Jesus, my husband and I have noted how sexual experiences outside of the God-ordained context carry an especially high level of shame for people. Why is this?

1 Corinthians 6:18-20 holds the answer:

"Run from sexual sin! No other sin so clearly affects the body as this one does. For sexual immorality is a sin against your own body. Don't you realize that your body is the temple of the Holy Spirit, who lives in you and was given to you by God? You do not belong to yourself, for God bought you with a high price. So you must honour God with your body." (NLT)

Sexual experiences were designed to be enjoyed in the covenant of marriage between one man and one woman. Sex is not just a physical act; when people unite sexually, it binds them together—physically, emotionally, and spiritually—even if they are unaware of it at the time. Sexual sin is not just outside the body; it is a violation of God's design for this deep part of who we are. Though the experience may be pleasurable in the moment, soon the sin catches up with people and many begin to feel deep regret and shame about their choices.

Not only does our shame come from within, but also throughout history, there has often been a social stigma attached to sexual sin. According to Webster's dictionary, the word *stigma* means, *"a mark of disgrace associated with a particular circumstance, quality, or person."*

This makes me think of the Nathanial Hawthorne novel, *The Scarlet Letter*, which I read in high school. This is a fictional tale of a woman who was forced to wear a red letter "A" stitched onto her clothing, identifying her as an adulterer—someone who had sinned sexually by getting involved with a married man. Though Western society no longer goes to these extremes to ostracize offenders, many people, inside and outside of the church, still sense the seriousness of sexual sin. They may sense a stigma—a mark—on their life, either from the things that they did, from things that they are tempted to do, from things that were done to them, or even from things that their family was involved in. Regardless of the cause, it leaves them susceptible to the accusing voice of shame.

Shame whispers,

"You're the only one."

"If anyone found out about what you did, they'd think you are disgusting."

"You should have known better."

Shame tries to convince people that they are alone in their sin and that they have to run and hide, just like the first man and woman did all those years ago in the garden. But just as God called out to Adam and Eve and didn't leave them to figure it out on their own, God calls out to us in the middle of our shame, opening His arms out wide, offering grace and forgiveness. That is why, in Christian tradition, the word *stigma* is also used to refer to the marks left on Jesus' body by the crucifixion.

Two thousand years ago, when Jesus felt the sting of the whip on his back, when the nails pierced through his hands and feet, and when the crown of thorns was thrust upon his head, he literally took upon himself the *stigma*—the marks of our sin. When He was raised back to life on the third day, He appeared repeatedly to his followers and would show them the evidence of His great love, pointing to the scars that remained on His resurrected body. He chose to keep the *stigma*, an eternal reminder that we could be free from ours.

Moms and dads all over the world and throughout the centuries have experienced the stigma of sexual sin that seems to lurk in the shadows of their past. Many parents feel disqualified and silenced on matters of godly sexuality because they don't know what to do with the details of their own story. I've spoken to many people who accept that they have been forgiven by God, but still live afraid that their children will find out their testimony. Others serve endlessly, striving like they are a slave, as though they could somehow prove to God how sorry they are, or pay him back for the wrong things they have done. They feel like they are running on a treadmill—a lot of movement, but not much progress in the direction of freedom. They are trying to cover over the scars and stigma from the past, so the idea of opening up a conversation with their kids about sex looks like a minefield.

I am persuaded that even as Christ pointed out the scars on his hands, feet and side as evidence of the resurrecting power of God, we are mandated to allow our testimonies, however messy, to be a witness of that same power available to others.

Before my dad came to Christ in his early twenties, he made unhealthy choices that led to heartache and sexual shame. When I was a teen, there were a couple of occasions when he would share aspects of those difficult parts of his story with my sister and me. I remember seeing him struggle to find the right words. I know he felt awkward. He wanted to be honest without oversharing or violating our innocence. Now, years later, I don't remember details of what he shared, but I do remember feeling grateful that he was willing to be vulnerable before us, to expose the destructive lies of the evil one while pointing to the kindness and forgiveness of God.

My dad pushed past the shame and cautiously shared his testimony, all in the hopes of protecting his daughters. I believe that his humility, coupled with his investment of time and care for us over the years, became a sort of shield that guarded me from having to learn those same lessons the hard way. Now when I think of the testimonies of salvation and restoration from my parents and grandparents, I see that they are a part of a spiritual inheritance that can be passed down to my children.

I can't guess at the details of your unique story, but I know that the Scriptures promise us,

> *"God causes all things to work together for good to those who love*
> *God, to those who are called according to is purpose."*
> **Romans 8:28**

All things?! Even the things that we are most ashamed of? Can God turn even those dark memories and secrets for good?

Yes. He is that good.

As we learn to surrender all things into His hands and allow the light of disclosure to break through the darkness, we are storing up a spiritual inheritance for our own families in the hope that when it comes time to build again, they will be inspired to build differently.

5

—

A TIMELESS RESPONSE TO MODERN PHILOSOPHIES

The blind lead the blind along paths of a winding labyrinth.
The loudest mouths gather the largest crowds. The maze is full of dead-ends and deep pits.
They can't see what step to take, they don't know what they are stumbling over.
The Way seems too narrow, the Truth too rigid.
Yet the cross remains, our signpost, and those who choose it find Life.

In March 2023, the question, "What is a woman?" flooded our social media feeds. Though I live in Canada, the algorithm suspected I'd be interested in the inquiry between United States Senator Marsha Blackburn and Judge Ketanji Brown Jackson. Blackburn had asked Jackson one simple question: "Can you provide a definition for the word 'woman'?"

Clearly trying to dodge the question and avoid public outrage, Jackson replied, "No. I can't. I'm not a biologist."

Many people were shocked. *Did it now take a biologist to define what was once agreed upon as common knowledge? What led to this hotbed of debate about matters of gender ideology, sexual orientation, and human identity? How had the cultural landscape been transformed at such a disorienting rate?* And it led many parents to question, *What will the world look like for our children in the future?*

As followers of Jesus, we need to recognize that when we step outside our front door, we are stepping out as the ambassadors of a heavenly kingdom with a fundamentally different culture than that of this world. In 2 Corinthians 5:20, Paul writes:

> *"We are therefore Christ's ambassadors, as though God were making his appeal through us. We implore you on Christ's behalf: Be reconciled to God."*

Like all commissioned ambassadors, we must find ways to work effectively with those around us. We need to seek to understand the language and culture of those who are citizens of 'the world'. That's what this chapter is about. By examining some key secular philosophies that have shaped Western culture over the last three hundred years, in both subtle and sometimes shocking ways, we will be able to offer thoughtful responses as we engage with our society—and teach our children to do the same.

ROMANTICISM: THE ELEVATION OF SELF-EXPRESSION

In the second century, just as the early church was beginning to spread through the Roman Empire, an ideology arose called "Gnosticism". Gnostics proposed that the inner person, the non-material self, was superior to the physical body. The physical body was considered 'base', even gross or offensive. The ideal, in their thinking, was to subdue or restrict the physical body in preference for expanding and elevating the mind.

This philosophy found its voice again in modern history with the rise of Romanticism in the late 1700s to mid-1800s. At that time, Jean-Jacques Rousseau, a Geneva-born political philosopher, often considered the "father of Romanticism", contributed greatly to the philosophy by promoting the idea that the truest form of an individual is the inner self.

With the emphasis on being 'true to oneself' came the rise of what some philosophers began to call *expressive individualism*—with a focus on personal happiness and self-actualization. Until then, it was assumed that the family, tribe or community were to take priority and that individuals would find their fulfillment and purpose in contributing to the common good.

Rousseau famously said, "Man is born free but everywhere is in chains." He went on to claim that humans, in their 'natural state' are good, but have been restrained and repressed through cultural expectations and social pressure brought on by the state, the church, and the family. He advocated for liberation from social obligation—celebrating all things that felt 'natural' to the individual.

DARWIN: THE DISSOLUTION OF DIVINE DESIGN

In the nineteenth century, a multitude of voices arose, collectively inviting a revolt against 'intelligent design'—the idea that God is the Creator of our universe. In the realm of natural science, Charles Darwin presented the theory of evolution. He proposed a world that was not divinely inspired but rather was here by matter of chance. Evolutionary theory did not (and could not) offer a solution to the question of the origin of the universe, but it did call into question the idea that humans were designed in the image of God, on purpose, for a purpose. It proposed that humans were simply highly adapted animals. In rejecting a Creator, these scientists and philosophers rejected divine design and subsequent accountability. Humans could therefore resist the need to comply with anything beyond themselves.

MARXISM: THE DISTRUST OF AUTHORITIES

In the realm of political economics, Karl Marx began to assert that history must be seen in light of how oppressors took advantage of the weak. Marx called religion, "the opium of the masses". He believed that religion was invented by the dominant class (or authorities) as a tool to control crowds. He said that only the feeble-minded would accept religion as a crutch they could lean on in order to soothe their consciences. Marx saw the issue as primarily political and framed all relationships as a wrestle between the oppressor and the oppressed. He believed that freedom was only possible with the dissolution of religion.

NIETZSCHE: THE ERADICATION OF MORAL ACCOUNTABILITY

Friedrich Nietzsche, a contemporary of both Marx and Darwin in the mid to late 1800s, was a philosopher who also believed that humans had invented the concept of God. Though he was a Nihilist, believing that life is meaningless and rejecting all religious or moral principles, Nietzsche at least had the intellectual honesty to admit that adopting his philosophy had difficult implications for society. He recognized that without a god of any kind, all moral obligations or transcendent ethics would be erased. In his infamous *Parable of the Madman*, Nietzsche poetically describes a world without God:

> Have you not heard of that madman
> who lit a lantern in the bright morning hours,
> ran to the marketplace, and cried incessantly:
> "I seek God! I seek God!"
> As many of those who did not believe in God were standing around just then, he provoked much laughter.
> "Has he got lost?" asked one.
> "Did he lose his way like a child?" asked another. "Or is he hiding? Is he afraid of us? Has he gone on a voyage? Emigrated?"
> Thus they yelled and laughed.
>
> The madman jumped into their midst and pierced them with his eyes.
> "Whither is God?" he cried; "I will tell you.
> We have killed him—you and I.
> All of us are his murderers.
> But how did we do this?
> How could we drink up the sea?
> Who gave us the sponge to wipe away the entire horizon?
> What were we doing when we unchained this earth from its sun?
> Whither is it moving now? Whither are we moving?
> Away from all suns?
> Are we not plunging continually,
> Backward, sideward, forward, in all directions?

Is there still any up or down?

Are we not straying, as through an infinite nothing?

Do we not feel the breath of empty space?

Has it not become colder? Is not night continually closing in on us?

Do we not need to light lanterns in the morning?

Do we hear nothing as yet of the noise of the gravediggers who are burying God?

Do we smell nothing as yet of the divine decomposition?

Gods, too, decompose.

God is dead.

God remains dead.

And we have killed him.

How shall we comfort ourselves, the murderers of all murderers?

What was holiest and mightiest of all that the world has yet owned

has bled to death under our knives:

Who will wipe this blood off us?

What water is there for us to clean ourselves?

What festivals of atonement, what sacred games shall we have to invent?

Is not the greatness of this deed too great for us?

Must we ourselves not become gods simply to appear worthy of it?[4]

Must we ourselves not become gods simply to appear worthy of it? With this 'elimination of God', Nietzsche proposed that the world would become a place where each person could be free to create and form themselves as they preferred. Each sat at their own potter's wheel, shaping themself into an image of their own choosing. There would be no declaration of universal, objective truth, only a societal determination that people should be true to themselves.

---

4   author's emphasis

Oscar Wilde: The Glorification of the 'Authentic Self'

Oscar Wilde, an Irish poet and playwright, is a prime example of what self-expression meant in the mid-1800s and early 1900s. Following the paradigm of Nietzsche and the ideals of Romanticism, Oscar Wilde resisted socially enforced morals and advocated that all that mattered is for a person to realize the perfection of the soul that is within him. All imitation in morals and life was wrong.

Oscar Wilde was notorious for his unique fashion choices, artistic expression, and persistent wit. The well-known quote, "Be yourself; everyone else is already taken," depicts his lifestyle and worldview.

But he wasn't the only one to cast off all social norms. Around the same time, many authors, poets and artists began to call for an unrestrained, 'authentic' lifestyle that allowed people to behave in accordance with their inner desires. Such unrestrained expressions of 'self' caused some to raise their eyebrows, but Oscar Wilde asserted that this was the price you pay for being an authentic self.

Freud: The Supremacy of Sexual Identity

Rousseau elevated self. Darwinian theory eliminated a Creator. Marxism rejected religious order. Nietzschean thought erased transcendent purpose or moral obligation. In embracing all of these worldviews, all that remained was the individual's right to self-expression and pursuit of happiness.

It was at this point that the psychologist Sigmund Freud stepped onto the stage of history and declared that a person's deepest satisfaction and primary identity was found in sexual pleasure. Though a large portion of his work was rejected by peers in his lifetime, this theory has since infiltrated modern thought.

In *Civilization and Its Discontents*, Freud wrote,

"Man's discovery that sexual (genital) love afforded him the strongest experiences of satisfaction and in fact provided him with the prototype of all happiness, must have suggested to him that he should continue to seek the satisfaction of happiness in his life along the path of sexual relations and that he should make genital erotism the central point of his life."

Freud proposed that our sexual urges are at the very core of our identity, with many desires so deep in our psyche that we haven't even unearthed them yet. While sex used to be an activity that people *did,* now it was to be considered *who we are.* He is quoted as saying, "The only unnatural sexual behaviour is none at all."

Freud knew that some sexual expressions would be culturally frowned upon and even potentially harmful to society, but in his opinion, there were no grounds to evaluate or judge anyone's sexual preferences as good or bad, right or wrong. Followers of Freudian theory went so far as to claim it is offensive to disagree with someone's sexual choices and lifestyle, because countering someone's sexual expression is countering their core identity, their freedom of expression, and their right to the pursuit of happiness.

A lesser-known but perhaps even more concerning theory Freud proposed is found in his book, *Three Essays on the Theory of Sexuality.* Here, he introduced the concept of 'infantile sexuality', arguing that sexual identity begins at birth and undergoes different developmental stages through childhood. A characteristic of one of these stages was what Freud called the 'Oedipus complex', where he described and normalized a child's subconscious desire for sexual involvement with their parent of the opposite sex.

REICH: THE DISSOLUTION OF FAMILY AND THE SEXUALIZATION OF CHILDREN

Following in the footsteps of both Freudian and Marxist thought, Wilhelm Reich, an Austrian psychoanalyst and doctor of medicine, took things to a whole other level.

Reich's childhood was marked with various kinds of tragedy—he was sexually molested repeatedly as a pre-teen, his mother committed adultery and then suicide, and his father was a harsh authoritarian who died of tuberculosis when Wilhelm was only seventeen years old. These experiences clearly left a mark and influenced Reich's theories and practices, as you will see.

Because he held to the Marxist thought that most authorities were oppressive, Reich resisted the structures of society that enforced any moral code regarding sexuality. Because he saw the traditional family as the basic building block of this oppressive society, he was particularly critical of it and called for its end as we know it.

In his book, *Children of the Future,* Reich wrote:

"This sexual suppression of the children by their parents, to which is added the intellectual suppression by the school, the spiritual stultification by the Church, and finally the material suppression and exploitation by employer of employee, is the primary source of youth people's emotional and sexual misery."

Echoing the thoughts of the Romantic era of the previous century, he said:

"These [future] children will have to choose their own ways and determine their own fates. We must learn from them instead of forcing upon them our own cockeyed ideas and malicious practices, which have now been shown in every new generation to be most damaging and ridiculous. Let the children themselves decide their own future. Our task is to protect their natural powers to do so."

In Reich's opinion, it was oppressive for parents to stand in the way of a child's sexual expression. He called for the State and its servants in the public school system to intervene and assist children in finding their true selves. He asserted:

"Every physician, teacher or social worker who will have to deal with children must show proof that he or she … is sex-economically healthy and that he has acquired an exact knowledge of infantile and adolescent sexuality. That is, training in sex-economy must be obligatory for physicians and teachers." [5]

---

5 Wilhelm Reich, *Children of the Future: On the Prevention of Sexual Pathology.* Translated by Derek Inge. Farrar, Straus and Giroux, 1985.

THE PEOPLE OF GOD IN THE TWENTY-FIRST CENTURY

And this is where we find ourselves today. We're just average moms and dads looking out the window provided to us by social media, entertainment, and emailed newsletters from the public school. We know things have changed, but we are shocked at how quickly. We are left wondering what the likelihood is that it can go back to normal by the time our great-grandchildren are born.

The convergence of these various philosophies has established somewhat of a laboratory where a mass social experiment has been introduced that is attempting to erase the definitions of reality. The ideas that would have once been considered scientifically absurd by the general public have been embraced as authentic, expressive, and liberating.

Many today would claim that we have evolved to a place of greater acceptance of one another's orientations and attractions, and that those who choose to limit their sexual expression are prudish and old-fashioned. The reality is that culture has vacillated between views of morality for centuries. The early church that Jesus commissioned was birthed in the Greco-Roman era and faced many of the same moral issues that we do today. During that time, in the name of their religion, people routinely engaged in orgies, in pedophilia, in homosexual relations, in cross-dressing, in adultery, in fornication, and in bestiality. There is nothing new under the sun. We are not evolving into anything.

In those times, Christians were called 'pagans' because they were monotheistic and refused to worship at the plethora of temples. In accordance with the teachings of Jesus and the apostles, Christians held a high view of the marriage covenant and sexual faithfulness between one man and one woman, so they would not engage in the sensual worship practices common to the Roman or Greek culture of their time. Those on the outside looking in at the Christian community were astounded and skeptical of a people who would have such countercultural views around sex.

One man, a Roman historian named Diognetius, wrote concerning the Christians, "They share their tables with all, and their beds with no one."

He respected their great levels of kind hospitality but marvelled at their sexual abstinence. I wonder if Peter had this very thing in mind when he wrote to the early church:

"Live such good lives among the pagans that, though they accuse you of doing wrong, they may see your good deeds and glorify God on the day he visits us."
1 Peter 2:12 NIV

In this modern time, we can rest in the sure foundation of a Biblical worldview that reminds us that our identity is bestowed on us by a heavenly Father, a masterful Creator. He created male and female and declared this to be very good. Our wise God established the marriage covenant as a lifelong commitment between a husband and wife, and for the power and beauty of sexual expression to rest securely in this relationship.

A Biblical worldview reminds us that our desires are not the sum total of our identity—just because we *feel* it, doesn't mean we *are* it. Just because we want it doesn't mean we can or should act on it. We aren't called to satisfy the lusts of the flesh as a demonstration of our individuality or authenticity, but to be led by the Spirit of God, keeping our passions and desires in check as we walk in love and faithfulness, in sacrificial service to others.

Through Christ, our attractions, sins and behaviours no longer primarily define us. "The old has passed away, behold all things have become new," Paul wrote in 2 Corinthians 5:17. Our identity is as a son or daughter of God who is being sanctified and conformed to look more and more like Jesus through the work of the Holy Spirit.

I'm reminded of Jesus' words as recorded in Matthew 7:24-27:

"Therefore everyone who hears these words of Mine and acts on them may be compared to a wise man who built his house on the rock. And the rain fell, and the floods came, and the winds blew and slammed against that house; and yet it did not fall, for it had been founded on the rock. Everyone who hears these words of Mine and does not act on them will be like a foolish man who built his house on the sand. The rain fell, and the floods came, and the winds blew and slammed against that house; and it fell—and great was its fall."

Imagine a neighbourhood with a dozen homes lined up, each with a good-sized lot and a decent grassy front yard. The kids play street hockey together on weekends. The adults give a little nod and wave at one another as they head out to work. Over time, relationships grow. Neighbours make small talk about summer holiday plans and remind each other that garbage collection day is shifting because of the long weekend. Work. School. Groceries. Taxes. Hobbies. Everyone living their lives. Above the surface, everything seems the same.

But then a storm comes. The rains fall . . . and keep on falling. Water begins to build up. The soil begins to erode away, exposing the foundation of each of those houses. Any foundations that were not constructed with trustworthy materials are destroyed. The homes are under threat.

This is what Jesus was saying: any life that is built on the philosophies of mankind cannot stand. Because the storms will come. The winds will blow and the rain will fall, but the lives that are built on and fortified by the ideas of God will hold up even under the pressure.

Consider again the neighbourhood in the middle of that storm. As the flood waters rise and the faulty foundations are exposed and eroded, I can picture men, women and children, escaping from the collapsing homes and seeking refuge in whatever structures remain nearby. The homes in the town that were built on sturdy foundations now have the opportunity to provide refuge for the drenched, shaken individuals. It reminds me of the hymn, *My Hope is Built*, written by Edward Mote in 1834:

> *My hope is built on nothing less*
> *Than Jesus' blood and righteousness*
> *I dare not trust the sweetest frame*
> *But wholly lean on Jesus' name*
> *On Christ the solid rock I stand*
> *All other ground is sinking sand.*

As Jesus explained, the storms of life will come against each one of us. The modern philosophies explained in this chapter reject both the idea of objective truth and morality, as well as the loving God who established those realities. Though these trending worldviews may seem bold and alluring, they simply can't offer the reassurance that Christ gives. They are sinking sand.

If we will build our lives on the teachings of Christ—the Christian worldview—we will be able to weather the storms of life. Though our building strategy may be criticized or misunderstood at times, if our homes are built on the love and principles of the kingdom of heaven, they will become the safe places where others can find refuge and learn for themselves how to build a lasting legacy.

With this is mind, let's turn our attention to the real-life way that these ancient truths can inform our everyday home-life and conversations with our children.

THE CONVERSATIONS

6

A CONVERSATION ABOUT THE ROLE OF PARENTS

"Be firm."
"Be gentle."
"Be a steady presence."
"Don't hover."
"Do more."
"Do less."

We are parenting in an era of mixed messages, aren't we? If you visit the parenting section in any local bookstore, you will find a multitude of books, all by experts, none of whom seem to agree with one another. How do we know who to trust?

I love what Jesus said in Luke 7:35, "Wisdom is proved right by all her children" (NIV). He was saying, "Look at the results of a decision or a lifestyle. You'll be able to tell if it is wisdom if the resulting fruit is good."

Even before I was married or had children, and still to this day, when I meet families who have a depth of relationship with one another *and* godly character, I take notes. I ask questions. Ultimately, I want to know, "How did you raise children like that?"

When I ask, most of these parents emphasize some key principles: consistency, prayer, patience, keeping your marriage healthy, being involved in a church community, and relying on the grace of God. If someone were to ask me for advice, I would echo their wisdom. However, I've witnessed another foundational principle at work in each of those beautiful families, and it is imperative for this generation to walk in it: We need to understand our role as a God-ordained authority in the life of our child.

A LESSON OF LEADERSHIP

Authority can be an intimidating word. Very few people hear that word and think of something positive. Perhaps there is a misunderstanding of what authority is, or maybe people have experienced the devastation that comes when leaders abuse their role. Throughout history, power-hungry leaders have caused despair and sometimes great trauma. Not only that, in a world that focuses on free speech, personal rights and self-actualization, the very idea of authority sounds archaic and restricting. The Scriptures prescribe what healthy authority looks like—and they acknowledge times when authority went horribly wrong, in the hopes that we will learn from their mistakes.

Proverbs 29:2 says it this way:

> "When the righteous are in authority and become great, the people rejoice;
> But when the wicked man rules, the people groan and sigh." (AMP)

When we remember that God is the ultimate Lord of all leaders, the King of all kings, we can learn to rest in His sovereign care. Romans 13:1 tells us:

> "Let every soul be subject to the governing authorities. For there is no authority
> except from God, and the authorities that exist are appointed by God."

Our goal should not be to throw out the concept of authority altogether. Instead, we should learn to follow well *and* lead well, wherever God places us.

Each of us is impacted by different types of authority. There are varying levels of authority in government, within our homes, schools, and workplaces. As followers of Christ, we are also called to submit to leaders who have authority within churches. At all times we are invited by God to use our minds and discern which worldviews are being heralded by those in authority, what culture is being formed, and what is being asked of us. If these do not line up with the ultimate authority of the Lord Jesus Himself, we will need to make the difficult choice to obey Him rather than human authorities (Acts 5:29).

When my husband and I were in our early twenties, even before we were married, we both began serving among the youth and the young adults within our local church. After we were married, we led a Sunday School class for ten- to twelve-year-olds and volunteered in a young adult discipleship school at our church. Even with those years of experience, when our lead pastor asked us to consider becoming a part of the eldership team, I was somewhat terrified.

> *"I don't want people to think that I think I'm better than them."*
> *"I don't want people to think that **I think** I have it all together."*
> *"I don't know how to lead people who are older than me!"*

Of course, I was honoured, but I was timid. I knew the verse, "Don't let anyone look down on you because you are young, but set an example for the believers in speech, in conduct, in love, in faith and in purity" (2 Timothy 4:12 NIV). Even so, I was double-guessing my abilities. I see now that I was wrestling with my perception of authority.

One day, I was driving to the gas station in our silver minivan, listening to a sermon podcast. I'll never forget the preacher's explanation of authority because it settled my heart so dramatically. He explained that a good leader's aim is simply *to protect people* and *to empower people*. Immediately, I envisioned a leader's hands, one scooping from below in order to lift people up, and the other hand covering from above, to create a shelter.

I breathed a sigh of relief that day. I genuinely wanted to do both and was committed to learning how to do so. True, righteous authority desires to protect and to empower. When Jesus was discussing this truth with His disciples—young leaders who were all a little power hungry—He told them:

> *"You know that the rulers of the Gentiles lord it over them, and their high*
> *officials exercise authority over them. Not so with you. Instead, whoever*
> *wants to become great among you must be your servant, and whoever*
> *wants to be first must be your slave—just as the Son of Man did not come*
> *to be served, but to serve, and to give his life as a ransom for many."*
> **Matthew 20:25-28 NIV**

As parents, we need to recognize that our God-given role is a call to servanthood and sacrifice, not dictatorship. We are called to empower our children and protect them. Walking in our authority as parents isn't about having certain credentials or experience, but rather it is a combination of:

a) the appointment of God, and

b) the desire to protect and empower.

Here are a few keys that I'd encourage you, as a parent, to remember as you navigate leadership within your home.

1. You are called

Maybe you are at a place where you are questioning your own qualifications or abilities as a parent. Maybe when you were growing up, you didn't have a healthy example of what a parent's role should look like, and so you feel intimidated. Or perhaps you are feeling disqualified because of yesterday's mistakes and failures. If you are a single parent, a step-parent, or a foster parent, that can make things particularly complicated.

No matter where you are at, I want to assure you—*God has appointed you to be the parent of your child.* His heart breaks to see vulnerable little ones without someone there to guide and watch over them. (This is why the Bible includes so many emphatic instructions for God's people to take care of orphans!). We cannot afford to abdicate our role as guardians over the next generation. Our children need us. We are essential to their security and success.

Theologian G.K. Chesterton once said:

"If families will not be responsible for their own children then officials will be responsible for other people's children. The care of all such things will pass into their hands; because there will be nobody else alive to notice such a 'trifle' as a living soul born alive into the world. The total control of human life will pass to the State; and it will be a very totalitarian State." [6]

We are living in a time when cultural messages threaten to undermine our God-given authority as parents. Many are trying to take the responsibility

---

6 G. K. Chesterton, *The Collected Works of G.K. Chesterton,* Volume 37: The Illustrated London News, 1932-1934, ed. Lawrence Clipper and Denis J. Conlon (San Francisco Ignatious Press,1991), 131.

for raising children away from parents, in favour of giving this role to the "professionals" who claim to know better. When parents begin to doubt themselves, believing that they are not equipped for the job, they end up slowly rescinding the role they are called by God to take.

Day-care workers, nannies, school teachers, pastors, coaches, counsellors, school board trustees, medical professionals and politicians can never replace *you* in the life of your child. As parents, we may need to call on these people for support—praise God for individuals who study and serve to that end—but beware of the temptation to relinquish familial authority in the name of submission to external authorities. God *Himself* positioned the father and mother as the leaders of their children, the chief mentors, and the primary role models. Stay firmly planted in that place.

2. You cannot control your children

Our goal is not to use our authority to control our children, but rather to lead them into maturity. Maturity is not about our kids parroting back to us what we've told them or being on their best behaviour while we are watching but rejecting our values as soon as we leave the room. What we want for our kids is for each of them to keep a soft heart, to internalize wisdom, and to fulfill their God-given purpose. In this maturation process, we don't want to manipulate or shame them, but we must disciple them in the way that they should walk.

So, what does it mean to disciple others?

Hebrews 12:5-11 speaks of the discipling process that our heavenly Father undertakes with us, His children. This portion of Scripture helps us understand how the parent-child relationship is designed to work and what the benefits of being under authority are.

> "Have you forgotten the **encouraging words** God spoke to you as his
> children? He said, 'My child, don't make light of the Lord's discipline,
> and don't give up when he corrects you. For the Lord **disciplines those**
> **he loves,** and he punishes each one he accepts as his child.'
> As you endure this divine discipline, remember that God is treating you
> as his own children. **Who ever heard of a child who is never disciplined**

*by its father? If God doesn't discipline you as he does all of his children, it means that you are illegitimate and are not really his children at all . . . God's discipline is always good for us, so that we might share in his holiness. No discipline is enjoyable while it is happening—it's painful! But afterward there will be a **peaceful harvest of right living** for those who are trained in this way." (NLT)*

Discipline is essential for the maturing process in every one of our lives. We all need to be coached and taught in order to experience a harvest of right living and peace!

This is not about using fear tactics or manipulation, neither can we swoop in and rescue our children from the consequences of their own decisions. Not all choices should be rewarded or affirmed. Not all feelings are based in reality. Not all opinions are life-giving. Sometimes the answer must be, "No." No matter how much they fuss or sulk or fume, if we know that something is not good for our children, we must step in to protect them from their own immaturity (Hebrews 5:14). The goal is that they would learn to discern what is *healthy*, what is *loving*, and what is *wise*.

That being said, we are not to control our children, their decisions, or all the outcomes of this journey. What we *can* control are the consequences, opportunities and permissions we provide our children with. These can serve as motivators so that our kids can learn to make healthy decisions. We can unapologetically use our parental place of authority to maintain order, to establish healthy relational boundaries, and to develop a family culture that is enjoyable for everyone.

3. Your example is crucial

Have you heard the old parenting adage, "Do as I say, not as I do."?

This kind of hypocrisy in a leader is a massive stumbling block for us as adults, and it is no different for our kids. We need to ask ourselves, "Do we walk in the principles of honour and submission? Or do we just demand it from our kids for the sake of convenience?"

As parents, we should be modelling submission to our leaders—this means employees to employers, congregants to church leaders, constituents to governors—and speaking respectfully about them (even if we do not agree with them). Then children get a live example to learn from. We can also set an example of speaking honourably about our biological parents (the grandparents), even when the relationship is strained or their lifestyles are not healthy. We do not honour others necessarily because they have earned our respect, but because we are people of honour. We are called to show our kids that we submit to authority figures because of their position, not their perfection.

THE TWO-FOLD GOAL OF PARENTING

I recently flew to Toronto from where we live in western Canada. As a busy mom, I was anticipating a good chunk of time to be alone with my thoughts and to dig into a good book. When a young mom with her baby boy walked down the aisle of the plane and took a seat beside me, I wondered if my expectations were about to be shifted. Sure enough, within moments we were engaged in friendly conversation, first about the joys (and mysteries) of mothering boys, but soon also about faith and Christianity. I was surprised by how openly and eagerly she was asking questions: "What if all these religions are all the same? What if people are just using different names for the same God? What if all paths lead to the same place?"

She emphasized how many religions seemed to be in agreement, in that they were seeking to help make people *good* and to help make the world a better place.

Of course, there is a lot to be said about core differences between religions and their gods—more than I could speak to on that flight, and more than I will address in this book. Sitting there with the young mom and her squirming eight-month-old, a scenario suddenly came to my mind:

"Imagine that your son grows up to become one of the best-educated, most successful men in our country. Imagine that he is influential, wealthy, and a philanthropist. He is healthy and well-liked, surrounded by friends. But, the thing is, he doesn't answer the phone when you call. And he won't come over to your home to have dinner with you. Not at Christmas, not ever. You are estranged from one another. Would that satisfy you?"

I could tell that she was gripped by the suggestion. She replied, "No, of course not!"

I shared with my newfound airplane friend that just as our goal as parents is for our kids to fulfil their potential *and* remain in a loving relationship with us as they mature, so also our heavenly Father desires these two things for us. In fact, psychologically speaking, the former is very difficult to achieve without the latter. Though we barely knew one another, tears spilled from our eyes as we shared that tender, God-ordained moment. We were a couple of moms who were in awe as we considered the idea that God loves *us* even more than we love our own boys.

Near the end of the Gospel of John, we read Jesus' vulnerable instructions to His disciples. He told them:

> *"Abide in Me, and I in you. As the branch cannot bear fruit of itself*
> *unless it abides in the vine, so neither can you unless you abide in Me.*
> *I am the vine, you are the branches; he who abides in Me and I in him,*
> *he bears much fruit, for apart from Me you can do nothing...Just as*
> *the Father has loved Me, I have also loved you; abide in My love."*
> **John 15:4-5, 9**

True maturity, the fruitfulness that Jesus spoke of, comes from remaining deeply connected in relationship with God. This *"abiding"* is about learning to enjoy one another, learning to linger with one another, and naturally, learning to listen to one another. Just as the tallest, strongest trees must be deeply rooted in order to endure and produce fruit of any kind, we too must be securely attached in relationship in order to become who God has called us to be.

Over our seventeen years of parenting, my husband and I have come to realize that having a depth of relationship with our children has longer-lasting and deeper-reaching effects than any consequence or reward system we can invent. When we are spending time with our children, listening to them, asking them questions, playing with them, and hugging them longer than they asked for—that's when we find that our kids are more ready to follow and to trust us. Somehow all the years of indoor Nerf gun battles, deluxe nachos, family movie nights and cramped-in-a-van road trips have translated in their souls as "abiding". Slowly, slowly, *slowly*, the fruit of maturity is growing in their lives. And to be honest, I can't think of a sweeter sight in all the world.

Our influence in the lives of our children is not meant to evaporate when they hit puberty or even when they graduate. We must learn to graciously and gradually transfer more decision-making power to our kids as they are growing up (Lord, help us!), but as parents, we remain in their lives as trusted counsellors, supporting and praying for them as they choose a vocation, start searching for a spouse, and even begin a family of their own.

Of course, our role of authority in their life will have to adapt. We have even spoken with our boys about how one day they may have a calling from God that will bring us, their mom and dad, under their leadership role. It could be a role within the government, city, or church, that we would then need to honour. Their eyes widen to think of such a possibility, but if we truly believe in God's delegated authority, we will have the grace to make that transition.

REFLECTION QUESTIONS

1. What was your childhood experience with authority? Were your parents present and involved? Authoritarian? Overly permissive? What methods did they use that you want to carry forward? What things would you want to exchange for a better way?

2. Do you struggle submitting to the current authorities in your life? What is one thing that you could do differently to model honour to your kids?

3. Are there things in your life that you feel discredit you from standing in your God-given role as a mother or father?

4. Is there anything standing in the way of your ability to *abide* with your children? Is the pace of life too busy? Are there habits of disrespect that hinder vulnerability with one another? Take a moment to consider—what is something you can do this week to communicate your love to your child(ren)?

7

A CONVERSATION ABOUT MEN, WOMEN, AND ROLES WITHIN MARRIAGE

Relationships between men and women are simultaneously some of the most common (in that they are a part of our daily existence) and the most complicated parts of life. Any significant interactions with men or women, especially those that happen in our formative childhood years, will shape our opinion of and resulting behaviour towards men and women. We suspect that our experience is the rule.

I remember speaking with a young woman whose dad left the family when she was very young. She had grown up living with her mom and sister, and shared with me about her hesitation to be around men because she just wasn't used to a masculine presence.

I think of a young man whose relationship with his mom is particularly strained. Because of unhealed trauma from her past, substance abuse and mental health complications, he grew up without a healthy example of feminine strength or beauty in his home.

Then there was the young lady whose father was like the Dr. Jekyll and Mr. Hyde archetype. In front of the congregation he pastored, he demonstrated compassion and conviction, but behind closed doors, his children and wife received his fury and blows. I remember the young woman asking me with disbelief in her voice, "Are you telling me that your husband has never hit you? Not even one time?!"

The reality is that most people have had experiences that mentally tie them up in knots when it comes to masculinity and femininity. In a world that has distorted what it means to be male or female, it is imperative that we as parents do the hard work of aligning our thoughts with God's kind intention for His creation so that we can contribute to healthy interactions and honourable atmospheres within our homes.

CREATING AN ATMOSPHERE OF HONOUR

Years ago I attended a large conference in Calgary, Alberta. Thousands of believers were gathered to worship and listen to the guest speakers as they opened the Scriptures. In one particular session, a seasoned female preacher stood up to share, but she began in an unforgettable way.

She spoke about the way men and women were often at war with one another. She went on to speak of the great respect she had for men and the vital role they played in leading their families, standing as protectors against evil, and giving themselves to what God had called them to. Then she asked the men in the audience to stand.

"Ladies, will you join me in applauding these men and expressing our gratitude for them?"

The room immediately erupted with the sound of cheering female voices and thunderous applause. We did not quiet down for many minutes. The atmosphere after that was tangibly different.

Then the speaker asked the men to take their seats and the women to stand.

She commended these women for trusting in Christ, for the way they sacrificially gave to their families and communities, and for courageously stepping out into their God-given assignments.

"Men, will you join me in applauding these women to express our appreciation of them?"

Instantly, the men began to roar, clapping and cheering. They continued on. And on. And on. The ladies stood, some smiling, others blushing, receiving the blessing of that affirmation.

Even now, years later, tears come to my eyes at the memory of what it was like to be in a room with that much honour. So much of life is lived in the everyday moments, in the common tasks, and even in the monotony of servitude. We can't give out standing ovations and gold trophies every day, but I wonder what it would feel like increase honour by even a few degrees and cultivate an atmosphere like that in our homes?

WE'RE EQUAL, BUT NOT THE SAME

In Galatians 3:27-28, we read:

> *"For all of you who were baptized into Christ have clothed yourselves in Christ. There is neither Jew nor Greek, there is neither slave nor free man, there is neither male nor female; for you are all one in Christ Jesus."*

Unfortunately, this verse has been used to claim that gender differences are eradicated because of what Christ did. But, just as this isn't a directive to ignore ethnic or socio-economic realities, this isn't a call to eliminate male and female. A contextual reading of this verse shows us that we all have equal standing and equal access to our inheritance in Christ. When this letter was written, that claim would have sounded ridiculous! At the time, slaves were not given any rights at all, and women were generally considered inferior. New Testament writers and church leaders boldly confronted these cultural norms, leveling the spiritual playing field for all these social groups by saying that all were of equal value through the work of Jesus.

The question remains, what does it look like for men and women to be equal before God, but different physiologically, divinely equipped for our unique contributions within the home? The scriptures inform us that men and women were never designed to be in competition but to operate as counterparts. We see this in the earliest chapters of the Bible. Together, Adam and Eve were given a blessing and an assignment from God. His heart was that they would work together, sharing dominion over the earth, stewarding its resources, and developing culture and infrastructure.

When we come into the New Testament, the apostle Paul speaks clearly about the inter-dependence of men and women:

> *"... in the Lord, neither is woman independent of man, nor is man independent of woman. For as the woman originates*

> *from the man, so also the man has his birth through the*
> *woman; and all things originate from God."*
> 1 Corinthians 11:11-12

Paul is reminding the Corinthians that as men and women, we need one another. We rely on one another for our very existence. There is no new life without the father's sperm or the mother's egg. Though some may say that "the future is female", logically speaking, the future belongs to both male *and* female ... or to no one at all! Understanding this interdependence is crucial if we are to maintain mutual honour between men and women in our respective God-ordained roles.

GOD-DIRECTED ORDER IN THE HOUSEHOLD

Ephesians 5:22-30 powerfully lays out the ideals that God intended for our marriages and families:

> **"Wives, be subject to your own husbands, as to the Lord.** *For the*
> *husband is the head of the wife, as Christ also is the head of the church,*
> *He Himself being the Saviour of the body. But as the church is subject to*
> *Christ, so also the wives ought to be to their husbands in everything.*
> **Husbands, love your wives, just as Christ also loved the church and**
> **gave Himself up for her,** *so that He might sanctify her, having cleansed*
> *her by the washing of water with the word, that He might present to*
> *Himself the church in all her glory, having no spot or wrinkle or any such*
> *thing; but that she would be holy and blameless. So husbands ought also to*
> *love their own wives as their own bodies. He who loves his own wife loves*
> *himself; for no one ever hated his own flesh, but nourishes and cherishes it,*
> *just as Christ also does the church, because we are members of His body."*

Men and women have each been given a significant measure of authority within their home. Both are called to serve as a righteous leader over their children and over any aspects of household management, growing in their individual gifting and capabilities.

No matter how bold, educated, strong and experienced a woman is, she cannot—and need not try to—escape her feminine assignment. Likewise, no matter how bold, educated, strong and experienced a man is, he cannot—nd need not try to—escape his masculine assignment.

The Role of Women

What are the bounds and responsibilities of a wife? Ephesians 5 says, "Wives, be subject to your own husbands, as to the Lord." This does not read, "Women, submit to every man." Nor does it say, "Wives, be a doormat to your husband."

In our culture, widely impacted by modern feminism, the instruction for women to submit to their husbands can cause the hair on the back of our necks to bristle. But for the believers in Ephesus, immersed in the culture of the Roman Empire, the instruction to husbands to be loving and sacrificial would have been the truly shocking part. From their perspective, wives were considered to be not much more than property—a useful acquisition so that men could gain an heir.

The idea that women should submit was not a new concept, but the instruction that she should be treasured was completely counter-cultural. These days, the church is often accused of being oppressive toward women, but history has shown that wherever the church spread, the status of women has increased!

The Greek word that has been translated in our English Bible as "be subject" or "submit" relates to "ranks and order within the army". It is not that a wife is inferior or has less intelligence; rather, she has been given a different rank and assignment. A wife who submits to her husband is acknowledging that there is something bigger going on. She knows that their marriage is about more than their individual experience; it is a portrayal on earth of the relationship between Christ and the church. Just as Christ is the head of the church and the church is His body, communicating with and receiving direction from the Head, so also a wife's function is designed to flourish in interdependence with her husband.

When I think back to the way the serpent tempted and deceived the first woman, I am surprised by one thing in particular: Why didn't Eve pause in the Garden of Eden to confer with her teammate, her husband—who we read was standing right there with her—about the monumental decision she was about to make?! (Genesis 3:6). When a woman practices yielding her heart to her husband, she is resisting the temptation to act independently. She is modelling the interdependence in marriage that God intended.

The Role of Men

When we look at the bounds and responsibilities of a husband in Ephesians 5, it is easy to conclude that he gets the better part of the deal. After all, he gets to be the "head of the home." But Scripture is emphatic that the responsibility of the head of any home is to be the *head servant*. (Remember the two-fold role of all authority—to protect and empower!) Just as Jesus suffered and sacrificed for His bride, so every man is called to suffer and sacrifice for the sake of his wife. He doesn't get to do whatever he wants. He is called to love His wife as Jesus loves the church.

What does Jesus do for His bride? He speaks words of blessing and encouragement to her, He provides for her, inviting her perspective and participation. He responds to her requests and is relationally available to her. He watches over her spiritual and physical well-being, and He intercedes for her. When a husband does these things, it is not so difficult for his wife to submit.

THE UNIQUE VULNERABILITY OF WOMEN

The Book of 1 Peter holds a fascinating instruction for husbands:

> *"Likewise, husbands, live with your wives in an understanding way, showing honour to the woman as the weaker vessel, since they are heirs with you of the grace of life, so that your prayers may not be hindered."*
> **1 Peter 3:7 ESV**

God clearly values His daughters and holds husbands to a high standard of leadership in the home: live with women in an understanding way and show them honour. If they don't? God warns that their prayers will actually be impeded! But what about the fact that this verse calls women "weaker"? At first glance, this sounds offensive. But what if Scripture is simply pointing out a biological reality and helping men understand how they can respond?

One aspect of being the 'weaker vessel' means that the average woman can't bench press as much as the average man. Because of their higher levels of testosterone, men have roughly sixty percent more muscle mass than women! The biological reality is that most men are physically stronger than most women. Of course, in the presence of cruel or dishonourable men, this leaves women peculiarly vulnerable, but in the presence of God-fearing, honourable men, she remains safe, secure, and valued for who she is.

Another aspect of a woman's physiology that lends to vulnerability is her menstrual cycle. On average, the healthy female will experience the ebbs and flows of hormones for forty years of her life! Her anatomy and corresponding hormones give her the incredible privilege and ability to carry a child in her womb and bring life into the world, but they also contribute to decades of significant challenges.

Ask the average woman how she feels in the first days of her period, and she will admit that she is dealing with physical and emotional weakness. Ask her about her experience with morning sickness in the early months of pregnancy or the days following childbirth while she bleeds and heals and waits for milk to come and fill her breasts. Ask her about the months of nursing a hungry infant or soothing the toddler who cries for her in the night. Ask her about the night sweats of perimenopause. She is well-acquainted with the vulnerabilities of her body, but again, in the presence of an honourable man, she need not be afraid or ashamed of her weakness. She knows that she will be protected and supported. God's directive to a husband is that as the head of the home, he will take his wife's needs into consideration, caring for her throughout their marriage.

Is Chivalry Dead?

For many years, my husband and I were involved in leading the young adult group in our church community. We deeply enjoyed the spontaneous games nights and the evenings spent out on the back deck of our house, chatting about life's mysteries with twenty-somethings under those strings of lights. We loved the worship and prayer gatherings and shared many meals together.

Because we were aiming to cultivate a spirit of honour between the men and women, whenever we hosted meals at our home, whether summertime BBQs or winter-time spaghetti dinners, my husband would announce, when it was time to start piling up our plates along the buffet line: "The food is ready! Ladies, you go ahead and eat first!"

The pattern stuck, and still today when we host large groups, this small gesture remains. You better believe that our sons took notice. One of them, ten years old at the time, asked me, "Mom, if men and women are equal, then why do we always let girls eat first?"

It was such a valid question. This is how I explained it to him:

"Son, you know about how in history women have not always been treated well? For many years, people thought they shouldn't be allowed to vote, or even read. Women have been treated as objects rather than as people. Still today, in many countries, women are treated like slaves. And sometimes, even men who are physically stronger than women don't use their strength to protect girls. So, when you open a door for a lady, or let her go ahead of you in a food line-up, or look her in the eyes and listen to her opinion, it's just a little way of saying that you are going to protect her and respect her, not hurt her or hold her back."

"Anything You Can Do, I Can Do Better"

When I was a little girl, there was a television advertisement that was particularly catchy. I don't remember what the advertisers were trying to sell, but I can clearly recall the jingle. It was a remake of the old song, *Anything You Can Do, I Can Do Better.* Essentially, two characters, male and female, were going back and forth, boasting about their superiority. I thought it was hilarious and soon began singing it around the house.

My mom quickly put a stop to it! She explained to me that we were not going to cultivate competition between men and women. God made us equal, and, as women, we were not to try to belittle men, but to show them respect. Though I stopped singing the song, it took me years to realize the significance of what she was telling me that day.

Men and women are not meant to live in competition but in cooperation. When we understand that God's design for male and female is fundamentally good, we can rest in our own design and begin to honour one another, modelling for our sons and daughters how to do the same.

More is Caught than Taught

Like most married couples, my husband and I have certainly endured a bumpy road as we tried to figure out how to honour God and the Scriptures within our relationship! I have re-read Ephesians 5 countless times during a season of conflict or tension, turning to it with a prayer in my heart: *"Remind me, Lord. Remind me of Your way."*

The day-to-day interactions of a mother and father establish the atmosphere for their children. As the old saying goes, "More is caught than taught." Our kids are watching and absorbing. Do mom and dad prioritize their relationship, giving time, attention and affection to one another? Do they communicate respectfully, or do they undermine one another? Do they humble themselves and ask for forgiveness in the case of offense?

We will never be perfect, and there is no need to feel condemned by our failings, but the hope is that our sons and daughters will be able to witness *growth* in our lives as the Spirit of God leads us, heals us, and transforms us.

Reflection Questions

1. When you were a child or teen, what did you witness as normal behaviour between men and women? Did you see routine competition or animosity between the genders, or did you see cooperation and honour?
2. Have you ever read those verses in Ephesians 5 and 1 Peter 3 about God's ordained order for the family? Was there anything in particular that stood out to you from this chapter on that topic?
3. What is one thing you can do to cultivate greater respect between the males and females in your home?

8

A CONVERSATION ABOUT BOYS AND GIRLS

My husband and I had been married for only three months when we discovered—with great excitement—that we were expecting. We were young but loved the idea of getting started right away on our family! Weeks later, at my first ultrasound appointment with the wand and that blue goopy jelly, pressing on my growing abdomen, the technician raised her eyebrows in surprise, then turned to me and asked, "Did you know about this?"

She adjusted the screen she was looking at to show me what she was seeing—the image of two little skulls and two little bodies. *Twins.*

Not only that, but *identical twins!*

We had decided to keep their sex a surprise until the moment of birth, so Bryan and I were left wondering, "Will they be two boys? Or two girls?"

Thirty-eight weeks into my pregnancy, my water broke and we headed to the hospital. Even after a relatively short labour, the moment of delivery was both a relief and a joy. Two healthy babies! *"Thank you, Lord!"* And immediately the question followed: *"Boys or girls?"*

They were boys!

The first declaration spoken over each human is almost always one of identity—whether we are male or female, son or daughter. When our twins were born, I never would have guessed how contested this concept of binary sexes would become in the years ahead. In much of the Western world this binary declaration of "boy" or "girl" has now been deemed narrow-minded, insensitive, or terribly presumptuous to an individual's self-determination.

I find it intriguing that a growing number of young people are experimenting with the idea that they can alter their gender, or invent a new one altogether, yet at the same time, our youth are reporting high levels of anxiety, depression, and suicidal ideation . . . with mounting evidence that gender reassignment does nothing to solve those issues.

It does not make us hateful or repressive to acknowledge what science has repeatedly confirmed—males and females are different. Not just externally because of our genitalia, but internally as well. Every single cell within our bodies resolutely carries either the XY or the XX chromosomes, and no amount of hormone therapy can undo what God has placed in our DNA. We are created as integrated people, three parts yet one: body, soul, and spirit. Our male-ness and female-ness are not merely a part of this bodily 'earth-suit' that we will one day shed. The sex we are born with is an integral part of our humanity.

With that in mind, I'd like to emphasize three things that we as parents can do to support our child's God-given gender identity.

1. Learn about the biological differences between male and female, and relay that truth to your child

The presence and absence of testosterone and estrogen really does make a difference in the body. Scientists who study mammals around the world can confirm this fact. One study found that female chimpanzees, even in young adolescence, more often opted to cradle and nurture sticks, while male chimpanzees would more likely use those same sticks as tools or weapons. These primates are certainly not prone to social stereotypes but rather are operating according to their biological design, physiology, and impulses.

Another study revealed that male infants, only hours of birth, more often turned to look at mechanical items, while female infants opted to look into the eyes and faces of people into the eyes and faces of people. Those infants were not influenced by social norms or peer pressure. (In this particular study, to prevent their own potential biases from impacting the experiment, the ones administering the test were not privy to the gender of the baby.)

As our children grow, it is fun to be able to teach them about the unique design of men and women in a way that honours the differences. Here are a few features you can share:

- Males' eyes have a higher number of rods in the retina compared to females, making them more capable of tracking movement and slight actions; while females' eyes can more easily differentiate shades of colour. If you ever hear a woman saying, "It's teal, not green!" there's good reason for this. It's because women have a higher number of cones in the retina! When we are watching a hockey game on TV as a family, I laugh because I can barely track the hockey puck, while my boys are calling out who made the assist and what type of shot it was. The rods in their eyes are doing the job!

- Most females have a greater sensitivity to smell, particularly when it is a scent she has experienced before.

- Their higher levels of testosterone mean males have a greater tendency for risk-taking (and experiencing physical thrill from it), whereas the average female is more risk-averse (to the point where the same risks can make them feel nauseous!).

- Females' brains have a higher number of neurological connections between the right and left hemispheres, resulting in greater integration of logic with emotional processing. This leads to what is often coined, 'women's intuition', and it may also lead her to be more easily distracted from a task. Males' brains have a greater number of connections between the frontal and parietal lobes, allowing them to have laser-sharp focus, but also making it more difficult for them to pick up on non-verbal communication.

- Men tend to use the hippocampus portion of their brain for navigating, whereas women are more likely to use their cerebral cortex. This difference accounts for why men tend to prefer cardinal directions and measurable distances, whereas women more often navigate using things that can be tangibly experienced, such as landmarks.

There are many other fascinating differences, and I welcome you to research scientific journals online for yourself! The take-home message is this: talking with our children about the amazing features of male and female bodies is a great way to honour God's good design for us all.

2. Celebrate your child's God-assigned gender

In the beginning, when God created man and woman He declared over them, "It is GOOD." As parents, we are commissioned to echo heaven's sentiment to our children, over and over again. Statements like, "I love that you are a boy," or, "I'm so glad that God made you a girl" set the foundation for self-respect and the ability to embrace who they are, even with all the unique challenges of their gender.

Our family is uniquely blessed with all boys, but I can tell you that there are those who do not share the sentiment that a multitude of boys is a blessing. When they were young, trips to the grocery store or any public place were routinely met by strangers' comments.

> *"Oh! Poor mom! I feel sorry for you!"*
> *"What?! All boys? You must have been trying for a girl."*

Some comments probably came from good-natured people who were just trying to make conversation, but others carried a sting. Regardless of their motivations, I could see the furrowed brows or the twinge of pain in my boys' eyes as they heard these negative sentiments. I always did my best to stand as a shield before them and expressed my joy at having so many sons. Yes, it is a lot of work. Yes, our hands our full. Yes, we understand that they eat a lot. But also, we are grateful to have every single one of them.

Of course, comments can be directed towards girls as well . . . and in some nations, it doesn't end with words. Evidence shows that sex-selective abortions are more common than we may have realized. One article reports:

"A huge analysis of worldwide population data suggests sex-selective abortions have led to at least 23 million fewer girls being born. The majority of these 'missing' girls are in China and India. Many societies value sons over daughters. As people around the world increasingly have fewer children, there has been a rise in families choosing to abort female fetuses in an effort to have at least one son. Normally, 103 to 107 boys are born for every 100 girls. But an analysis has found evidence of an unnatural excess of boys in 12 countries since the 1970s, when sex-selective abortions started becoming available." [7]

Sex-selective abortions are committed against boys too, but not at such a startling rate. There needs to be an adjustment in the hearts of parents everywhere to see that when God said both male and female are *very good*, He meant it.

3. Avoid socially constructed gender stereotypes

A stereotype is defined as "a widely held but . . . oversimplified image or idea of a particular type of person or thing." We have to fight hard to resist oversimplified ideas of what it is to be a man or a woman, while acknowledging that some stereotypes exist because of the natural attributes that are found in males and females around the world and throughout history. For instance, one common stereotype is that boys tend to be more bold, while girls have a tendency to timidity. We can ask ourselves, *"Was this just an idea introduced by a patriarchal society to convince boys to be the leaders and train girls to think that being brave would make them less desirable?"*

In her book, *The Toxic War on Masculinity*, researcher and thought-leader Nancy Pearcey offers some valuable insight:

"Most people do not realize that females are biologically programmed to experience more fear than males. *Research shows the single biggest sex difference in emotions is in the frequency and intensity of fear*, write marriage counsellors Patricia Love and Steven Stosny. *Girls and women both experience and express far more fear, as measured in social contexts and in laboratory experiments*—even experiments with newborns (using a sudden noise to evoke a startle response).

---

7 Debora Mackenzie, "Sex-Selective Abortions May Have Stopped the Birth of 23 Million Girls," New Scientist, April 16, 2019, www.newscientist.com/article/2199874-sex-selective-abortions-may-have-stopped-the-birth-of-23-million-girls/

A greater sensitivity to fear makes biological sense as a survival mechanism because the world is more dangerous for women than for men. Women are physically smaller and weaker, as well as more vulnerable to sexual assault. They are also neurologically programmed to be aware of threats to their children—the Mama Bear. So it is logical that women are more sensitive to fear."[8]

Any woman who is an athlete could tell you that she will have to work significantly harder to get comparable results to the men in her world. That doesn't mean that she is destined for weakness, but that she has natural obstacles to overcome. Similarly, when we understand that science indicates a female's greater tendency towards fear, we can celebrate when she steps out in courage, knowing the greater effort she has had to exert. Conversely, we can celebrate expressions of gentleness in a male, knowing that this doesn't necessarily come naturally to them.

Acknowledging these tendencies or common traits should never place a limitation on our sons and daughters. Traditionally narrow gender stereotypes have led many boys and girls to wrestle with insecurity if they don't fit neatly within our cultural expectations. In a 2024 article entitled *The Data Behind Gender Stereotypes*, writer and journalist Ilana Reimer explains:

"We are not lopsided beings, with only some traits available to us. Training, formation, and personal choices all contribute to developing our best selves and helping us fulfill individual vocations. Perhaps then, it is factually incorrect to call a girl a tomboy or encourage a man to get in touch with his feminine side. A man who patiently comforts his crying child is not showing motherly instincts, but fatherly ones. A woman who takes charge of a crisis and directs others how to respond is not showing a kind of male assertiveness, but a female one. Thinking this way affirms the full range of emotions and skills women and men are capable of."[9]

8 Nancy R. Pearcey, The Toxic War on Masculinity: How Christianity Reconciles the Sexes (Grand Rapids, MI: Baker Books, 2023), p 235

9 Ilana Reimer, "The Data Behind Gender Stereotypes," Substack, April 17, 2024. https://ilanare-imer.substack.com/p/data-behind-gender-stereotypes

As parents, we need to be able to walk a fine line, respecting innate differences between male and female while not succumbing to the unique cultural pressures we face in our generation.

STEREOTYPES THAT MEN FACE

What does it mean to be a man? One of the characteristics of stereotypical masculinity is that he must be rough-and-tumble. The phrase "a man's man" is held up as an ideal, and those who don't fit into that mold can be made to feel inadequate. If a guy doesn't want to hunt or chug beers and throw a football around, then he is considered less manly. For some boys, being an artist, designer, or musician would result in rejection from their peers or even from their own father. Boys who are more reserved or less competitive may even be called "mama's boys".

It's interesting to consider that in centuries past, men have been greatly respected for their artistic ability. In the Old Testament, there was great honour given to the artisans who crafted the tabernacle and temple, and to the musicians who served there—the majority of whom were male. King David, a key figure in Israel's history, was heralded as an excellent leader. The biblical account tells us that David knew how to show up on the battlefield, but that he also knew how to hide away with an instrument, pouring his passionate emotions out in song.

During the Renaissance, artists like Leonardo da Vinci and Michelangelo impacted the world with their skills. We look back on them with respect, even veneration, and yet somehow over the years, culture has developed limiting archetypes that we expect all men to fit into. Boys who love to paint or write or compose music are at risk of feeling like they are stepping into a feminine domain. But we need to be careful not to swing too far. We also need to show respect for any son who desires a physically laborious job, like a framer, a farmer, or a mechanic. The real measure of manliness is not in his hobbies or career choice but in the content of his character.

Jesus is the ultimate example for men to follow. He came to earth and modelled an amazing combination of gentleness, self-sacrifice, servanthood, and boldness. Being a man means using one's strengths to protect and support the people around him. This definition of masculinity makes room for every variety of personality and passion.

STEREOTYPES THAT WOMEN FACE

What does it actually mean to be a woman? Is it about her sex appeal, personality, or domestic aspirations? Often, if a girl exerts leadership, she is labeled as bossy. If she is bold or speaks her mind, she can be called a 'know-it-all'. Traditionally, there are certain activities that are considered girl-typical, but what if your daughter would rather dissect insects or collect rocks than play with dolls? What if she is an entrepreneur who is always coming up with business ideas, or an athlete who loves to spend time on the soccer field?

Because of narrow stereotypes, these kinds of passions can make her feel like something is wrong with her, as though she isn't as 'good at being a girl' as her peers. So much work has been done in the past decades to normalize these types of expression, but quickly rising ideologies suggest that if a girl expresses that she "feels different", this could be an indication that her biology is misaligned to her "true gender".

The Bible shows us that variety in female personalities, preferences and vocations is God-ordained. For instance, in the Old Testament, Judges chapter 4 highlights a woman named Deborah who was honoured for her incredible leadership ability. She was a married woman who served her people as a judge. As a protective 'mother' over the people of Israel, she was not seen as power-hungry. Instead, she was honoured for the way she rose up when the nation was under threat, fulfilling her mandate as a leader and labouring for the betterment of others.

Throughout history we can read of other influential women who sacrificed personally for the sake of reform, serving the needs of nations. Harriet Tubman was one such woman. In the mid-1800s, after escaping from slavery, she planned and executed thirteen rescue missions, served as a spy for the Union Army during the Civil War, and was honoured as the first woman in the United States to lead an armed military operation.

Florence Nightingale is another example. In the mid-nineteenth century, she shocked her affluent family when she refused a marriage proposal and rather chose to serve as a nurse, caring for the wounded soldiers of the Crimean War. Her emphasis on hygiene and sanitation saved lives and ended up revolutionizing the medical world! To this day, awards are granted in her name to medical professionals who show exceptional courage and devotion.

These women did not fit into the cultural expectations for women in their day but used their God-given passion and abilities to fill a desperate need in the world.

LOOKING BEYOND STEREOTYPES

God has a unique calling for each of our kids. In Ephesians 2:10 we read,

> *"For we are God's handiwork, created in Christ Jesus to do good works, which God prepared in advance for us to do." (NIV)*

As parents, we would do well to ask God for wisdom. "What is the pathway that You have intended for our child? How can we guide them and give them opportunities to grow?"

We get to be in the front row of our children's life, cheering them on as they step into God's purposes for their lives. As they face pressure regarding their male-ness or female-ness, we are the hopeful voice countering the messages of our culture. "How God made you is very good! There is nothing wrong with you! We love who you are!"

In future chapters, we will look deeper into the complex issues surrounding transgenderism, ensuring we are ready for honest conversation with our kids about the unique challenges of their God-given sex, encouraging them to trust our Creator, and praying that they will see the great glory in their masculine or feminine design.

REFLECTION QUESTIONS

1. When you were growing up, did you feel like you fit into the stereotypical norms for your gender? If not, how did that make you feel? Did anyone particularly support you in your unique interests, or did you face embarrassment? Please take a moment and invite the Lord into that situation and consider what He might say to you about that circumstance.

2. Are you able to recognize the difference between God-given boundaries for males and females, and those that society has invented? Is there something you still need to pray about, search the Scriptures on, or get counsel about?

3. Is there something you can do or say this week to affirm your child's God-given gender as male or female?

9

A CONVERSATION ABOUT DELAYED GRATIFICATION

Because our identical twin boys and our third son were born within only a year and a half of each other, it meant that all three of them were in varying stages of potty training at the same time. An experienced mom warned me, "If you try to potty-train kids before they are ready, all you are doing is training *yourself* to be in charge of their bladder!" She was right. Even when my boys showed interest in using the potty like Mom or Dad, if they couldn't unzip their pants and get up on the toilet by themselves, I was still the one sliding across the kitchen floor, running to plop them on the seat.

Even when our children were certifiably out of diapers, all the celebratory ice cream had been eaten, and we were rejoicing at how much money we were going to save each month on those bulk-sized packs of diapers and wipes, there was still a window of time when we, the parents, were a little bit on edge. Before we headed out the door for a trip to the playground, we'd still find ourselves asking the boys,

"Do you need to go potty?"

"Not even a little?"

"How 'bout we just empty out, okay?"

A drive across town had me nervously looking in the rear-view mirror at my toddlers, wondering if we'd make it in time.

At this point, our youngest son is four. There are still occasional accidents, but the adrenaline rush of an average outing is nothing like it used to be. As these kids are growing up, they are increasingly able to govern their own impulses and natural functions. They are learning to control themselves—in more ways than one.

In a previous chapter, we talked about the way our parental authority is essential in supporting the maturation process. Part of that maturity is growing in self-governance. In Galatians 5:22-23, the apostle Paul instructs:

> *"The fruit of the Spirit is love, joy, peace, patience, kindness, goodness, faithfulness, gentleness, **self-control**; against such things there is no law."*

How wonderful that even though God is all-powerful and all-knowing, He doesn't desire to control us. Instead, He gives us His Spirit to lead us and help us learn to walk in *self*-control. Similarly, as parents, our hope should be that our kids will learn to be internally guided by wisdom, rather than being externally restrained by fear of consequences.

THE EFFECT OF SELF-CONTROL IN OUR LIVES

One element of self-governance that we need to teach our children is that *no one gets whatever they want, whenever they want.* Some of our desires can never be fulfilled, while others will come to pass only after waiting, sometimes for months, other times for years. The adult or child who has yielded to this reality will have a significantly greater amount of peace in their life. Some scenarios are simply outside of their power to change. The sooner our children accept this, the fewer 'temper tantrums' they will have. And goodness, there are certainly still adults who know how to throw a fit, aren't there? Silent treatment, road rage, shopping sprees, food and alcoholic indulgences can all be adult versions of a temper tantrum.

When our children are young and demand a snack, their hunger may be real, but for the most part, asking a preschooler to wait twenty minutes until dinner time is not cruel or unreasonable. If anything, it is a real-time demonstration of the fact that waiting is not the same thing as dying. Through patient endurance, they will inherit the promise! (Hebrews 6:12)

I remember when one of our sons was six-years old. He'd been given some money to spend on whatever he liked. It was as if the money was burning a hole in his pocket! Every day for an entire week, he begged me to take him to the store so he could spend some of his money on a specific toy that he had his mind on. His desire was real. And he made his requests known.

On Monday, when I told him "no", he whined. I told him we'd work on a plan. On Tuesday when I told him "no", he cried and accused me of not loving him. I held firm. It simply would not work to go that day. On Wednesday morning when I told him "no", he sighed, but yielded. I told him the plan: *Dad would take him at the end of the week.*

Through that week, our son discovered that delayed gratification would not kill him. Temper tantrums did not get him what he wanted, but patience and trust carried him through to Friday, when, sure enough, off he and his dad went to the store.

As our boys mature, their desires will mature too. When they are teenagers, they will no longer cry for candy or new Transformers action figures. I anticipate that they will naturally begin to desire companionship, sexual expression, and intimacy with a woman. The desires are good, but timing and setting are everything. It's in the early years that we set a foundation for life, reminding them that *nobody gets whatever they want, whenever they want.*

In his book "Mere Christianity", C.S. Lewis wisely explained:

> "Every sane and civilized man must have some set of principles by which he chooses to reject some of his desires and to permit others. One man does this on Christian principles, another on hygienic principles, another on sociological principles. The real conflict is not between Christianity and nature, but between Christian principles and other principles in the control of 'nature'. For 'nature'…will have to be controlled anyway, unless you are going to ruin your whole life." [10]

The reality is, not all of our desires are good or healthy. Sometimes we're tempted by things that could absolutely devastate us if we give them access in our lives. Yet many people today believe that if a person desires something, it would be inauthentic for them to deny themselves.

---

10 C.S. Lewis, *Mere Christianity*. New York: HarperCollins, 2001. p. 58.

Proverbs 25:28 (NLT) says, "A man without self-control is like a city broken into and left without walls."

Think about the role that city walls had in ancient times. Yes, walls were for protection from enemy armies, but they also served as a checkpoint through which the imports and exports of the city passed. A handful of gates provided access to the city, with line-ups of travellers seeking to come in or get out. The city without a wall was a city that could not regulate the comings and goings. It was vulnerable to unauthorised and potentially harmful influences.

The man, woman, or child who does not have self-control is like a city without walls. Without personal boundaries, they are susceptible to indulging in practices that will cause brokenness and shame.

THE EFFECT OF SELF-CONTROL ON OTHERS

One of the first portions of the Bible that I coached our boys to memorize is found in Philippians 2:3-7:

> *"Don't be selfish; don't try to impress others. Be humble, thinking of others as better than yourselves. Don't look out only for your own interests, but take an interest in others, too. You must have the same attitude that Christ Jesus had. Though He was God, He did not think of equality with God as something to cling to. Instead, He gave up His divine privileges; He took the humble position of a slave and was born as a human being."*
>
> **Philippians 2:3-7 NLT**

I love that line: *Be humble, thinking of others as better than yourselves.* Over the years, we have often asked this question in our home, "Who is most important?" It is technically a trick question, because the answer is "everyone". Regardless of someone's age, gender, ethnicity, religious or political views, wealth, capabilities or appearance, Jesus considers each of us as "most important". He doesn't call us to degrade ourselves or become doormats, but to love people and lift them up. Sometimes, this means denying or delaying our own desires.

As parents, we want our kids to treat others with respect, remembering that each of us has been made in the image of God (Genesis 1:27). We should consider others and love them, remembering that every person is worthy of dignity.

This truth about the intrinsic worth of every human being is useful in defusing fights about who gets to hold the remote or who has to pick up the toys. It also has the strength to dismantle damaging cultural trends, such as we find in the pornography industry or sex trafficking.

Both pornography and trafficking rely on a base of consumers who do not consider the fundamental worth, personhood, rights, or well-being of those caught up in the industry. These consumers are often unaware of the wider issues. Generally, they are only focusing on what they can get for themselves in that moment. The porn stars and trafficked victims, men and women alike, never dreamed of the torturous lifestyle they are trapped in. I can guarantee you that as little boys and girls they did not hope to be objectified, wanted only for their sexual performances or physical appearance. Statistically, most of the victims are self-medicating with substance abuse, numbed out, in order to survive.

By teaching our children that *nobody gets whatever they want, whenever they want,* and that *we are all 'most important',* we are empowering our children to become defenders of the weak instead of siding with the oppressors.

When it comes to sexuality and relationships, we all need self-control. It is the muscle that allows us to refuse crude joking or sensual entertainment. It gives us the strength to walk in sexual chastity before marriage and then faithfulness to our spouse within marriage. It even gives us the mental fortitude to resist fleeting thoughts and temptations that try to distort our personal identity.

As parents, we are leading our children towards self-governance, one day, one conversation at a time. At the same time, we as the adults are determining to live with integrity, setting an example as those who walk, not according to the desires of our flesh, but by the leading of the Holy Spirit. Because no one gets whatever they want, whenever they want it—not even us.

REFLECTION QUESTIONS

1. How can that concept of "nobody gets whatever they want, whenever they want it" apply to your own life as an adult? If you had to evaluate your own patience and self-control on a scale of 1 to 10 (with 10 being best), what would you say?

2. Are you comfortable saying "no", setting boundaries for your children and allowing them to sit in discomfort or disappointment? If they are young children or even in their teen years, do you cave under the pressure of various kinds of "temper tantrums"?

3. What is the atmosphere in your home like? Is everyone shown equal respect, regardless of their age, gender, or ability? What is one thing you could work on to improve your home's culture of respect?

10

A CONVERSATION ABOUT BODY PARTS AND MODESTY

In the youngest of our sons and daughters, we catch glimpses of the innocence that Adam and Eve had in the garden. Toddlers have no problem being naked and unashamed! They usually don't mind stripping down or running nude after a bath. There's a delightful naivety regarding their bodies. Of course, this allows us as parents to care for them in practical ways, unhindered by unnecessary shame, but the day soon comes when self-consciousness kicks in. They ask us to close the door so they can get changed or go to the bathroom. After a shower, they wrap a towel around their little body and call out, *"Don't look!"* They have noticed that not everyone is walking around naked, and now they are thinking that maybe they don't want everyone seeing them in their entirety either.

What part of covering up our bodies comes from a natural sense of modesty, and what part comes from 'body shame' or a fear of ridicule? It is a question we can each ask ourselves, and one that we need to guide our kids through as they grow.

CELEBRATE GOD'S GOOD DESIGN

Let's start by talking about what it means to have a healthy body image. There are some aspects of our appearance that we can do something about, and that we must therefore take responsibility for. I am regularly reminding our boys, "You only get one body for your entire life! Take good care of it!" But there are also plenty of physical characteristics that simply come down to our genetic code. Every single human could find something to complain about in that regard. When I see a photo of my side profile, I am still surprised by how pointy my nose is! Others moan about how their ears stick out, how tall they are, the size of their legs, the colour of their hair, or the freckles sprinkled over their face. The lesson of accepting yourself can be a hard one to learn.

When I was around seventeen years old and had a steady part-time job, I decided to use some of my paycheck on a monthly membership at a gym. I found that I really enjoyed the exertion of getting on a treadmill and lifting some weights. Prior to this, I had never done anything beyond occasional walks and hikes with friends. After a few months of consistency at the gym, I began to see results and was in better shape than ever before in my life. Oddly enough, at the same time, my self-esteem was plummeting! It didn't make sense to me!

I had the presence of mind to invite Holy Spirit's counsel into the situation. "Why am I suddenly dealing with so much insecurity?" I prayed. Within moments, a clear response surfaced in my mind.

The fitness magazines.

I knew what the Lord was pointing out. When I began working out, I also began habitually flipping through female health and fitness magazines from the gym. Every time I walked on the treadmill, I pored over articles, learning how to make my body look more like the model posed on the front cover.

"Oh yeah. My calves could use some work."
"I wonder if I could get my abs to look like that?"
"Next week I'll add some reps to build up my glutes."

I thought I was finding inspiration, but I was actually unlocking the door to insecurity through comparison.

The kind conviction of the Holy Spirit guided me to abandon those magazines. If I wanted an education in fitness, I'd have to find it another way. To this day, whenever I work out at the gym, I use the time to listen to Scripture or worship music—something that will spiritually build me up and remind me that exercise is more about stewarding my body and cultivating health than about keeping an appearance.

Even though I overcame that obstacle as a teen, it wasn't until I was in my late twenties that I was finally able to find rest in God's diverse creative expression. He made us all different on purpose. We do not need to despise our genetic predisposition! I remember seeing a female friend of mine in a new light as she walked up to me one day. She has a naturally long and lean frame, and in that moment, I suddenly realized, "No matter how much I work out or watch over my nutrition, my body will never look like that!" And that is more than okay.

Psalm 139:14-15 reminds us of God's intentional and personal design of every one of us:

> "I will give thanks to You, because I am awesomely and wonderfully made; wonderful are Your works, and my soul knows it very well. My frame was not hidden from You when I was made in secret, and skillfully formed in the depths of the earth."

As parents, when we are comfortable in our bodies, we are modelling confidence to our children. Growing up in a culture that worships "flawless" bodies, our kids will still have their own battles to face, but we can teach them to recognize the poisons of comparison and envy. We can help them discern which entertainment sources, social media content, or relationships will only fuel insecurity.

Our attitude toward food and exercise will also impact body image and the environment of our homes. Do we punish ourselves when it comes to food? Or do we turn to food to avoid processing our emotions? God is inviting all of us to govern over our appetites, to give our bodies the fuel they need to be strong, and to enjoy good food with gratitude (1 Timothy 4:4).

The same applies to physical activity. Do we avoid it at all costs? Or does shame drive us to work out harder and harder, pushing for greater visible results? When we look in the mirror, do insults flood our minds? Do we say of ourselves what He says of us? That we are made in His image, that we are His valuable children? God reminds us in 1 Corinthians 6:19-20 that our body is a dwelling place (a temple) of the Holy Spirit. We are called to glorify God *with our body*, and this includes stewarding our health, doing the best we can with our abilities in our season of life. He doesn't insult us to motivate us or shame us towards strength. He motivates and leads us with kindness. As we celebrate and steward our bodies, we are showing our kids how to live beyond the cultural pressures that surround them.

TALKING ABOUT 'PRIVATE PARTS'

As we recognize the goodness of God's design, it is important to note that in very young children, though their genitalia are indicative of their sexual identity, they are not yet mature to the point of having a sexual function. As parents, we often project our awareness of genital function to our kids, and this can make us feel awkward. It's reassuring to know that our toddlers aren't thinking like us at all! God granted children this precious innocence. They are *female*—but not sexualized. They are *male*—but not sexualized. This is why they can so easily be "naked and unashamed". They are blissfully unaware.

As they start to grow up, however, they will naturally become more conscious about their bodies, including their genitals. We want to make sure our kids know that these parts are not for everyone's eyes—but that just because they are *private*, doesn't mean that they are *bad*. Every single inch of a child's body was designed by God, and we do not want to attach a dirty connotation to it.

God didn't blush or laugh when he gave Adam a penis and scrotum, nor when He gave Eve her vagina, vulva, and breasts. Instead, when He gave them each a gloriously functional anatomical design, He called them "good". We don't give nicknames to our ankles or triceps, so why should we avoid the accurate names for our private parts? Too often, the slang words we use carry a sense of crudeness or shame, when what we really want to do is communicate honour.

As our kids begin to ask questions about their anatomy, let's speak encouragement and blessing about our children's bodies—from head to toe!

THE MYSTERIOUS 'OTHER'

Children are naturally curious—and maybe more so if they do not have opportunities to see what the private parts of the opposite sex look like (as in the case of having a young sibling who they see in the bath or having their diaper changed). I think every one of our boys has asked me if I have a penis! When I told them *no*, they inevitably asked, "Then what *do* you have?" They were asking for biological information, so that is what I gave them.

I encourage you to use accurate terminology with very young children, but also to include simple terms that can describe function. You could tell a little girl that, "Boys have a penis, which is kind of like a hose with a little hole in it that empties the pee out of a boy's body." You could tell your son, "Girls have a vulva, which has a hole in it, like a tunnel inside her that opens up to let pee out." You may also want to draw a simple sketch so that they can understand the concept. (Personally, I wouldn't use Google or an internet search with my children. I'd rather get the information for myself and pass it on.)

As awkward as it is to face their questions, let's be glad when our children come to us! As the child gets older and begins to ask about sexual intercourse, pregnancy and childbirth, they will certainly need more specific information, but I've found that the questions in the early years have more to do with "pee and poop" than with sexuality or the reproductive system!

When Children Touch Themselves

Before having kids I didn't realize how common it was for young children to touch their private parts! When our young boys would inevitably reach for their genitals, we learned to light-heartedly say to them, "Yes, that is your penis! God gave that to you to take care of. You're going to grow to be a great man!"

A more experienced mom once shared with me about how she responded when her young kids would touch their private parts. She linked touching their private parts to the possibility of a need to go to the bathroom. Before kids start potty training, their bulky diapers often prevent the habit, but once they are in undies, the habit can begin to develop. At this point, if I saw my children touching their private parts, I would simply ask, "Oh! Did you have to go potty?"

For the most part, I've found this gentle question brought them enough awareness to stop the action without implying shame. If a child continued to touch their genitalia even as they got older, I explained how that could naturally draw other people's attention to their private parts, and I knew that wasn't what they wanted! Our goal isn't to shame our kids about these parts of their body, but we want to help them build self-restraint. Just because it feels pleasurable doesn't mean it is the right time or setting.

THE WEIRD STUFF THAT KIDS DO

I recently initiated a giant rearrangement of bedrooms and roommates amongst all the boys.

Every one of our six boys loaded up their belongings into bags, boxes and laundry baskets. We cleared out closets, we cleaned under beds, we wiped dusty baseboards. (Okay, let's be real. I was the only one who wiped baseboards). But let me tell you—we found weird things. Because kids do weird things for weird reasons. Random items in random places.

"How long has this been here?" I wondered, sweat on my brow as I madly sorted.

A fork. A screwdriver. A dirty sock with a gaping hole in the heel. A half-empty can of flat, "sparkling" water that our four-year old had tucked away "for later". And so much LEGO in places LEGO need not be.

The point is that sometimes, kids do weird stuff, and when you ask them "Why did you do that?" they really have no reasonable answer. If you are a parent, you know that this principle applies to more than just dirty socks and LEGO. Sometimes kids will say things and do things that we understand to have a sexual connotation, but they actually have no clue. It's not lust informing their choices—it's curiosity. Depending on their age, this is a great chance to coach them towards appropriate behaviour and language.

Many adults today are dealing with a subtle sense of shame because of the "weird" things they can vaguely recall from their own childhood. I'm not even talking about anything illegal or predatory—just interactions that may have happened between siblings or friends—where the children involved had no idea that what they were doing was sexually inappropriate.

Yet, because we are integrated beings, when that physical boundary is crossed, a sense of shame descended like a fog. The temptation, even from a young age, is to keep that 'weird' experience a secret.

Even though you could not have understood the full ramifications of your actions at the time, I want you to know that God made a way for you to be free from the sense of shame that you've been carrying. Just like a parent who is sorting through the toy bins or the dresser drawers, God wants to help you sort through what you can take responsibility for and what was only the naivety of a child.

Honest Talk About Masturbation

Because God designed sexual experiences to be pleasurable for both men and women, the parts of the body that are designed for sex are loaded with additional nerve endings. Many kids will figure this out on their own; a large number of them will touch their private parts long before they go through puberty. At a young age, this behaviour is rarely sexual in nature (though it can be an indication of early exposure or abuse, which is good for parents to be aware of).

The Scriptures do not explicitly say 'thou shalt not masturbate', leaving room within the Christian community for debate and conversation on the matter. Is masturbation intrinsically connected with lust, or is it just a natural function of the body that happens to feel good? We know where Jesus stands on the matter of lust—Matthew 5:27-28 says,

> "You have heard that it was said, 'You shall not commit adultery.'
> But I tell you that anyone who looks at a woman lustfully has
> already committed adultery with her in his heart." (NIV)

That sounds pretty clear. Jesus cares a lot about what is happening in the hearts and minds of men and women. Lust is a hunger that dishonours others, reducing them to an object for our 'consumption'. Any activity that stirs up lust in our hearts is a no-go in the kingdom of God.

But what about a young child who tries it out of curiosity or a preteen who begins masturbating simply out of boredom? Is *that* 'wrong' or sinful? In the case when no lust is involved, rather than asking a 'right or wrong' question, we would do better to ask if masturbation—as a 'feel-good' anatomical function—is 'wise or unwise'.

The truth is that though modern 'experts' have sought to normalize masturbation—and have even introduced curricula into schools to teach elementary children how to do it in the name of 'sexual self-care'—masturbation almost always leads to complications and confusion later in life. Here are a few scenarios that we as parents can be aware of as we help our kids navigate the matter of masturbation.

1. Recognize that masturbation is often used as a coping or escape mechanism

In recent years, we've heard many stories from young adults—male and female alike—who said that as a child, they would touch their genitalia as a form of self-comfort in times of anxiety. Most people say that they didn't even know what this action was called or that it was connected to their sexuality at all—it just felt good. Yet, they still felt shame about it, didn't know how to stop, and most wished that a parent had initiated a conversation about it, because they had no idea how to bring up the topic. One young woman told me that when she was a little girl, the atmosphere in her home was often hostile. As she lay in bed at night listening to her parents yell at one another, she would use masturbation to find comfort and tune out the situation happening downstairs.

In these kinds of cases, we want to help our kids in two ways: by doing our best to establish atmospheres of peace in our homes, and by normalizing conversations about tough emotions.

Stress and frustration are inevitable in all of our lives; if we don't find a way to access and process those feelings, pressure will build up. And when that pressure stays high, with no healthy outlet, some choose masturbation as a distraction. The problem is that it builds a neurological pathway of escapism, masking the deeper needs and fears that our heavenly Father wants to heal.

I'm often surprised by the level of emotional intelligence that my kids and teens are capable of—but it is a skill that has been cultivated. As parents, Bryan and I intentionally made room for their emotions by regularly asking, "How is your heart doing?", "What is the deeper issue here?", or "How does that make you feel?" Sometimes all of us sit together around the dining room table, processing sorrow or conflict. Other times it'll be in a one-on-one conversation, leaning against the kitchen island late into the evening, helping our teens find language—and their tears, if necessary—to express their emotions about a situation.

2. Be alert to the addictive nature of masturbation

Because having an orgasm dumps a load of dopamine—the pleasure hormone—into the brain, a child may feel better during masturbation. But this same hormonal pleasure can also lead to an all-consuming habit that is hard to break. What may have started in a moment of boredom, can easily become an obsession.

There are many ways to get a dopamine release—eating delicious food, exercising, spending time with good friends, and labouring to achieve goals. However, we can also get a hit of dopamine through junk food, gambling, scrolling on social media, video games, drinking alcohol, or binge-watching a TV show. In our house, we've started a saying: "Work hard for your dopamine". It's a reminder that not all dopamine is equal. It is better to seek that pleasure hormone by engaging in healthy activities that enable us to develop into well-rounded people, free from addictions.

3. Communicate the relational obstacles that masturbation can establish in the future

People who are accustomed to 'taking care of their own sexual needs' will generally be less motivated to pursue sexual interdependence with a partner. There are already plenty of obstacles that husbands and wives have to overcome in order to find rich fulfillment in the bedroom. Masturbation (which is often accompanied by fantasy or pornographic content) only complicates the situation and erodes trust further. God designed sexual pleasure to be experienced within the giving-receiving relationship of a marriage. Self-focused pleasure-seeking distorts this sacred space of mutuality.

If we want to protect our children from the shame and addictive power of masturbation, then we need to keep the door open for honest conversation, asking them questions and sharing about having a greater vision for restraint.

THE NATURE OF 'MODESTY'

When we are talking about body parts and body image, the topic of modesty inevitably comes up. In our current culture, this topic can be a bit of a minefield. If all we talk about are 'rules', the issue becomes polarizing, but when we talk about the principles, we can more readily agree.

I'm surprised by how mad people can get about this topic. Some rage against the not-so-distant era of 'purity culture' in churches that perpetuated body shame and wreaked havoc in so many people's sexual relationships. Others call for no restraint, no parameters around modesty at all.

I assure you that we are not going to go anywhere near those damaging messages. The reality is, modesty should never have been framed as just a women's issue. We must remember that true modesty is not about measuring how many inches of skin are showing. It is about carrying oneself in such a way that is not attention-seeking or pretentious. There are those who are covered from head to toe yet have a seductive demeanour that is silently yelling, "LOOK AT ME!"

Modesty comes from a heart that is quietly confident. It's the opposite of showmanship. Again, it comes down to what is appropriate in the setting. It would be as "immodest" to wear full-body scuba gear to a wedding as it would be to wear a three-piece suit to the beach. Both options create only one outcome—to draw excessive attention to the person. It might create a funny moment, but technically, it would not be modest. In our culture of egocentric behaviour, we want to help our kids find the balance of showing up fully themselves, yet not hogging the limelight.

Just as I'm not willing to give the general public access to the most vulnerable, private parts of my heart, I also am unwilling to give the general public access to all of the vulnerable, private parts of my body—not because they are *shameful,* but because they are *valuable* to me.

GUARDING OUR CHILDREN'S INNOCENCE

When our children are very young, they are naive to matters of sexuality. Even after they have learned the facts about where babies come from, they are still experientially innocent, and rightfully so. God has commissioned us as parents to be guardians over our kids, protecting their innocence. Some parents may argue that because sexuality is a *natural* part of life, it is reasonable to expose children to sexual content. Some would even say 'the earlier, the better'.

I'm reminded of a conversation I read in *The Hiding Place*, by Corrie Ten Boom, where she described the close relationship she had with her father in the early 1900s. It is a reminder that some things in life—though natural—are complex and heavy, unsuited for young ones.

> "Once, I must have been ten or eleven, I asked father about a poem we had read at school the winter before. One line had described 'a young man whose face was not shadowed by sexsin'. I had been far too shy to ask the teacher what it meant, and Mama had blushed scarlet when I consulted her. In those days just after the turn of the century sex was never discussed, even at home.
>
> So the line had stuck in my head. 'Sex', I was pretty sure, meant whether you were a boy or a girl, and 'sin' made Tante (Aunt) Jans very angry, but what the two together meant, I could not imagine. And so, seated next to Father in the train compartment, I suddenly asked, "Father, what is sexsin?"
>
> He turned to look at me, as he always did when answering a question, but to my surprise he said nothing. At last, he stood up, lifted his traveling case from the rack over our heads, and set it on the floor. "Will you carry it off the train, Corrie?" he said. I stood up and tugged at it. It was crammed with the watches and spare parts he had purchased that morning.
>
> "It's too heavy," I said.
>
> "Yes," he said. "And it would be a pretty poor father who would ask his little daughter to carry such a load. It's the same way, Corrie, with knowledge. Some knowledge is too heavy for children. When you are older and stronger you can bear it. For now you must trust me to carry it for you."

And I was satisfied. More than satisfied, (I was) wonderfully at peace. There were answers to this and all my hard questions. For now, I was content to leave them in my father's keeping."[11]

In our culture today, girls and boys are inundated by sexualized content, often accidentally. Media, music, and advertisements intended for an adult audience somehow slip through. Around the world, some schools are racing to introduce mature vocabulary and concepts through sex-ed curriculum and literature—all in the name of education.

Many parents are feeling the tension. They long to 'carry the heavy knowledge' for their kids for as long as possible, but they also want to tell them about God's design before the culture feeds them distorted information laced with an agenda. This is where we must turn our hearts towards each of our children, praying for wisdom regarding the specifics of what to share—and when.

We need to be alert to the content our children are exposed to, but protecting their innocence has to do with more than filtering content, though we will address that further in an upcoming chapter. Recent statistics in Canada show that before age eighteen, one in four girls and one in six boys will experience sexual molestation or abuse. We do not need to live afraid, but these statistics serve as reminders of why we want to be alert regarding in-person and online dangers, watching out for those who would exploit our children's vulnerability.

Here are some practical things we can do to guard their innocence:

1. Always accompany young children to the bathroom when in public places

As they age, you may not always be the one going in with them, but don't send them into public bathrooms alone. Have an older sibling or a caregiver that you trust go with them.

---

11 Ten Boom, Corrie, John Sherrill, and Elizabeth Sherrill. *The Hiding Place.* New York, NY: Bantam, 1971.

2. Encourage young children to have discretion about how they dress, sit, or play

As we model this lifestyle of keeping our "precious parts" private, I believe most will naturally follow suit, but we should also have purposeful conversations with them about it.

3. Be alert to online predators and teach your kids to do the same

Do not post content of children online that could be accessed and altered by people with malicious, perverted intent. Yes, little toddler bums are adorable, but they are not for the public domain. And as they get older and spend time online themselves, we must train them to look for suspicious activity. Set boundaries on apps and video games so that kids cannot chat freely online with strangers. Remind them to never share private info, and to watch out for secretive behaviour—anything that would try to isolate a child from their family.[12]

4. Ask the Holy Spirit to help you discern any atmospheres or individuals that are potentially unsafe

As our children get older, they will likely begin to spend time at friends' homes, without us there. Their world naturally will expand beyond us! Proceed with caution, asking questions, and communicating with whoever the supervising adult will be. *Who is going to be at the event? Who will be in the home? What activities will be happening? Will there be unsupervised screen time?* We need to be ready to politely refuse invitations. As a friend of ours recently explained to us, "I'd rather insult someone by saying no than have to look into the eyes of my daughter later and ask her forgiveness for not protecting her."

---

12 Ally Global and ExEd have partnered together to develop *The Prevention Project*, a great online resource with videos and conversations starters for parents and educators to help children recognize warning signs of online predators. Ally Global's vision is to end exploitation and child trafficking, while restoring those who have been targeted.

In our family, we rarely allow sleepovers for our kids. It's just not a thing our family does. As our kids get older, they know that we're up for late-night hanging out, but they also know that we'll be nearby.

5. Have regular conversations with your kids about 'tricky people'

Years ago, we took the advice of Pattie Fitzgerald of *Safely Ever After,* who said that we need to stop villainizing strangers for simply being strangers. Rather, we can teach our kids to look out for what she calls "Tricky People". Tricky people will try to separate children from their parents, either physically or psychologically, by inflicting shame or asking for secrets to be kept. Tricky people may approach children under the guise of needing help from them. These are big clues that we can teach our kids to watch for.

In our family, we talk A LOT about showing people honour and kindness, so their eyes widen in wonder when I tell them that they have my full permission to throw away all their manners if they ever sense danger or feel threatened! "Kick! Bite! Scream! Twist and scratch! Do whatever you need to!" I've told them.

Even when they were as young as two and three years old, I invited them to practice raising their hand, palm outward, encouraging them to say, "No" in a firm way if they felt uncomfortable with someone's attention or affection. I would run through practice imaginary scenarios with them, inviting their responses (ie, if someone tickled them and they didn't feel comfortable, or asked them into their house to help with their hurt puppy, or tried to show them a picture that they knew was not appropriate).

6. Remind them, "You can tell me anything."

Children who have experienced a sexual violation often feel afraid to tell their caregivers; they may feel ashamed to even speak about it. They may also fear burdening their parents with the issue. We like to remind our kids, "Because God has made us your leaders, He has given us the strength to handle any bad news you may have. We can handle more than you think we could. What is most important to us is that you don't feel alone if something is hurting you."

If you are noticing that your child is repeatedly saying or doing things that have a sexual connotation, it may be a red flag that your child has been exposed to content or an atmosphere that is planting ideas in their minds. This is a great opportunity to ask your child some gentle questions—not panic or over-react—and find out where they are getting these ideas from.

7. Support your children's boundaries

We need to respect the boundaries our children have regarding physical affection and allow them to say "no" if a situation makes them feel uncomfortable.

There will be innocent, kind-hearted people who approach your kids, asking for high-fives and hugs. Children with a more reserved disposition may recoil and hide sheepishly behind our legs, while others may have no problem with it at all. Either way, we get to be there to watch the interactions, reminding our child that their body belongs to them and not to anyone else. If they choose to politely say "no", we will back them up.

RESTORED INNOCENCE

Years ago, I taught a class at our church to young adults about sexuality and relationships. In our first meeting together, I gave a brief introduction of the scope of the coming lessons, and then invited them to submit any topics or questions that they would like me to address in our weeks together. As I opened up those scrap pieces of paper with scrawled handwriting, one question stood out above all the others: "Can I be innocent again?"

I knew who the writing belonged to—a young man who had very recently come to Jesus. This young guy had brought with him the piles of brokenness and regrets and confusion that he had collected over the years and he was asking if the shameful memories would fade and stop haunting him. He wanted to know if his heart could be healed from those things that had been done to him.

The short answer to his question was "Yes. Yes, you can be innocent again."

The long answer? Yes, Jesus can make all things new. He can bind up the brokenhearted. In fact, it is one of His specialities. He can cleanse the conscience, wash our mind, and separate our heart from our history.

I mention this now because even very diligent parents have been grieved to learn about a violation of their child's sexual innocence—either through sexual content or molestation. If this is your story, I urge you to seek professional, faith-based, trauma-informed support, for you as the parent, and for your child. Even though it may be difficult, it is important to always report criminal activity.

And remember that the Lord is a Restorer and a Comforter. Jesus delights to take the very things that the enemy meant for evil, the secrets that cause us the most grief, and somehow, miraculously, make things new. The story is not over.

REFLECTION QUESTIONS

1. When you were growing up, did you feel like you fit into the stereotypical norms for your gender? If not, how did that make you feel? Did anyone particularly support you in your unique interests, or did you face embarrassment? Take a moment and invite the Lord into that situation and consider what He might say to you about that circumstance.

2. Are you able to recognize the God-given, physiological differences between males and females, versus the expectations that your community has invented? Is there something you still need to pray about, search the Scriptures on, or get counsel about?

3. Can you see something in your son or daughter that may not fit into a stereotypical norm, but is a unique aspect of God's design for them as a male or female? What is something you can say to them today or this week to encourage them in that part of their personhood?

11

A CONVERSATION ABOUT THE NATURE OF PORNOGRAPHY

"Those pictures pull my eyes like they are magnets."

Our sons were seven and nine years old when they explained the way they felt walking through the checkout aisle at the grocery store. I was surprised by the angst in their voices as they expressed their frustration with those fashion and entertainment magazines. The models were so beautiful, their bodies posed to allure, inviting a second glance or a long stare.

Those pictures do pull us like magnets, don't they? Even as "mature grown-ups", we have to be honest that there is an innate beauty in the human body. It is attractive. Unfortunately, because of our sinful nature, that acknowledgment of beauty can quickly turn to lust, and attraction can quickly turn to seduction. Images like the ones my boys were drawn to are all about objectifying people, trying to alter our mindsets regarding the role of sexual expression. The sacred is being dragged out into the public arena to be stared at and trampled over.

But our young kids don't understand that yet. All they know is that the images "pull on their eyes like magnets."

I am a loud proponent of internet filters that stop the influx of sexual content coming into our homes, and I am appreciative of the growing library of resources that acknowledge the damaging neurological and relational effects of pornography. But as parents, we first need to understand the way that pornography uniquely targets our sons and daughters and how it is contributing to their distress.

I want to share some language that has enabled our kids to be on the offensive when it comes to pornographic content, not just on the defensive. As we share with our children about the dangers of pornography, we need to keep a compassionate and redemptive tone, because our aim is to raise children who can reform culture, not just retreat from it.

A Broader Understanding of Pornography

When I use the word 'pornographic', I'm not just referring to porn sites, sending nudes, or a box of dirty magazines down in the basement. I'm referring to the cultural onslaught that is coming at us from every direction. It is in the song lyrics of the Top 10 charts, it is in the fashion choices of the rich and famous, it is in pre-teen fiction, and it is in advertising tactics.

The word 'pornography' is made of two Greek words, *porneo* and *graph*. *Porneo* means 'to be bought, purchased, to traffic, to sell', and *graph* means 'to write, to draw'.

As this etymology indicates, the problem of pornography is not merely in explicit photos or videos; it is in a culture that is pushing us to sell ourselves.

In Proverbs 4-6, we gain insight about this matter of avoiding seduction, laid out in a discourse from parents to their son. Throughout these chapters, they are imploring him, "Guard over your heart! Don't fall into seductive traps! Don't go after the harlot or the adulteress woman!"

> *"Do not desire her beauty in your heart, nor let her capture you*
> *with her eyelids. For on account of a harlot one is reduced to a loaf*
> *of bread, and an adulteress hunts for the precious life . . .*
> *Can a man take fire in his bosom and his clothes not be burned?*
> *Or can a man walk on hot coals and his feet not be scorched? So*
> *is the one who goes in to his neighbour's wife; whoever touches her*
> *will not go unpunished. Men do not despise a thief if he steals, to*
> *satisfy himself when he is hungry; but when he is found, he must*
> *repay sevenfold; he must give all the substance of his house."*
> **Proverbs 6:25-31**

I find it fascinating that both the 'harlot' and the man who uses her are described in this passage as hungry—even starving. The harlot reduces a man to a loaf of bread (v. 25) while the man is only stealing to satisfy a hunger (v. 30). Though their desire may be legitimate, the Scriptures are showing us that the way they choose to *satisfy* those desires is illegitimate.

When we think about our sexuality as merely filling a hunger, it becomes transactional, void of love, tenderness, and commitment to a multi-dimensional person with their own intrinsic worth. This is the essence of prostitution, which in turn, is the essence of pornography.

It is the kingdom of this world that exploits the human body, proclaiming that sexuality is about doing whatever you need to do to get your hunger met. It turns sexual experience into buying and selling, a simple trade: "I'll give you this, if you give me that. I'll perform for you if you perform for me."

But the kingdom of heaven says, "Do not buy and sell one another. Commit to one another, embrace each other, then give and receive freely. You do not have to perform or keep up an illusion of perfection. You can be known for who you really are and truly loved."

Though the pornography industry is very much in the visible realm, we have to remember that our primary wrestle is in the unseen realm where our spiritual enemy is scheming to destroy the image of God in humanity. And one of the most nefarious schemes, formulated in hell, is to trick people regarding their bodies and sexuality.

One of these tricks, which we have already noted, is *to disintegrate an individual, convincing them that the most important part of who they are is either their physical, material self or their inner perception of self.*

As our children grow a little older, and they start to feel that magnetic pull of sensual content, it is good for them to know that the enemy of our soul is always trying to get us to fall for the lie that "the physical part of us is the most important." But Jesus made us with a body, soul and spirit, and every part is important! Not only that, but every part directly affects the others.

How We Satisfy the Hunger

Many people live as though their body, appearance, and sex appeal—which could be deemed as one's "power to attract"—are the most important part of who they are. We see the results of this deception in the loud, flashy ways that people try to gain attention and affirmation. Like the woman mentioned in Proverbs 6, their hearts are hungry, so they do what they can to draw people in. They reduce one another to loaves of bread in the attempt to satisfy their longing for significance. They dress provocatively. Their facial expressions and demeanour are seductive and bold. Women and men alike are seen as playing some kind of game, luring and prowling. Pornography is everywhere, and it is trying to communicate a message to our children about what they need to do and how they need to look in order to be accepted, to be 'normal', or even what it means to have healthy sexual experiences.

Your child's heart is designed for relational connection and is naturally hungry for the blessing and verbal affirmation that God intended to be theirs through their family and extended community. In an ideal world, moms and dads, grandmas and grandpas, aunts, uncles, and other caring adults all help to solidify a child's self-esteem and non-sexual identity as innately valuable, *not* contingent on their physical appearance or sexuality. Every time we give appropriate attention, affirmation, and affection to a child, we are satisfying an inbuilt natural hunger within them.

When you encourage a six-year old boy, "Wow, you are so good at kicking that soccer ball!", you are helping him be established in his multi-dimensional personhood.

When you take a moment to engage in conversation with that eleven-year-old girl in your neighbourhood, asking her about her hobbies or interests, you are reminding her that she has value far beyond her physical appearance. These small, seemingly insignificant interactions are strengthening children to stand against the ploys of darkness.

Unfortunately, countless young men and women are not surrounded by this kind of positive attention and affirmation. Their empty hearts leave them particularly susceptible to the scheme of Satan that pushes them to *overemphasize* their external appearance.

SUNDAY SCHOOL STORY MEETS
CULTURAL REFORMATION

In Judges 6, we find the account of a man named Gideon. He was an Israelite who lived at a time when the people of his nation had become dualistic, forsaking faithfulness to their God. Having slipped into compromise, the Israelites were attempting to simultaneously worship God *and* the gods of the surrounding nations.

It wasn't long before this led to nationwide oppression—a neighbouring enemy tribe, the Midianites, moved in and began raiding Israel, taking the crops as they were being harvested.

It was at this dire moment that God came to Gideon and called him to rise up as a deliverer.

> *The LORD looked at him and said, "Go in this your strength and*
> *deliver Israel from the hand of Midian. Have I not sent you?"*
> **Judges 6:14**

Gideon was intimidated, and told God about all his disqualifying features, but God did not relent. Finally, when Gideon submitted to the call, God gave him his first strategic assignment:

> *"Take your father's bull and a second bull seven years old, and pull down*
> *the altar to Baal which belongs to your father, and cut down the Ashram*
> *that is beside it; and build an altar to the LORD your God on the top of this*
> *stronghold in an orderly manner, and take a second bull and offer a burnt*
> *offering with the wood of the Asherah which you shall cut down."*
> **Judges 6:25-27**

Gideon gathered some men, and under the cover of night they tore down Gideon's father's idols. The men of his tribe were straight-up angry, ready to destroy Gideon for his reforming deed, but when Gideon's father intervened in his defence, they backed down.

Knowing what we do about Baal and Asherah worship and how they were linked to explicit sexual experience, we can see that Gideon's act was one of personal and familial consecration, demonstrating a return to covenant with God. Though unpopular with his neighbours, this was an essential part of God's strategy, overthrowing the Midianites and bringing a miraculous victory to the entire nation of Israel (Judges 7).

In all my childhood years of attending Sunday School, and in every children's Bible that I have ever seen, Gideon's victory on the battlefield is included, but the behind-the-scenes tearing down of those idols is usually not. One day, when our twins were around six years old, this often-forgotten aspect of Gideon's story became a key in conversation.

I was washing dishes in the sink, towel over my shoulder, looking out through the window down at the backyard. Nearby, the twins were at the round glass kitchen table colouring in their superhero colouring books. At one point, I glanced over and saw that one of the boys was working on a picture of Wonder Woman. Like most comic-book depictions of women, this illustration had Wonder Woman posed seductively in skin-tight costume, with clear emphasis on her breasts. I caught the eye of my son. He instantly blushed.

I slowly took the towel from my shoulder, dried my hands, and walked over to crouch beside his chair.

"Hmmm. What do you notice about this picture?"

A little more blushing.

"What do you think the artist was trying to get you to notice about Wonder Woman?"

He clutched his crayon and briefly pointed at her chest with it.

"Yes. I think you're right."

At that point, I gently invited the boys to come and sit with me on the couch in the living room. And there, I told them the *complete* story of Gideon. I didn't explain in detail what Baal and Asherah represented, but I told them about the "tricks of the enemy" and about how Gideon's first act of courage was actually when he broke down the idols that convinced people that what was on the outside of a woman was most important.

By the grace of God, it clicked for them; they understood. So, together we flipped through the colouring book, and every time we found a picture that portrayed a character in a sensual way, I invited them to be courageous with me and tear out that image. They enthusiastically agreed. Somehow their young spirits could easily identify when sexuality was being emphasized. Sadly, there was only one page of a female character that could remain.

The story of Gideon is a wonderful example that we can point to, inviting our kids to think like reformers, ready to courageously pull down the idols and images that oppose faithfulness to God's design and loving boundaries.

Not too much later, I was in a doctor's office with one of the boys. In the magazine rack on the wall nearby, I noticed a *Cosmopolitan* cover that featured a young woman, poised somewhat seductively—low cut jeans, midriff bared, hands on her hips, and "that look" in her eyes. It was not nearly as scandalous as most covers are, so I left it alone instead of drawing any attention to it. But, my son noticed it too. I heard him gasp, and I wondered what he was thinking.

"Oh no, Mom. She fell for the trick."

I was profoundly impacted when I saw that even at a young age, my son could sense the deeper reality of a common magazine cover—more accurately than most adults could. His tone of voice was full of compassion. He was not judging her—but he could see beyond her luring posture to recognize that this young woman had been lied to. She was a daughter who needed to be reminded of her true value.

REFLECTION QUESTIONS

1. What has been your personal journey or battle with pornography? Was it an acceptable resource in your family of origin? How did it shape your perception of sex or relationships? If you are still struggling with the impact or influence of porn in your life, who can you reach out to for help? What is a step you can take today towards freedom?

2. Have you ever considered the biblical story of Gideon in this context before? What stood out to you from the Scriptures?

3. If your children are at an appropriate age to understand, what is a conversation you need to have with them to help them contextualize the seductive images they may be seeing in advertising or online?

12

A CONVERSATION ABOUT PORNOGRAPHIC CULTURE

She sees the images everywhere.
The way she stands. The way she moves. That look in her eyes.
The way he looks at her. The way he wants her.
She's told that it is normal.
"If you want to be loved, if you want to be chosen, this is what you must do."
Little does she know that he doesn't want her the way she hoped. If she stands like that . . . if she moves like that . . . if she lets the light go out of her eyes like that, she won't be any closer to her dreams coming true.
He sees the images everywhere. It appeals to something powerful within him. He dreams of coming near that kind of beauty. He hasn't yet tamed his strength so that he can hold flora without crushing it. He hasn't yet found the courage to look in the eyes of the Father and say with certainty, "Yes, sir, she will be safe with me. I will not use her and forsake her. I give you my word."
And so, the tigers come at night and tear their hopes apart. Their dreams are turned to shame.

Males and females are different, and thus, pornography affects our sons and daughters differently. Knowing this, we can better equip them to resist the lure.

The Unique Design Of Daughters

Jim Anderson, author of *Unmasked: Exposing the Cultural Sexual Assault*,[13] is a US-born father of eight (six of them being girls!). As a pastor, he has travelled the world for over thirty years, speaking about the original design of our sons and daughters. From Russia to Kenya to the Philippines, and within his own home, he has observed that daughters were designed by God for relational safety, security, permanence, and commitment. There is not a girl on this planet who dreams about giving herself sexually to a man just for him to discard her or move on to someone else. Little girls vary in their personality and aspirations, but they all have this in common: their hearts thrive in atmospheres of steady, honouring love.

Every daughter has something like a 'fuel tank' in her heart that God intended to be satisfied by the tender-hearted, non-sexual love of her father and mother. She was designed to be seen, considered and celebrated during her formative years, before adolescence, when her body changes and that sexual aspect is awakened in her personhood.

God's design for sexual expression is that it would be enjoyed within the context of a marriage covenant, when a loving husband has publicly made a lifelong commitment to her.

The messages behind pornography target daughters with the idea, "If you want to get love, you are going to have to sell this part of who you are and learn to perform." The lie to young women is, "What you offer to a man sexually is the most important part of who you are. This is what all men want. This is your path to security."

Our daughters need to know three things:

1. **Pornography has created an illusion of unattainable, unsustainable physical 'perfection'.** A certain level of insecurity is common among all young people as their bodies are changing and they are attempting to find acceptance among peers, but the pornography industry has fuelled extreme levels of insecurity and even self-hatred for many girls. As parents we can stand guard against this pressure by initiating conversations about the

---

13 Jim Anderson, *Unmasked: Exposing the Cultural Sexual Assault.* Carpenter's Son Publishing, Cincinnati, 2012.

unrealistic—and often digitally altered—images that are portrayed of women in advertising and entertainment. By speaking words of blessing over our daughters, we are reminding them of their innate beauty and value, pushing back the darkness on their behalf.

2. **A woman is valuable for who she is as a person, not just what she can do for a man sexually.** Mothers specifically have an opportunity to model to their daughters what it is to cultivate physical beauty without letting the sacred, sexual component of life take over their entire persona. There are many mothers today who need to be reminded of this same lesson: *You are valuable for who you are as a person, not for what you can do for someone sexually.*

   Some women spend years of their lives ingesting the messages of culture, developing a flirty persona or sex appeal, because they believe that their greatest value comes from how they perform in the bedroom. When those women inevitably begin to age, they often fear the wrinkles and the sagging because they wonder if they will still be cherished once the flower of youthful beauty has faded. God loves to reassure all of His daughters of His Fatherly affection—our identity as His treasured daughter can not be taken away. And there is an unfading beauty that endures in the heart of a woman who chooses to trust in Christ (1 Peter 3:3-4).

3. **She has permission to say no.** Every daughter needs to be reminded that if she ever feels uncomfortable or unsafe, she can and should either say something or remove herself from the situation. Too often, a girl will stay quiet because she is afraid of insulting or hurting a man's feelings. She doesn't know that she has the power to say "no". Modern pornography has become increasingly degrading, training boys to think that vulgarity is acceptable and training girls to think that it is their only option. Mothers and fathers need to have straightforward conversations with their daughters, reminding them of their value and the lies of porn-culture.

A father has a crucial role in his daughter's life, helping her know what appropriate, respectful masculine attention is like. A dad's presence is a gift to his daughter; she needs quality and quantity time with him. Many dads find it easier to be involved in their daughters' lives when they are young, and may wonder what their role should be once they see their little girl morphing into a young woman. Fathers, you need to know that no matter how mature and capable your daughter becomes, she still needs your smiles, your hugs, and those conversations that communicate how you cherish her. A father's love serves as a shield for his daughter, giving her confidence and strength.

In the book of Esther, we see the dedication of a man named Mordecai who, in the spirit of adoption, fathered his young orphaned cousin, Esther. When she was conscripted into a competition to determine who would be the new queen of Babylon, she was brought to live in the palace. Yet, even then, Mordecai's fatherly care remained consistent:

> *"And Mordecai walked every day in front of the court of the harem, to know how Esther was and what was happening to her."*
> **Esther 2:11 ESV**

He checked on her every single day! After a year of living in the king's harem, in an atmosphere likely fraught with competition between the women, the king chose Esther as his new queen. What was it about Esther that caused her to stand out among all the eligible virgins? Esther undoubtedly had physical beauty, but I suspect there was a unique beauty, an inner confidence about her that came from the steady presence of her father-figure, Mordecai.

Not only did Mordecai remain relationally connected to Esther even in her new role as queen, he also emboldened her when she was afraid, and offered wisdom to her seemingly impossible circumstances.

Fathers, your daughter needs you.

THE UNIQUE DESIGN OF SONS

Jim Anderson often says that men were designed by God to look in the mirror and see someone they respect. They need relational attachment, as women do, but men are also more eager to rise up as a warrior and defender. Men are designed to do what is right, not what is easy. When that drive is cultivated, our sons have an amazing capacity to sacrifice for the people or cause that they care about.

All men—young and old—are also fuelled by honour. There are many things that can bring fitting honour to a man—he can receive honour from a healthy marriage and family, from physical strength or heroic efforts, from economic success, or from a role of social influence.

Pornographic messaging tells sons that the primary measure of their masculinity is in sexual conquest. Instead of choosing a healthy pathway to honour that involves selflessness, pornography trains men to believe that women and sexuality should revolve around them, and be all about the fulfilment of their desire. Pornography is 'free of risk'. A man doesn't have to fear rejection from pornography. The women on the screen are always happy to see them, flattering them. But this is a counterfeit honour.

Our sons need to know four things:

1. **God does not despise a man's sexuality**—He is the one who designed it! God is inviting every man to walk in surrender in this area of his life, because these desires were never supposed to rule over him. Through the grace of God and the sanctifying work of the Holy Spirit, men can learn to govern their sex drive even in the midst of a pornographic culture.

2. **They will never be satisfied by counterfeit or 'shortcut' honour.** The honour that will fuel our sons is found on the journey of humility and suffering. Philippians chapter 2 lays out how Jesus emptied and lowered Himself, serving and sacrificing for those whom He loved. Only then did the Father elevate Jesus to the place of highest honour. 1 Peter 5:6 reminds young men specifically, "Therefore humble yourselves under the mighty hand of God, so that He may exalt you at the proper time."

3. **They were made for true intimacy.** In porn culture, which focuses on physical pleasure, men are led to believe that sexual release is all they need. Our sons need to know that they are not one-dimensional beings. Men and women alike are made for relational fulfilment and deep soul-satisfying friendships.

4. **Hell is warring against every daughter, trying to get her to emphasize her sexuality above all other things.** While porn culture says that women are objects to be consumed, a religious system will say that women are objects to be avoided because their beauty is 'too tempting'. As parents, we are not asking our sons to run and hide, but to step up into the fight. They are not to be predators but protectors.

   I believe that every little boy dreams of being 'the hero', a protector who uses his strength to defend those he loves and to put an end to 'the bad guy'. In a healthy childhood, as a part of community, boys get frequent chances to spend time with sisters, cousins, mothers, aunts, grandmothers, and female friends. He sees that they are multi-dimensional individuals with unique features, personalities, and skills. He learns that they have feelings and deserve respect.

   If a neighbourhood bully ever messes with his sister or if ever someone talks badly about his mama, a boy naturally longs to put an end to it. This is where our sons must be encouraged to embrace that identity of a protector, learning how to stop those small-scale injustices against girls with non-violent means. They will not aspire to disarm the perversions of pornography if boys believe they just need to stay on the defensive.

Fathers who show respect for women, are demonstrating the pathway to true honour. A son needs to have a deep relationship with his dad. When a father enters the world of his sons, encouraging and coaching them in becoming good men, it gives those boys a fighting chance against the traps of lustful behaviour. That relationship needs to be strong enough—and vulnerable enough—so that their conversations about women, pornography and sexual desires can be a little less awkward.

A mother's feminine presence in the life of her son demonstrates that women have greater depth than just their sexuality. When sons experience her loving, non-sexual care on a daily basis, they are imprinted by feminine strength and beauty. It teaches them how to interact with women in a respectful way.

As parents, we are not only having conversations with our sons and daughters—we are setting an atmosphere, creating a safe space, a sanctuary against the pornographic storms that are raging against this generation.

THE AGGRESSIVE NATURE OF PORN IN OUR DIGITAL AGE

The introduction of the internet to the general public in 1993 brought incredible benefits to society. Comparable to the Industrial Revolution of the 1700s, there have been widespread effects, many of which are worth celebrating. We have the opportunity to harness technology for good, for the spreading of the gospel, for staying connected with loved ones, and for finding freedom in education.

Unfortunately, as you know, there is a dark side to the internet. The same roads paved to carry shipments of blessing have also been used to spread pornography. With the internet as it is, and algorithms designed as they are, the pornography industry is able to aggressively take advantage of whole populations, intent on cultivating addicted consumers. Spell something wrong in a search engine, and you could end up on an explicit site. Fall for the clickbait on a pop-up ad, and there's a good chance you will be assaulted visually. The pornography of the last century, the dirty magazines with 'pin-up' centrefolds, is fading in the shadows of the mountainous amount of pornographic content that is now available online.

All pornographic content is detrimental to the development of the brain, of one's self-identity, and of healthy, realistic relationships, but the hardcore, violent nature of mainstream pornography is alarming. According to a 2021 study, nine out of ten porn videos contain acts of physical aggression or violence, and 97% of the time these acts are against women.[14]

---

14 Vera-Gray, F., McGlynn, C., Kureshi, I., & Butterby, K. *Sexual violence as a sexual script in mainstream online pornography.* The British Journal of Criminology, 2021.

Given that an increasing number of young people admit to using pornography as one of their primary sources of "sex education", and those who watch porn are often influenced to believe that the sexual behaviours they see are normal, we should be alert to the societal ramifications of porn exposure. One study conducted in 2016 by Middlesex University in London asked adolescents aged 11-16 if online pornography was giving them ideas of the types of sex they could try out. Of the 1,000 respondants, 29% of girls and 44% of boys agreed.[15]

The negative side effects of pornography are certainly being talked about in the mainstream, and not just from a moral or spiritual perspective. *Fight the New Drug* is a non-religious, non-legislative, non-profit organization that exists to educate people on the harmful effects of pornography. Their website offers hundreds of articles and resources that support individuals and families who wish to arm themselves against this unwanted content.

Clay Olsen, co-founder of *Fight the New Drug* said, "Average age of (initial) exposure has traditionally been quoted as eleven years old, but we are seeing studies now showing that it could be as young as nine years old." In a recent interview by Kansas City News, *Fight the New Drug* was quoted as saying, "The point is that this is not a question of if they will be exposed, but when and to what degree." [16]

STANDING UP AGAINST PORN'S INFLUENCE

The widespread presence of porn doesn't mean that we should fold our hands and let it have its way in our hearts and homes. There are plenty of precautions we can take.

Daniel Principe is a youth advocate and consent educator in Australia seeking to reverse the damage being done in young men's lives by pornography. Principe shares openly about how he did not receive a healthy

---

15 Elena Martellozzo et al., *"I wasn't sure it was normal to watch it…": A quantitative and qualitative examination of the impact of online pornography on the values, attitudes, beliefs, and behaviours of children and young people.* London: NSPCC, 2016, p. 3, https://assets.childrenscommissioner.gov.uk/wpuploads/2017/06/MDX-NSPCC-OCC-Online-Pornography-Report.pdf.

16 Christa Dubill, *'Fight the New Drug' Helps Parents Understand the Prevalence of Pornography,* Kansas City News, November 15, 2019, https://www.kshb.com/news/local-news/fight-the-new-drug-helps-parents-understand-prevalence-of-pornography.

sexual education at home or school, and instead got a "comprehensive education" when he was exposed to pornography at age eleven:

> "It was an education that lasted ten years and shaped my attitudes towards men, women, bodies, violence, respect, intimacy, consent and pleasure. I didn't recognize the influence it had on me until I stopped consuming the content."

Principe now spends his days communicating with young people, particularly boys, on the dangers of pornography.

> "Now as an educator, I give young men an opportunity I never had— to recognize this indoctrination instead, and consider the benefits of embracing healthy masculinity and sexuality grounded in empathy and respect. I'm motivated by the urgent need to humanize women and girls, who many of us tragically came to believe are 'sluts', 'whores' and worse, thanks to the billion dollar porn industry algorithms. Porn shaped the perspective that women are objects who exist for male entertainment."

The world needs more advocates like Daniel, who will educate the next generation—starting with our own sons and daughters. As a parent, you may never stand in front of middle schoolers in a school assembly, but you can initiate some crucial conversations with your son or daughter in your minivan or at the dining room table.

PRACTICAL ADVICE ON PORNOGRAPHIC CONTENT

1. **Have intentional conversations when you come across sexual content.** In our family, when we encounter those images, we take a few moments to have a conversation: *"What did you notice about that picture? What do you think the artist or photographer is wanting you to focus on? When you see a picture like that, is it hard to remember to think about that woman (or man) as more than just a body?"*

2. **Have conversations about how to guard your eyes and mind.** It is inevitable that we will come across seductive content or end

up in a compromising setting, possibly interacting with someone whose dress or behaviour is intentionally provocative. We need to take responsibility for what we choose to look at and what we choose to think about. We've often shared this Martin Luther quote with our sons: "You can't stop a bird from flying over your head, but you can stop a bird from building a nest in your hair."

3. **Use internet filters or parental controls** that allow you to put time boundaries on the internet. For instance, the filter we have in our home allows us to turn the wi-fi off from 11:00pm-8:00am every day.

4. **Secure devices with passwords.** Do not allow kids to use screens in private locations, like bedrooms or bathrooms.

5. **Use media review websites** such as *Plugged In Online* or *Common Sense Media* to give you an idea of what type of content is in video games, movies and TV shows before you permit your child to engage with it.

6. **Don't allow young kids to play around unsupervised** on YouTube or other platforms that allow unmonitored uploads; unfortunately, there is exploitative material hidden under innocuous-looking titles.

7. **As your children get older and have their own devices, set strong boundaries and expectations about usage.** If you want to prevent social media's influence or device addiction, but still need a way for them to communicate with you, consider starting them out on an old-fashioned flip phone. Keep those filters in place, and consider giving their phone a 'bedtime' outside of their room at night.

8. **Communicate regularly and ask questions boldly, with a compassionate tone:** "Have you seen anything sexual on your phone lately? What could you do if a friend tries to show you a video with sexual content? How would you handle that?"

9. **Reinforce ways to show respect.** As parents, we teach our children that when we meet someone in person who is dressed in a particularly sensual way, we show them respect by looking

them in the eyes. We want to see everyone for who they are as people, and never to reduce them to their physicality only.

10. **Equip your children to guard their eyes.** If we see an advertisement or a picture of someone dressed or behaving in a way that brings obvious sensuality, we've encouraged our boys to close their eyes or look away. This will not insult that person in any way and will help them be on guard against the message that this part of who they are is commonplace instead of sacred, to be reserved for the marriage covenant.

The goal isn't to shame them into darting their eyes, but to keep reminding them of the bigger picture. Sexualized images of the human body are a powerful thing. Neurological science shows us that the brain is altered by these kinds of images, and so it is wise to talk openly with kids about what to do when we encounter them. In a pornographic culture, these images can pop up all over the place. Bus stop advertisements, YouTube commercials and murals at the mall all provide opportunities to talk about the messaging behind the images.

INVESTING IN WHAT WE CAN CONTROL

I remember when our boys were toddlers and preschoolers—innocently playing with blocks, building forts, and dressing up in costumes—and hearing someone speak of the predatory nature of pornography and how exposure was inevitable. Something rose within me, something like a mama-bear: "I will protect them." I imagined that if I was diligent enough, if I prepared them enough, if I prayed protection over them enough, and if we had enough common sense boundaries around devices, then surely we could avoid this plight. I'd *make sure* that we would dodge the statistical prediction.

It wasn't long before I realized that pornography is not just something people actively search for. Pornography is something that is, algorithmically-speaking, searching for our kids, preying upon them. Even with a pile of precautions in place, even after countless conversations, pornography has still infiltrated our home, impacting our sons' lives at times over the years. Each time, though we were grieved, we were also grateful that the Lord was watching over our children, ensuring that the incident didn't remain a secret. We were also thankful for all the conversations we had with our kids when they were young, which laid a foundation of understanding. The brokenness of porn culture affects all of our lives, in one way or another, but our presence in the lives of our kids strengthens them to resist—and ultimately, reform—the world around them.

I find comfort in the biblical story of a young man named Timothy. He grew up with a Jewish mother and a Greek father, as a citizen of the Roman Empire. The empire was notorious for its acceptance and vulgar celebration of sexual perversions. Timothy would have been regularly confronted by sexual images carved into the doorways and walls of public places. It was ancient pornography, on display for all to see. When Timothy became a young pastor of a large church congregation in the port city of Ephesus—located in modern-day Turkey—his exposure to sexual content in those city streets would have only increased. People traveled to Ephesus from around the ancient world to worship at the temple dedicated to the goddess Diana (also known as Artemis), who was worshipped with cult sexual rituals.

Timothy didn't have a God-fearing biological father to teach him about righteous living, but Paul stepped in as a spiritual father, mentoring him on how to live and lead in that broken culture:

> *"Don't let anyone look down on you because you are young, but set an example for the believers in speech, in conduct, in love, in faith and in purity."*
> **1 Timothy 4:12 NIV**

Paul knew that Timothy needed to stand strong, and that part of his witness would be found in how he carried himself sexually. Later in the same letter to Timothy, Paul offered some guidance in how to treat women in a culture that routinely objectified them:

> *"Treat older women as you would your mother, and treat younger women with all purity as you would your own sisters."*
> **1 Timothy 5:2 NIV**

Though Timothy was surrounded by the presence of temple prostitution and pornography, he did not succumb to its lure. No doubt, Paul's example and admonition gave him the courage to stand firm. This reinforces what studies are confirming today. Clay Olsen, co-founder and president of *Fight the New Drug*, notes:

> "Study after study is helping us understand that the number one thing that helps teens or youth avoid inappropriate content or dangerous content online is the strength of their relationship with their parents."

In a world full of sexual content that is far beyond our control, our relational investment in our kids' lives is something that we *can* control.

REFLECTION QUESTIONS

1. What practical boundaries can be established in your home to diminish the risk of your kids being exposed to pornographic content?
2. What is your child's relationship with technology like? What changes would you like to make?
3. How can you apply the information given in this chapter about the unique motivations and struggles of daughters and sons? Did this information help you understand your child better?

13

A CONVERSATION ABOUT SEXUAL ORIENTATION

When I was twenty years old, I got a job working part-time for Starbucks. Nowadays, I prefer to visit small, locally owned coffee shops, but at the time I happily wore that green apron and served innumerable caramel macchiatos. Together with my fellow baristas, we built a really special working environment that we loved being a part of. One day, as I was standing at the coffee grinder, I overheard a couple of co-workers chatting:

"Hey! Did you hear we are getting a new assistant manager?"

"Oh, really?"

"Yes, and he is just as much a girl as Emma is!"

Emma was a bright-eyed, engaging, co-worker who was 'feminine' in many of the stereotypical ways—big purses, flashy sunglasses, and a great sense for fashion.

My co-workers went on to describe how gay our new manager was.

I grew up in a fairly conservative city—this was my first chance for consistent interaction with someone who was openly homosexual. The wheels in my head were spinning—I prayed for wisdom.

The Holy Spirit was clear with me, *"If you see him only according to his sexual choices, you are making it his entire identity. You would be falling for the enemy's lie."*

The instruction felt clear and straightforward. Show love. Treat him as a brother. Remember that he is more than his sexuality. With that in mind, I was able to see him as a hard worker, a confident leader, and a good listener.

It became clear that he cared deeply about his family, his responsibilities, and the people around him. I learned a valuable lesson through that Starbucks scenario, and it set precedent for how God wanted me to see all people, homosexual or not—as a *son* or a *daughter*—not reducing anyone's identity to that of their sexuality.

THE SHIFT IN OUR GENERATION

In a relatively short amount of time, we have seen a huge shift in our societal norms. Whereas at one point, this was an issue that was generally hidden, now it is demanding our attention. Everyone seems to know someone—and love someone—who identifies with the LGBTQ+ community. Reasonably so, this raises urgent questions about how a follower of Jesus should navigate matters of sexual orientation and identity.

Our children are growing up surrounded by constantly changing definitions and an ever-expanding spectrum of sexual options. Understandably, many people still aren't totally sure what they think about it. We've moved from a time when to 'tolerate' was the highest goal. "Love is love!" was the rallying cry in the early 2000s. "As long as it is between consenting adults, it's not hurting anyone."

Before we knew it, the messaging had shifted again. Now we were being called to *celebrate* everyone's sexual desires. Here in Western Canada, LGBTQ+ flags were proudly raised on school grounds, baristas began wearing rainbow pins, and the front doors of downtown shops were adorned with decals. Today, what was intended as a symbol to communicate "everyone is welcome here" has quickly morphed into a public service announcement: "Those who don't stand with us are now the outsiders."

It's gone even further, and now young people are being 'unofficially recruited' to explore a variety of sexual expressions—to the point where some feel under increasing pressure to adopt sexual orientations that go against their honest convictions and desires, for fear of being considered homophobic or hate-filled.

We need to know God's thoughts. Only then can we help our children settle the matter in their own hearts, even while the ground is moving under their feet. Taking the time to study Scripture and learn some history on this issue can help us as parents find our voice and be ready to guide our sons and daughters through these tumultuous times.

THE SHIFT FROM HOMOSEXUAL BEHAVIOUR TO GAY IDENTITY

Before we revisit the Scriptures, let's look at the way that cultural perspectives have rapidly changed in the last sixty years. Homosexuality has shown up in historical records from ancient times—for millennia it was regarded as an act or a lifestyle (previously called 'sodomy'). Today, however, it is considered an inbuilt part of a person's identity (such as 'gay' or 'lesbian'). It is interesting to consider the steps that brought us to this point in modern culture.

In the West, prior to the 1960s and 70s, men and women who identified as gay or lesbian were often treated harshly. Those who came 'out of the closet' reported injustice, abuse, job loss, arrest, and sometimes aversion therapy in an attempt to cure them of their 'deviancy'.

The Stonewall Riots in New York in 1969 were key in bringing civil rights for homosexuals onto centre stage in North America. The homosexual community began to seek legal protection under the Charter of Rights, and they knew that the only way to achieve this was to convince society that sexual orientation was a genetically established trait, much like skin colour or race.

At that time, some gay and lesbian voices pushed back against the strategy, arguing that homosexuality was not a fixed identity, but a matter of preference. They saw sexual desire to be a fluid attribute, based on choice not genetic assignment. However, they conceded that to change the cultural mindset, achieving legal protection was their first priority.

At the time, the American Psychiatric Association (APA) categorized homosexuality as a mental illness. Clearly, this was a key obstacle that needed to be overturned in order to achieve gay liberation. Barbara Gittings, a prominent activist, shares openly about their strategy:

"I was... very involved, along with many other people, in efforts to get the American Psychiatric Association... to drop its listing of homosexuality as a mental illness. Psychiatrists were one of the three major groups that had their hands on us. They had a kind of control over our fate, in the eyes of the public, for a long time. Religion and law were the other two groups that had their hands on us. So, besides being sick, we were sinful and criminal. But the sickness label infected everything that we said and made it difficult for us to gain any credibility for anything we said ourselves. The sickness issue was paramount." [17]

In 1973, after facing three years of disruption and intimidation from pro-gay activists, the APA took a vote to determine if homosexuality should be taken off the list of mental disorders. Only 32.7% voted in agreement, but with forty percent of the members abstaining from the vote, the ruling passed. That vote set in motion major societal changes within the United States.

The next step was for the homosexual community to gain official Minority Status, a move that could only be made by changing the Civil Rights Act. This required acknowledgement that homosexuals, like all official minority groups:

1. Had suffered a long history of discrimination
2. Needed support and protection as a community
3. Are born that way

It's this third point that changed the conversation. By declaring that sexual orientation was a fixed part of someone's identity—comparable to race or skin colour—the community could begin to claim equal rights and fight for further civil liberties.

In the early 2000s, the culture underwent a rapid shift, with homosexuality increasingly normalized through television sitcoms. Same-sex marriage was made legal in much of the Western world, and gay parades became a place for the general public to stand in solidarity and shamelessly celebrate what was now considered an intrinsic part of a person's individuality.

Simultaneously, scientists were searching for any genetic markers that could prove any predisposition towards homosexual orientation.

17 Eric Marcus, *Making History: The Struggle for Gay and Lesbian Equal Rights: 1945-1990: An Oral History.* Perennial 1993. p.221

Social media and mainstream news outlets regularly touted claims that scientists had *possibly* found DNA evidence. Throughout this time, despite disclaimers that 'further research was needed', most of the general public became convinced that some people were simply *born gay*. People began to wonder: "How can we oppose the gay lifestyle if those desires and behaviours are hard-wired?"

Naturally, this questioning reached into moral and religious territory. The orthodox view of sexuality, held by Christians since the advent of the early church, is that the sexual act is reserved for the relationship between one man and one woman who are in marriage covenant. Now this was being challenged. The accusation came against God. If people are born gay, and if someone's 'gayness' is immutable, how could a loving God oppose people for simply living in line with how *He made them*? What are the logical possibilities? That perhaps God *isn't* loving? That He doesn't *actually* have a problem with homosexuality? Or maybe people aren't *born* gay after all?

In recent years, these questions have been the fault lines along which churches and denominations have split . . . and many individual Christians have felt the heaviness and angst as they, too, have searched for answers.

Interestingly, the moment homosexuality became culturally accepted, all discussion about genetic inclination towards sexual orientation disappeared from the mainstream media. In its place, there rose a call for the acceptance of *fluidity* in sexual orientation. It was as if the whole argument was flipped on its head. Sexuality was not only "fixed from birth", it was also now supposed to be fundamentally changeable.

In August 2019, results from the largest-ever research project on genetics and homosexuality were published, and the chief takeaway was this:

"There is no single gene responsible for a person being gay or a lesbian…
The study of nearly half a million people closes the door on the debate around the existence of a so-called 'gay gene'." [18]

---

18 Nsikan Akpan, "There Is No 'Gay Gene.' There Is No 'Straight Gene.' Sexuality Is Just Complex, Study Confirms," *PBS NewsHour*, August 29, 2019, accessed October 11, 2025, https://www.pbs.org/newshour/science/there-is-no-gay-gene-there-is-no-straight-gene-sexuality-is-just-complex-study-confirms.

If people are not physically born gay—at least, not in the way that culture has led us to believe—then clearly, something else is at work here . . . something in the realm of our spirit and soul.[19]

"I Never Would Have Chosen This!"

I have not personally wrestled with homosexuality, but I am friends with people who do. Back when the message to those with same-sex attraction was "you're born this way", Bryan and I became quite close with a young woman in our church community who shared some aspects of her struggle with us.

This young woman was going through a tough time and needed a place to stay, so we invited her to come and live with our family. Through the months that followed, we got a close-up view of her incredible musical ability, her wit and humour, her generosity, and her giant heart of compassion. And as she shared her story with us—the joys and the traumas—we came to see her deep struggle with sexual temptation and identity. We had countless conversations about it all; we spent hours at the dining room table with cups of tea or coffee in hand. So many hours. Trying to grapple with questions of God's love, the nature of sin, and the possibility of ever being able to break free from the heaviness of shame that she felt.

"I never would have chosen this!" she yelled out one day.

My heart broke for her. I wish I understood things better then, so that I could have confidently shared with our friend what I know now—that the 'born gay' ideology was a hoax. Just because you *feel* it, doesn't mean you *are* it. But she didn't know this, and we saw her hope fade before our eyes. She became convinced that her sexual desires were the compass she was destined to follow.

Because for so long the church remained silent about the topic of homosexuality (or else lambasted it as though it was the 'sin of all sins'), young people who dealt with same-sex desires often felt ashamed and beyond help. If they did gather the courage to share their struggle with

---

19 You can read more about the strategies of the homosexual movement of the 1960's and 70's by Marshall Kirk and Hunter Madsen in their work, *The Overhauling of Straight America*, as well as *The Gay Manifesto* by Carl Wittman.

someone they trusted, they were often met by ill-informed responses—pastors and parents alike who were under-equipped or hadn't thought much about it.

Fortunately, conversations in the church about sexuality are becoming more common and people are getting more of the support that they need. Of course, there are those who embrace their homosexuality and claim no conflict between their sexual desires and their faith. But for those who do recognize the tension, and for those parents who are wondering how they can support their children, here are a few keys to hold onto:

1. We can teach our kids to recognize the ongoing wrestle between their spirit and their flesh.
2. We can love everyone without affirming everything.
3. We can proclaim that Jesus is the most inclusive of us all; His invitation is for anyone who is willing.

THE WRESTLE OF THE SPIRIT AND THE FLESH

It need not surprise us when people say, "As long as I can remember, I have felt this way." If we're honest, we've all wrestled with one thing or another—sometimes the battle is won and done in a short season of life, but other times there are battles that span our lifetimes. In these situations, we have to learn to patiently endure.

Some temptations may be sexual in nature—we are seeing a growing number of cases of bestiality, incest, polyamory, pedophilia (renamed "minor-attracted-persons" or "MAPS" to de-stigmatize the concept), and autogynephilia. Some temptations come from Satan—the enemy of our soul—who launches ideas at us like flaming arrows (Ephesians 6:16). Some of the temptations are stirred up by cultural pressures and vulgar pornographic content in the world around us. But we cannot forget that we also are at war with the desires of our own flesh.

The flesh is not merely our physical body, but a 'carnal nature' that desires things that are contrary to the Spirit and will of God for our lives. This carnal nature is like a genetic predisposition that has been passed down from one generation to another—beginning with Adam and Eve in the garden—affecting all people throughout the ages.

In the book of Romans the apostle Paul describes the struggle with sin that is common to all:

"For what I am doing, I do not understand; for I am not practicing what I would like to do, but I am doing the very thing I hate ... For I know that nothing good dwells in me, that is, in my flesh; for the willing is present in me, but the doing of the good is not. For the good that I want, I do not do, but I practice the very evil that I do not want ... Wretched man that I am! Who will set me free from the body of this death? Thanks be to God through Jesus Christ our Lord!"
Romans 7:15, 18-19, 24-25

The phrase "body of death" used in that final verse would have been familiar to the Roman church for a unique reason. The Romans at this time were experts at cruel punishment, and one well-known sentencing was to force a murderer to have their victim's corpse tied to their back. As that 'body of death' decomposed, it would begin to rot the criminal's skin as well—a putrid reminder of the crime which had been committed.

This is how it can seem for those who feel bound to the desires of their flesh. "Who will rescue me from this body of death?!" Isn't that the desperation we sense? "Thanks be to God through Jesus Christ our Lord!" Jesus! He is the answer. He is the one who has made a way for us to be saved—not just from the devil, or from the systems of this world, but also from the 'carnal' desires that can rise up within us. In James 1:14-15 we read:

"Temptation comes from our own desires, which entice us and drag us away. These desires give birth to sinful actions. And when sin is allowed to grow, it gives birth to death." (NLT)

When any of us faces temptation, we have a decision to make: will we entertain the idea and let it occupy a place in our heart, or will we deny it? Sin is like a fire—it is never satisfied and will take as much of our life as we allow.

You may have heard the legend of the two wolves, an old story which illustrates this wrestle perfectly:

"An old chief was teaching his grandson about life. He said, "A fight is going on inside me—a fight between two wolves. The Dark One is evil—he is anger, envy, greed, arrogance, self-pity, and lies. The Light Wolf is good—he is joy, peace, love, hope, humility, truth, and compassion. The same fight is going on inside of you, Grandson . . . and inside of every person on the earth."

The grandson pondered this for a moment, then asked, "Grandfather, which wolf will win?"

The Grandfather smiled and gave a simple answer, "The one you feed."

As parents, we need to coach our kids not to fix their eyes in a direction that they don't want to move towards. How many kids have been swept into a lifestyle or shifted their identity because they wanted to be entertained by trending videos or they let their curiosity lead them somewhere dangerous? The wolf we feed is the wolf who wins.

As parents, we can invite our kids to talk honestly about the struggles they are going through. By simply admitting the things that tempt them and receiving prayer from us, they are actively fighting their flesh. As my kids get older and spend more hours away from me, my prayer for them in this area, is for both God's protection over their lives, and for His wisdom to tip me off when something is going on that my kids need to get off their chest.

In the face of any kind of temptation, "...we take captive every thought to make it obedient to Christ." (2 Corinthians 10:5 NIV). This means that we teach our kids to *think about* what they're thinking about. Right from an early age, we've taught our kids that they can "grab the reins" of their own minds, and fix their thoughts on things that are lovely and excellent and honourable (Philippians 4:8). Then we pray together for God's grace to wash their minds of any foul imagination or thoughts.

This is the everyday Christian life, not prescribed for only one category of behaviours. As those who follow Jesus, we cannot play around with sin of any kind. We are called to be led by the Spirit, and as we do so, we will not succumb to the desires of our flesh (Galatians 5:16).

LOVE EVERYONE WITHOUT AFFIRMING EVERYTHING

For a generation that is in the midst of redefining human identity and sexuality, it can be difficult to accept that every mention of homosexuality within Scripture comes with either a negative description or a direct prohibition,[20] and every mention of marriage is listed as a relationship between a husband and wife.[21] That's not to say that homosexuality is elevated as the worst of all practices. In 1 Corinthians 6:9-10, we read:

> "Or do you not know that the unrighteous will not inherit the kingdom of God? Do not be deceived; neither fornicators, nor idolaters, nor adulterers, nor effeminate, nor homosexuals, nor thieves, nor the covetous, nor drunkards, nor revilers, nor swindlers, will inherit the kingdom of God."

Here we can see that homosexuality is listed right along with other practices that people don't usually take as seriously, such as drunkenness or coveting. But as we recognize ourselves in that list of behaviours, we can find comfort in the verse that follows:

> "Such were some of you; but you were washed, but you were sanctified, but you were justified in the name of the Lord Jesus Christ and in the Spirit of our God."
> **1 Corinthians 6:11**

The amazing reality is that God doesn't wait for any of us to get ourselves cleaned up before He will love us. In fact, He showed His great love for us in that while we are in the middle of sinning, Jesus went to the cross in order to offer us forgiveness and the cleansing of our conscience. And more than that! He shows His love for us by not leaving us as He finds us! He doesn't affirm all of our behaviours, but gives us an invitation to a new beginning. Jesus makes room for every one of us, regardless of our past or current struggles.

God is love (1 John 4:16). We cannot possibly love people more than He does. And since Jesus doesn't affirm all behaviours, it is possible that we can love everyone without affirming everything too.

JESUS, THE MOST INCLUSIVE ONE OF ALL

As we approach this conversation about sexual identity with our kids, remember that we are modelling how to live full of both compassion and

---

20 See Genesis 19, Leviticus 18:22, Leviticus 20:13, Romans 1:26-28, 1 Timothy 1:8-11, Jude 1:7

21 See Genesis 2:24, Matthew 19:1-12, Mark 10:6-9, 1 Corinthians 7:2, Ephesians 5:22-33

conviction. Often people will find that one of those virtues comes more naturally, while the other is neglected. There are some people who seem to have an extra helping of the gift of mercy; they easily empathize with the struggles of others. These individuals may be tempted to erase boundary lines around sexuality. They will need to intentionally ground themselves in the truth of Scripture, recalling that it is impossible to love people more than God does. God does not give us boundaries to ruin us or burden us, but to protect and empower us.

On the other hand, some people may have something like a "prophetic disposition"; they seek justice, they see the world in absolutes, and sense an urgency to end the perversions of our time. In one way or another, they are the ones who proclaim, "Come! Repent! Think differently! Now!" These are the ones who need to remember that the Lord is gracious and compassionate, slow to anger and rich in love—for everyone.

We must remember the example Jesus gave us. He knew how to dine and visit in the homes of notorious sinners, but He also didn't hesitate to call people to follow Him, leaving everything behind. This invitation is the same for anyone . . . and everyone.

In Matthew 16:24-26 we read,

> *Then Jesus said to His disciples, "If anyone desires to come*
> *after Me, let him deny himself, and take up his cross, and*
> *follow Me. For whoever desires to save his life will lose it, but*
> *whoever loses his life for My sake will find it." (NKJV)*

In the original language here, when Jesus says "whoever desires to save his life", He is using the Greek word, *'psyche'* which refers to the inner man, to the soul—the seat of feelings and desires. (This is where we get the word 'psychology' from.) Jesus is saying that if we try to hold onto a 'psyche' of our own making, we will ultimately lose. But if we will lay all of our 'psyche' at the feet of Jesus, surrendering the "self" and yielding to the identity we receive as a child of God, then, and only then, can we access the abundant life Jesus offers.

As our own children face the sexual confusion of the current culture, we want to remind them of this Gospel message: all are welcome, and all can find life when they lay down their psyche to follow Jesus.

REFLECTION QUESTIONS

1. Did this chapter influence your perspective on homosexuality? Do you tend to lean more to the side of "compassion" or "conviction"? How can you grow in the alternate virtue?

2. How frequently is your child being exposed to teaching or influence on the topics of LGBTQ+? Are there some changes (small or large) that you sense need to be made so that you can take that role as their primary educator on these topics?

3. What are your thoughts on the idea of homosexuality in regards to the levels of "having desires", "choosing behaviours", or "finding identity"?

14

A CONVERSATION ABOUT TRANSGENDERISM

When I was young, I often thought that being a boy would have been better. I don't know why. Maybe it was just a case of the grass looking greener on the other side. A few of my friends and I would boast about our desire to be tomboys and for others to think about us that way. If being a girl meant donning fashion only in the palette of pink, fearing any activity that would break a nail, or refusing to take risks, it seemed an inferior existence by far. "No, thank YOU!" was my attitude.

"Tom-boy" seemed like a more enjoyable route to go. I envied boys who could easily pee outdoors and go shirtless on a hot summer day. It wasn't gender dysphoria; I think it could more accurately be called gender *discontent.*

As I grew older, I still had a desire to be "one of the guys". I didn't really enjoy all the emotional roller-coaster rides of my female friends. Add in the struggle of monthly periods and the fear of the pain of childbirth, and you can perhaps empathize with me on why being a girl seemed like a bad deal.

When I was nineteen years old, away at Bible school, I had a life-changing encounter with God that shifted my view of myself. During a time of worship with my classmates, I was standing near the back of the room, with my hands held up as a sign of surrender. Suddenly I heard Him whisper to my heart, "I made you a girl on purpose."

This blessing brought me to tears, both of relief and humility. Relief that I was not a cosmic mistake. Humility and sadness at the way I had kicked against my own design for so long. That day, I determined to begin learning about the unique strength of my God-given femininity. That doesn't mean that I haven't wrestled with the restrictions of my gender, but in the years that followed, I found deep contentment and increasing confidence.

The grass looks greener everywhere else. A lot of children are being told that their biology should not be a hindrance—that we can 'remake ourselves' into whatever image we prefer. In a generation that is dealing with unprecedented levels of inner turmoil, more than ever, we need to know our Good Shepherd and allow Him to guide us. I believe that He will show us the green grass right there at our feet, and invite us to a place of rest.

When it comes to transgenderism, increasing numbers of people are telling their transition story, and while many feel a momentary relief, the inner conflict often remains. The experience of most is that the grass isn't necessarily greener on the other side.

What does this mean for families today? How can we recognize the authentic struggle, yet offer a solution that reaches deeper? As parents, it's important for us to understand the cultural moment we find ourselves in so that we can lead our children to a place of lasting peace.

GENDER DYSPHORIA AND THE REEMERGENCE OF GNOSTICISM

The Christian worldview states that man is a triune being—much like our Maker. We are made up of a spirit, a soul, and a physical body. These three aspects are not segmented but are interdependent—the health or suffering of one part influences the well-being of all parts. One of the first major heresies that the early church faced was Gnosticism—a belief that pushed against the sanctity of the human body. Gnostics believed that humans were "trapped in the material world", but that in seeking after a "secret knowledge" they would discover the divine spark within them—their inner, *authentic,* immaterial self.

The fact that Gnostics considered the body as base and inferior was a huge problem for the church for two reasons:

1. Gnosticism taught people to reject and limit the natural inclinations of the body as much as possible. The pleasures of food, rest, and sexual relations in marriage were looked down on.
2. Gnosticism questioned the physical incarnation of Jesus, because it seemed impossible that God would ever lower himself to that level. They proposed that Jesus had come merely as an apparition or an idea.

Early church leaders, like the apostles John and Paul spoke up against Gnosticism, because they understood the implications that this philosophy would have on the people. In 1 Timothy 4, Paul identifies that this doctrine is demonic in origin, and he offers a godly response:

> "But the Spirit explicitly says that in later times some will fall away from the faith, paying attention to deceitful spirits and doctrines of demons...men who forbid marriage and advocate abstaining from foods which God has created to be gratefully shared in by those who believe and know the truth. For everything created by God is good and nothing is to be rejected if it is received with gratitude."
> **I Timothy 4:1, 3-4**

Physical, natural things were given to humanity as gifts from God; we are encouraged to enjoy our embodied experience as believers, receiving them with gratitude. In 1 John 4:2-3 we gain further insights:

> "This is how you can recognize the Spirit of God: Every spirit that acknowledges that Jesus Christ has come in the flesh is from God, but every spirit that does not acknowledge Jesus is not from God. This is the spirit of the antichrist, which you have heard is coming and even now is already in the world." (NIV)

The writer, John, makes a bold statement—anyone who says that Jesus did not come in the flesh is connected to "the spirit of the antichrist". Gnosticism was pushing against a foundational belief within the church, and John could not stay silent about it. He had witnessed the physical nature of Jesus. In their years of ministry together, John had seen Jesus eat plenty of meals, had seen Jesus get tired and take a nap, and had seen Jesus' body be bruised and beaten at the site of his crucifixion. And most gloriously of all, John had seen Jesus's resurrected body with the scars still marking his hands, feet and side. Jesus had not belittled, bypassed, or despised the physical dimension of humanity. He had embraced it, and in doing so, He elevated the value of the physical and modelled how to honour God with our bodies.

In this modern era, Gnosticism has reemerged, this time in the form of transgender ideology. Men and women, young and old, are invited to look beyond the constraints of their biological design to find the deeper truth of who they are—to uncover their most "authentic self". The idea is that *only the individual* could ever know the inner mystery of their own true identity. Increasingly, children's literature and cartoon characters alike are used to propagate this exploration process. The ideology of 'the authentic self' is most often linked with the concept of gender, but now also extends to include the idea of trans-humanism. If a child determines that they are an animal, perhaps a cat, a raccoon, or some mythical creature, teachers and classrooms are expected to accommodate and never question this "secret knowledge".

Of course, most parents understand the joy of imagination that is present in their preschoolers. We've had a menagerie of zoo animals, superheroes, and favourite book or movie characters make their appearance in our home over the years—and I've certainly supported this kind of play! I've face-painted little tigers, and sewn superhero capes. We've made cardboard props together and I've played right along with them. Because it is fun to pretend!

The problem isn't pretending. The problem is when we blur the line between imagination and reality and call it enlightenment. The problem is when those of us who express hesitation are suddenly considered public enemies. Many parents are left wondering:

How did this ideological freight train pick up this much speed in such a short time frame?

Am I an unloving parent if I don't give a stamp of approval to social transition, to a name change, or to begin taking puberty blockers?

What do I need to know to help my children grow in confidence in the midst of a gender-fluid culture?

The Reality of "Gender Dysphoria"

Undeniably, some people truly sense a disintegration between their physical body and their personhood, and this is not something to be glossed over! Some describe feeling out of place in their own body, like a hand in a glove that just doesn't fit. When someone experiences distress about the incongruence between their biological sex and their perceived sense of self, this is referred to as "gender dysphoria"—formerly known as "gender identity disorder". Historically, gender dysphoria has been recognized and reported from as young as two years old, but in the majority of cases (70%) it would resolve itself without treatment after the tumults of puberty had settled.

In 2021, Canada became the first country in the world to include this concept of transgenderism in a census of their population. At that time, Statistics Canada reported that 0.33% of Canadians over the age of fifteen identified as either transgender or non-binary. Just a few short years later, we're seeing evidence that the rate is increasing—disproportionately among the young.[22] Some of those people may never go through transition surgery, yet they still live with a sense of disconnect between their "inner self" and their "outer self". Where does this sense of dissonance come from? Does transitioning really improve their life? If not, what hope do they have for finding peace?

Our Girls Are Not Okay

Whereas in the past gender dysphoria was more often experienced by boys, now for the first time in medical history, it is the girls who are leading the pack with what psychologists refer to as "rapid onset gender dysphoria." This is primarily occurring in a girl's early teen years. [23]

---

22 In this 2025 study, 23.1% of Gen Z in the United States identified as something other than 'straight': "LGBTQ Identity Growth in the United States," *USA Today*, March 13, 2024, accessed October 11, 2025, https://www.usatoday.com/story/news/nation/2024/03/13/lgbtq-identity-growth-united-states/72949630007/.

23 Madison Aitken et al., "Evidence for an Altered Sex Ratio in Clinic-Referred Adolescents with Gender Dysphoria," *Journal of Sexual Medicine* 12, no. 3 (March 2015): 756–63, https://doi.org/10.1111/jsm.12817.

In recent years, studies show that girls are experiencing a mental health crisis, with record high levels of anxiety and depression. Boys are struggling too, but the rates of clinical depression in girls have increased three times as much as the rates in boys since 2010. Rates of self-harm, suicidal attempts and eating disorders have also risen steeply in girls, which, as experts like Jonathan Haidt, author of *The Anxious Generation,* point out, is synchronous with the advent of the smartphone.[24] The introduction of this technology brought a steady diet of social media into the lives of our children—by 2015, young girls reported being on social media apps for more than forty hours a week. This has only added fuel to issues teen girls have struggled with for decades—insecurity about their own bodies, and comparison with others.

Add to this the fact that pornographic sites have become an online 'sex-ed class' that many young people are enrolling in, and we can understand why the interactions between boys and girls are becoming more adverse. Girls are being increasingly ogled, objectified, and assaulted. The advent of a feminine physique at puberty only makes it harder for girls to hide from the unwanted attention of men.

In her book, *Irreversible Damage,* Abigail Shrier, writer for the *Wall Street Journal*, makes a case for why girls are the ones identifying as trans at a disproportionate rate:

> "The adolescent girls currently identifying as transgender... make little effort to adopt the stereotypical habits of men... they flee womanhood like a house on fire, their minds fixed on escape, not on any particular destination. Only 12% of natal females who identify as transgender have undergone or even desire phalloplasty.[25] They have no plans to obtain the male appendage that most people would consider a defining feature of manhood... A common response I get is something along these lines:

---

24 Jonathan Haidt, *The Anxious Generation: How the Great Rewiring of Childhood Is Causing an Epidemic of Mental Illness* (New York: Penguin Press, 2024).

25 Def. *Phalloplasty:* The construction or reconstruction of a penis or the artificial modification of the penis by surgery.

'I don't know exactly that I want to be a guy. I just know that I don't want to be a girl.'" [26]

Surrounded by impossible standards of beauty, unwanted sexual attention and a high risk of assault, is it any wonder that a growing number of today's girls are uncomfortable in their skin? For girls, to become masculine in appearance—or even androgynous—is to camouflage oneself from certain dangers.

Our girls need parents who come close, dethrone social media, and speak words of blessing and affirmation. We want to ensure that every daughter grows up in an atmosphere free of pornography's poison so that she can rest confidently in her identity—*her design is good*, and her value extends far beyond her appearance or her sexuality.

THE SANCTIFYING WORK OF THE SPIRIT

For both females and males, the wrestle with gender dysphoria can be exhausting, leading many to wonder if gender reassignment will be their only relief. They need to know that there is hope beyond hormones. There is a God of peace who brings comfort and healing, whatever their struggle. This is the God we want to tell our children about! 1 Thessalonians 5:23-24 says it this way:

> *"Now may the God of peace Himself sanctify you completely, and may your whole spirit and soul and body be kept blameless at the coming of our Lord Jesus Christ. He who calls you is faithful; He will surely do it."*

Notice that God is a God of peace, not chaos or disintegration. Those who feel disorder within their own design can find comfort in a Creator who calls things into place. Even at the very beginning of time, Genesis tells us that the Spirit of God hovered over the chaos and called forth order and beauty.

Notice also that God Himself is committed to the sanctifying process in our lives. In the original language of Greek, this word "sanctify" means "to render as holy, to dedicate, purify, and renew". Those who have walked

---

26 Abigail Shirer, *Irreversible Damage: Teenage Girls and the Transgender Craze*, Swift Press, 2022, p. 7-8.

with the Lord for some time will testify that God faithfully works in our lives, day by day, step by step, helping us to find wholeness in our soul, in our relationships, and in our view of self. As we walk in relationship with Him, learning to trust His leadership, there is nothing that is beyond the capability of His sanctifying power!

Remember that in the life, death and resurrection of Jesus, He showed us the importance and the value of our human body. It was the Spirit of God who raised Jesus from the dead, reintegrating His spirit back into His physical body. The same Spirit is working in us today, and can bring life to our mortal bodies! (Romans 8:11)

THE PROCESS OF DETRANSITIONING

A friend of ours, Kyla Gillespie, has first-hand experience of the sanctifying work of God when it comes to gender dysphoria. By late 2023, multiple people had asked me, "Have you met Kyla yet? Have you heard her story? She was born female, underwent gender reassignment surgery, then six years later, she detransitioned. Now she's preaching about Jesus!" As most millennials would naturally do, I began following her on Instagram. It wasn't long before we had set up a coffee date—she wanted to hear about the work that we do . . . and I wanted to hear her story.

Kyla grew up in western Canada in a Christian family. As a child she attended church regularly with her mom, dad, and older brother—she loved Jesus. But she also recalls a shadow of unease with her female-ness from a very young age. She didn't want to be a figure skater wearing a tutu; she would rather be playing hockey with her brother and cousin! As a teen in youth group, the sense of angst only grew when she also discovered that she was dealing with same-sex attraction. This was in the 1990s, when conversation in the church about these topics was rare, so Kyla kept quiet about her inner thoughts about gender and sexuality. In reflecting on this time of her life, she says:

> "As a child, I was under the impression it wasn't okay to talk about these kinds of feelings. Amid the silence of everyone around me, I felt silenced. Looking back, I believe it would have made a huge difference if I had known my parents, teachers, friends, or church family would've been

open to listening to me and walking with me through these feelings, experiences, and struggles."[27]

In the midst of this struggle, at the age of fourteen, Kyla's parents brought a shocking announcement that they were getting a divorce; her world started to spin. Both of her parents soon remarried, and she began to spend more of her time and energy pursuing her dream of playing professional hockey. Though she eventually trained with the Canadian National Hockey Program, by her early twenties, her inner world was falling apart. Kyla felt increasing discomfort in her female body, and got involved in same-sex relationships. She soon turned to alcohol to cope and began drinking excessively.

When Kyla realized that she needed to get some help, she enrolled in an alcohol recovery program. While in the program, Kyla decided to transition from female to male. She went the whole way—hormone therapies, reassignment surgeries, even a legal name change. Kyla slowly disappeared, and in her place was "Brycen"—complete with a beard and a deepened voice. Despite of all these changes, Brycen did not feel content in his new body; there was always another step he felt he needed to take to make the transition more real.

It was Brycen who came back to a church setting and soon connected with a tight community of faithful Jesus followers, including the lead pastor, BJ, and his wife, Jess. Brycen was greatly impressed by their love for God, for one another and for the Scriptures. When Brycen eventually told the believers about the hormones and surgery that had altered his appearance, they were shocked—no one had suspected anything! Yet they didn't reject him at all. It was clear to Brycen what their position was on the matter of gender and sexuality, but he never questioned their genuine care and love for him. He kept coming to church services and Bible studies and slowly, slowly—over many months—with a lot of prayer and fasting on the part of his friends, Brycen began to surrender his gender into God's hands. One evening while in prayer, he felt God whisper to his heart, "Return to me, Kyla."

---

27 Kyla Gillespie, "Renewed & Transformed," KylaGillespie.com, accessed October 11, 2025, https://www.kylagillespie.com/blog/f/renewed-transformed.

After six years of living as a man, Kyla began the emotionally vulnerable and physically arduous process of detransitioning—surrounded and financially supported by a church family who walked with her every step of the way.

Today, Kyla praises God that the gender dysphoria that was once suffocating has been alleviated. It hasn't disappeared completely, but she has learned how to surrender those struggles to the Holy Spirit, allowing Him to bring comfort and healing to her as His daughter.

Kyla's story is a beautiful example of how the love of God, demonstrated through His people, can heal and restore members of the trans community. I believe there will be hundreds (and thousands) more stories like hers around the world in the coming years if families and churches are willing to walk patiently and prayerfully with people.

Is There Room in the Church for Trans-formation?

When the film, *Jesus Revolution* came out in the spring of 2023, we took our family to see the movie. I was moved to tears repeatedly throughout the film as I rejoiced in the true stories of what took place in that young 'hippie' generation of the 1970s. Psychedelic drugs, efforts to find peace, and promises of free love simply could not satisfy the longings of their hearts—but Jesus could.

The movie demonstrated how one traditional church and its pastor were radically impacted when they inherited a group of young hippies overnight. Some of the people who were already faithfully attending church refused to worship in the same space with the hippies—they did not know how to adapt in order to disciple this young generation. Others felt uncomfortable at first, but in time, they got on board and allowed the Spirit of God to guide them. The broken-hearted found healing, the lonely found a family, the addicted found freedom. When the movie was over and we were walking out of the dark theatre, one of our sons asked me, "Who do you think the 'hippies' of today are?" I knew what he was asking. "Who are the people that the church doesn't really know what to do with today?"

I knew right away—it is the people who currently identify under the LGBTQ+ banner. The hippies of a previous generation were hungry for identity and were shaping it for themselves through music, fashion, drugs, and sexually unrestrained lifestyles. That deep hunger is in this generation too. In a search for liberation we are seeing not only the rejection of what God says we can *do*, but also the rejection of who God says we can *be*. The culture is promising a young generation that if they 'liberate themselves' from the constraints of gender and committed heterosexual relationships, they will find true life. But this is a circumstance like Proverbs 14:12 describes, "There is a way that seems right to a man, but in the end it leads to death."

We are hearing a growing number of reports from those who once identified as trans but have since de-transitioned. They explain how they found ways to manipulate their caregivers and doctors to give them what they wanted, and are grieved now that no one questioned their decision. After the most extreme measures were taken, they realized that gender reassignment and hormone therapies would not heal the ache within them.

More and more psychologists and doctors are reevaluating the wholesale prescription of hormone therapy and the medically sanctioned sterilization of minors. The testimonies and lawsuits are piling up, and the statistical reports on negative side effects are demanding the attention of people in the secular arena. We now know that the rates of suicidal ideation are not diminished at all after gender reassignment. An article in *Forbes* recently acknowledged that, "longitudinal data collected and analyzed by public health authorities in Finland, Sweden, the Netherlands and England have concluded that the risk-benefit ratio of youth gender transition ranges from unknown to unfavourable." [28]

People are realizing that they've been lied to. Gender reassignment did not fix all their problems. Nations like Norway, Denmark, Sweden, Finland and the United Kingdom have already outlawed these measures being used on children. At the time of writing we are continuing to pray

---

28 Joshua Cohen, "Increasing Number of European Nations Adopt a More Cautious Approach to Gender-Affirming Care Among Minors," *Forbes, June 6, 2023*, https://www.forbes.com/sites/joshuacohen/2023/06/06/increasing-number-of-european-nations-adopt-a-more-cautious-approach-to-gender-affirming-care-among-minors/.

for breakthrough in nations like Canada, the United States, and Australia, which have been aggressively pushing children into this ideology.

Isaiah 56 speaks of a "promise of salvation" for the Gentiles—those who were once *not* a part of the nation of Israel, the children of promise. Isaiah was prophesying of a time when the dividing line between the ones who *could* belong and the ones who *could not* would be eliminated.

Listen to what verses 3-5 say:

> *"Do not let the son of the foreigner who has joined himself to the Lord speak saying, "The Lord has utterly separated me from His people"; nor let the eunuch say, "Here I am, a dry tree."*
> *For thus says the Lord: "To the eunuchs who keep My Sabbaths, and choose what pleases Me and hold fast My covenant, even to them I will give in My house and within My walls a place and a name better than that of sons and daughters; I will give them an everlasting name that shall not be cut off ... even them I will bring to My holy mountain, and make them joyful in My house of prayer ... for My house shall be called a house of prayer for all nations."*

In ancient times, a eunuch was a man castrated in order to serve within a religious cult or the courts of the king. There were numerous ancient religions whose gods were also depicted as castrated, androgynous, or gender-fluid, and so to be castrated or to have one's genitals crushed was seen as a sacrificial offering.

In the midst of this culture, Yahweh called to the Israelite people and laid out clear boundaries for morality and gender. In Deuteronomy chapters 22 and 23, we read that God didn't want His people to cross-dress or to enter the place of worship if their genitals had been crushed. What strange instructions! But, He was saying, "I don't want to be worshipped the way these other nations gods are worshipped!"

This promise of salvation for the eunuchs found in Isaiah 56 is particularly notable, because now the castrated man was being given an invitation to be amongst the people of God. Let's look again at those verses, and now I'll humbly offer a paraphrase:

"Don't let the gender-transitioned ones say, 'I am destined to be an outsider forever. There is no hope that I can bring life again.' No! The Lord says to them, "If you will enter into the rest found through My Son, if you will choose what pleases Me, and remain in covenant with Me, I will give you a secure place in My house, amongst My people, and in the kingdom. You may have switched your name and not know what name to use now, and you may not have children to carry on your name or legacy, but I will give you an everlasting name and I will not forget you."

There is room in the heart of Jesus for all people. Is there room in our hearts? Will we make space in our homes and our churches for those who have transitioned but have discovered that peace without Jesus is impossible? Will we welcome the young man who is wearing nail polish or feminine clothing? What about the young woman who still has traces of beard stubble? Will we open wide our front door and show hospitality, inviting them to know the love of God? Will we have patience for the unique sanctifying process that they are in?

WHAT OUR KIDS NEED TO KNOW

When I was young, I didn't face gender dysphoria, but I did experience gender discontentment. As I've had the chance to share my story with groups of all sizes, I've looked around the room to see heads nodding in agreement. We all know what it is to wrestle with the limitations of our physiology. Being male can be difficult. Being female can be difficult.

It was the writings of Elisabeth Elliot—a missionary and influential Christian writer from the 1970s—that gave me some language to describe what I had wrestled with. In her book, *Let Me Be a Woman,* she described how every creation in the world could certainly find something to complain about in its God-given design.

"Every feature of God is given something that could be called an inconvenience, I suppose, depending on one's perspective... The special gifts and abilities of each creature define its special limitations." [29]

---

29 Elizabeth Elliot, *Let Me Be a Woman,* chap. 8 "Weight of Wings". Harper and Row, 1976.

She noted that the mouse and the elephant alike could complain of their size, that the turtle could complain of the weight of its shell, and even the bird could complain of the weight of its wings. But if a bird would learn to trust its Designer and "come to terms with the necessity of bearing wings", it would find that those are the very things that would lift it into the heavens.

This is the lesson that every child needs to know. The weight or complexity of our design is the very thing that is meant to bring us freedom. We are not shape-shifters; we are among the created order. And like the birds, our children can also rise into freedom when they discover the purpose for the 'weight of their wings'.

REFLECTION QUESTIONS

1. Do you currently have relationships with people who are identifying as transgender? After reading this chapter, do you feel more equipped to relate to them?

2. What do you think churches can do to be ready to welcome victims of this ideology? Would you feel ready or comfortable in that?

15

A CONVERSATION ABOUT WHERE BABIES COME FROM

The time inevitably comes in each child's life when they begin to notice women with big pregnant bellies, and they will wonder, *How does the baby get out of there?* And equally reasonable, though exponentially more awkward, they may ask, "How did that baby get in there?"

Once, while I was largely pregnant with our fifth son, I was helping the other four get their teeth brushed before bedtime—just a regular gong-show night of antics at our place, with distractions at every turn for our twin five-year-olds, a four-year-old, and a two-year-old—when all of a sudden, out of nowhere, one of the boys posed the question:

"How is the baby going to come out of your tummy?"

We had heard this question before, but I had always kept it simple by saying that Daddy and I would go to the hospital and the doctor would help us get the baby out. I tried that answer again, but it didn't cut it this time. He nodded, but then repeated, "Yeah, but HOW?"

I swallowed hard. I had not prepared myself for this discussion. "One minute," I said calmly, holding up my finger. Then I turned and waddled down the hallway to where my husband was, and whispered in a desperate manner, "They want to know how the baby comes out! Should I tell them?!"

"Sure!"

Wide eyes, another strong swallow. Waddled back down the hall. It is funny how focused and still little boys can be when they get the feeling that they are about to get some top-secret information. I casually explained to them how my muscles would begin to squeeze the baby—kind of like how we squeeze toothpaste out of a tube.

"But how does the baby actually get OUT? Is it through your belly button?"

"Noooo . . . well . . . it's more like . . . one second, okay?"

I literally waddled back down the hall to double-check.

"Should I really, REALLY tell them?"

Yes, my husband affirmed again. Another waddling trip. Steady tone, calm expression . . .

"Well, boys, you know how Mommy doesn't have a penis? I actually have a tunnel from my womb—which is called a uterus—where our baby is, to the outside world."

I told them a bit about the contractions and pushing ("Does it hurt, Mommy?!", "Is there blood?!"), and about the happiness I experienced when I got to see them and hold them and smell them for the first time. I told them that each of them was worth the pain of the squeezing and pushing.

I smile now at my hesitation all those years ago. Why was I so nervous to tell them about God's beautiful design? I have friends who boldly share those details (and more!) with their young children. And when I think about how the vast majority of human history had been lived in a rural setting, surrounded by livestock that reproduce in that classic mammal way, I realize that most kids back then had a pretty vivid sex-ed curriculum—complete with live illustrations out in the fields. ("Why is the daddy cow trying to get on top of the mommy cow?")

"HOW DOES THE BABY GET IN THERE?"

As some of our boys started getting older, though they weren't necessarily asking for more information, Bryan and I knew that we wanted to have some strategic conversations with each of them. We wanted to be their first informant on the idea of sex, so that any new information would be held up against the framework of what we—the resident experts—had already shared with them.

When each of our sons was around the age of nine, my husband and I set up a time to have a forthright conversation with them about sexual intercourse. My husband and I were both involved. We opted for spaces that were less likely to be interrupted (ie, a coffee shop, the dining room table with siblings out of earshot). Honestly, each conversation was such an awkward, precious time. Some of their mouths dropped open in shock. I remember one of our boys' eyes darting back and forth between my husband and me in utter disbelief (and perhaps an element of disgust), no matter how heartily we emphasized the goodness of this design!

The timing and method of how we give kids this information is not formulaic with a one-size-fits-all approach, but I do have a few recommendations from our experiences:

1. Emphasize that God designed sex for both procreation and pleasure.

With each of our boys, the first lesson about sex was quite biological in nature. We're talking sperm production, erections, penetration, ejaculation, ovulation, fertilization, DNA strands, pregnancy. The whole deal.

I remember one son timidly asking with a stutter in his voice, *"Do . . . I . . . have sperm?"* At this point we were able to dive into discussion about puberty and the changes that would be coming his way in the years ahead. Almost all of them asked at one point or another, "If I want to be a dad, will I have to do *that?"*. . . to which we would reply with an explanation that by the time they were grown men, they wouldn't mind the idea quite so much and that it was a wonderful expression of love between a husband and wife—and it was God's idea to make it feel good too!

2. Ensure opportunities for follow-up conversations.

I often think that if we all dealt with sexuality once in our lives, then one conversation about it might suffice. But that's not the reality. As parents, we have the privilege of facilitating an ongoing conversation.

Practically speaking, at random times you can ask your kids, "Do you have any questions for me about sex? About the human body? About periods? About penises? About masturbation? About breasts?"

It could be on the drive back from hockey practice or piano lessons, or at the dinner table on any weekday evening. It will certainly keep them on their toes, and it will reinforce the idea that these topics are always open for discussion.

The other way you can initiate conversations is to share what you've learned over the years. It can be as simple as saying, "I remember when I was your age and I asked my mom what oral sex was. Have you heard of that before?"

Or you could pose a question, "Have I ever told you about in vitro fertilization?"

"What do you know about a woman's menstrual cycle?"

Feel free to speak candidly.

"Women have three holes, one for poop, one for pee, one for sexual intercourse and giving birth. Men have two holes. One for poop and another for pee and semen. Nope, pee and semen don't come out at the same time. The poop hole is called the anus. Haha, yes, it's very funny that there is a planet called "Uranus". No, we are not going to tell that joke over and over."

3. Instruct your child not to be the educator of their siblings or peers.

An important element we should communicate to our kids is that they are not meant to be the educators among their siblings or friends. Byan and I have told our sons that though it may be tempting to talk about sex with other kids, we want to allow each of their friends to hear about it from their own mom and dad. If other kids try to initiate conversations about sex with them, then we want our boys to do their best to deflect and redirect those kids back to their own parents.

4. Play it cool. You're the expert here.

As awkward as we may feel, as parents, we have to hold steady. Take a deep breath, and don't you dare run from those conversations! We want our kids to see us as a far more reliable source than YouTube or any of their friends. We want to reassure them, "You can ask me anything. I know all about bodies and sex!"

I recently saw a social media reel where men on the street were being interviewed: "How does a woman go to the bathroom if she is wearing a tampon?"

I was shocked by the number of men who supposed that they would have to remove the tampon in order to urinate. In a society that considers itself to be so liberated and advanced sexually, it's ironic that so many remain uneducated in the basics of reproductive anatomy! I suppose we are playing a part in remedying that problem every time we show up for awkward conversations with our kids, aren't we?

PUBERTY, PERIODS AND WET DREAMS, *OH MY!*

Puberty is defined as the period during which adolescents reach sexual maturity and become capable of reproduction. An adolescent has gone through puberty and is continuing to transition into adulthood. Dr. Gordon Neufeld, a Canadian psychologist and author of the book *Hold onto Your Kids*, describes the adolescent stage as the bridge between childhood and adulthood. He explains that the tricky thing about the process—which often baffles parents—is that our child does not simply walk across that bridge one day and set up camp in the new world of adult maturity. Rather, they unwittingly wander back and forth between the lands. One day, you are surprised and pleased by your child's maturity and wisdom, and the next day, you are exasperated, wondering, "Have we lost all progress?!"

Though puberty and this adolescent phase are a normal part of life, it is also a tumultuous experience for our children and for us as parents. But it helps to get an idea of what to expect so that from an early age, we can be talking about these changes with our kids.

Internally and externally, things will change. Hair will grow in new places, new oils and odours will be released, fat stores will grow, and bone structures will change. Voices will deepen, legs will lengthen, and reproductive organs will begin new operations like semen release and monthly menstruation. Interests will change, and emotions will become increasingly complex. Hormones will be released. New questions will be asked about "the self", about previously accepted beliefs, and about their place and purpose in the world.

Our family has found incredible value in being connected with other families through a church community. Whenever children are part of a multi-generational community, it gives them the opportunity to recognize changes happening in young men and women who are older than them. They see boys slowly morph into men and girls slowly transform into women. There are countless opportunities for conversation:

"His voice is starting to get deeper, hey, Mom?"

"Yes, it sure is. That's going to happen to you one day. Sometimes it might crack as your vocal cords stretch and thicken. Have you ever heard that happen to anyone before?"

"She is sure getting tall, hey, Mom?"

"Yes, often girls get big growth spurts a couple of years ahead of boys. Have you noticed that?"

Of course, some of the changes are private and internal, but we still need to have the conversations. To be real, one of the most awkward topics for me has been the conversation about nocturnal emission, aka 'wet dreams'. Years ago, I heard a story about a boy, twelve or thirteen years old, who thought he was dying because he kept waking to discover a mysterious liquid was leaking out of him. He was mortified but kept it to himself for months, and only discovered the truth when he confessed his 'terminal condition' to a counsellor. (Poor guy!) This was enough motivation for me to brave the clumsy conversation—and to double-check that my husband had also processed the concept with them. It is valuable for young men to know that nocturnal emissions are totally normal and that we won't make a big deal about any extra laundry that needs to be done.

There is also the matter of periods. When I was a teenager, my friends and I groaned about our monthly experience, at times jokingly referring to it as "the curse". While it certainly brought new difficulties, I wish I had understood better what was going on in my body and hadn't fallen for the lie that the period (or my female body) was the problem.

The average woman has a monthly cycle for forty years of her life. Our society could certainly benefit from understanding the four unique phases of this cycle—ovulatory, luteal, menstruation, and follicular—and the ways to naturally support those phases through proper nutrition, adequate rest, and varying types of exercise. I've been intrigued to learn more about this aspect of feminine health, and I'm hopeful that the next generation of girls can be more equipped to understand their God-given design and work with it, not against it.

With a household of boys, Bryan and I have attempted to give our sons insight into the female menstrual cycle, too. The reality is that they are going to be interacting with females for the rest of their lives and we want them to honour that unique design, not belittle or ignore it. As mothers, we have the chance to communicate with both sons and daughters about our own experiences, finding a way to be real and honest about the challenges, while not speaking negatively about this awe-inspiring process that carries the potential to bring life into the world.

Of course, the conversation about body parts, reproduction, and birth of babies, is linked to a concept far bigger than biology. It is the origin story of individual, unrepeatable souls who are made in the image of God.

Made with Purpose

When our sons were little, they loved to hear about how we prepared for their arrival, how we felt when we first held them, why we named them as we did, and the sweet moments during their early years. Ultimately, I think all children want to know that they are *still* wanted, all these years later. The way we talk about birth and babies and children in general can help secure their identity as a son or daughter.

How many young people in this generation are fundamentally wondering if they are wanted? Is there a purpose for their existence? The son or daughter who knows that they have a treasured place in the heart of their mother and father is less likely to seek the affections of a stranger who doesn't really love them.

So, while you are answering questions about sperm and penises, eggs and ovaries, remember that you also have the opportunity to communicate value and a God-given purpose to your child.

In our home, our kids have asked, "Where was I *before* God put me in mommy's tummy?" To this, we could honestly reply: "You were in God's heart, dear. He had the idea of you long before any of us were here on earth."

As the songwriter David says in Psalm 139:

*"For You created my innermost parts; you wove me in my mother's womb . . .
Your eyes have seen my unformed substance; and in Your book were written all
the days that were ordained for me, when as yet there was not one of them. How
precious are Your thoughts to me, O God! How vast is the sum of them!"*
Psalm 139:13, 16-17

What a comfort for us to know that, regardless of the circumstances surrounding our conception, and before we were born or even carried in the womb of our mother, we were first carried in the heart of God.

*Listen to me, O house of Jacob, all the remnant of the house of Israel,
who have been borne by me from before your birth, carried from the
womb; even to your old age I am he, and to gray hairs I will carry
you. I have made, and I will bear; I will carry and will save.*
Isaiah 46:3-4 ESV

In the church, we so commonly emphasise the role that fathers can play and affirm it as a reflection of our heavenly Father. Rightly so. But Scripture also honours the role of mothers and shows that they too, represent the image of God on earth.

The Significance Of The Maternal Nature

I am convinced that in our modern culture, the maternal nature is one of the least recognized, most underestimated forces on earth, and consequently, much of the Protestant church has ceased to celebrate mothers or help them cultivate and govern this instinct.

When I was about nineteen years old, before I had any babies of my own, I saw a painting of a mother and her young child that captured my heart. Up until this season of life, I had enjoyed kids, but never really wanted children of my own. I didn't know if I had what it took. I dreamed of traveling the world, and frankly, childbirth sounded horrifyingly painful. Something about that painting inspired me as I began to consider the possibility that one day maybe I *could* be a mom. However, I didn't write down the title of the piece or the artist's name. Years later, I thought of the painting again and naively wondered, *Maybe I can just search online and type 'mother and child painting' and be able to find it again.*

I had not considered the enormous number of artists throughout history who have attempted to capture the beauty of a mother with her child. My browser window was filled with oil paintings, watercolours and acrylics from past centuries. These weren't just moms asking for a family portrait session. It was a reflection of the sentiment of past generations; artists had devoted hours of their time to the subject because humanity was once convinced of the significance of motherhood. Across the board, we once treasured and honoured the years that a child could rest in the arms of its mother. We once saw a certain loveliness in the unchiselled body of a woman who sacrificed to sustain the life of her young.

On the contrary, in my early years of motherhood, it felt like I was regularly swarmed by an inner critic that was echoing the sentiment of society,

> *"You are wasting your life. Wasting your mind. Wasting your strength."*

I would try to swat the thoughts away and keep to the task at hand. Feeding. Changing diapers. Wiping faces. Patting backs. Finding soothers. Helping them walk up steps. Clipping fingernails. Pointing out colours and teaching them what elephants say.

The shadow of death always taunts,

> *"What's the point? Giving your life for these children who keep demanding from you. What reward will there be in that? Is this what you dreamed it would be?"*

I'd backhandedly push the demon off my shoulder and get back to work. Washing countless dishes. Teaching compromise and patience. Finding the missing sock. Catching the boys at the bottom of the slide. Reading the same story one more time. Washing the shampoo out of their hair. Trying to translate their babbling.

> *"This is a joke. You wanted to make a difference and experience the wonders of the world. Here you are, making pasta. Again."*

One day, for the first time ever, I turned around and took a moment to face that whisper:

"Stop. This is my choice. I will not give up. I believe in the significance of motherhood. I believe in the significance of a woman who will surrender for the sake of her children. Over and over again. I will tell my children over and over again that they are valuable to me. The whole world may not see the glory hidden in them, but I want them to know that the one who lives nearest to them believes in their worth. Enough to sacrifice for them. Over and over again."

That day was a game-changer, and strength began to rise in me for my task. I wonder how many mothers today feel torn, either because they are devoting their lives primarily to caring for their children and feel like they should be doing more, or because they are investing in a career when they truthfully would rather be giving more of their energy and time to their young children in the home. I know that every woman's path looks different, so this isn't a 'one size fits all' recommendation, but I would simply like to encourage you by saying that the role of the mother is irreplaceable to her child and within our society.

The poet William Ross Wallace (1819-1881) wrote a piece called *The Hand that Rocks the Cradle.* Here is a selection from that poem:

Infancy's the tender fountain,
Power may with beauty flow,
Mother's first to guide the streamlets,
From them souls unresting grow—
Grow on for the good or evil,
Sunshine streamed or evil hurled;
For the hand that rocks the cradle
Is the hand that rules the world.
Woman, how divine your mission
Here upon our natal sod!
Keep, oh, keep the young heart open
Always to the breath of God!
All true trophies of the ages
Are from mother-love impearled;
For the hand that rocks the cradle
Is the hand that rules the world.

I was always encouraged by this poem, because in the secret place of motherhood, especially in those labor-intensive, early years of raising children, it is tempting to believe that we aren't making a difference.

I was moved by the story of the missionary Amy Carmichael, a single woman who worked in India, rescuing children who were being sex trafficked within Hindu temples. In her biography, *A Chance to Die,* the author shares how she travelled throughout the regions of India for years, on rescue missions, bringing girls and boys home to Dohnavur Fellowship, a home for former child prostitutes. But the time came when she began to recognize that the children needed the stability and consistency of a mother on-site. The children needed the faithful care of her steady hands. She wrestled with the decision and wondered if God would actually be calling her to stay 'home' and continue her work in a new way. There was a common Indian proverb of the time, "Children tie the mother's feet," but Carmichael added, "We let our feet be tied for love of Him whose feet were pierced."

May that be the prayer of mothers all over the world. When we are given the honoured role of motherhood, may we rise to cultivate our God-given maternal instinct in our own unique ways. When a mother "lays down her life"—her time, her preferences, her ambition—for the sake of another, it is a picture of the sacrificial love of our Saviour. It is also a profoundly healing force in a world that so often seeks its own.

When we support and encourage mothers in their tasks, it gives them strength to continue pouring into the young generation. I think we have some work to do, especially in the Protestant church, to restore the honour due to the vocation of motherhood. In our home, I've told the boys regularly, "Always look out for the moms who have their hands full. Their arms may be burning, but they usually won't let on. It can be difficult for them to ask for help, so be ready to offer." I pity the society that pressures women to forsake their maternal instincts. The nurturing aspect of mothers is one of the pillars that sustains a civilization. Without her, the whole of society is at risk of toppling.

The Way We Talk About Sex

As our children have gotten older, Bryan and I have done our best to emphasize the truth found in Ephesians 5:3-4:

> But immorality or any impurity or greed must not even
> be named among you, as is improper among saints; and
> there must be no filthiness and silly talk or coarse jesting,
> which are not fitting, but rather giving of thanks."

The information our children learn about sex should not be turned into an opportunity for coarse joking or cheap laughs. In a culture that is full of foul and impure language, this may feel like an uphill battle, but it is one worth fighting for. We can supplement our instruction to our kids by being vigilant about the kinds of entertainment we allow into our lives, as well as setting an example of what pure conversation and humour look like.

The way we talk about sex matters. It is God's desire for us that we understand sex to be a sacred thing. It should not be treated as a profane thing or joked about in a crude way. Sex allows a man and his wife to come together as one flesh in intimacy, and it holds the potential to bring a new, unrepeatable life into the world.

Reflection Questions

1. How has the modern-day estimation of motherhood impacted your life and the choices of your family?
2. At your children's current stage of development, what do you suspect are the next conversations that you'll be having with them about procreation? Are there any aspects of these conversations that you've been avoiding?

16

A CONVERSATION ABOUT CHILDREN AND ABORTION

When we first talk to our kids about sex, the aspect of procreation is usually central to the conversation, but we also understand that God designed sex to be a pleasurable experience. In a world that glorifies sexual pleasure as basically the highest human experience, we need to remember that God never intended humanity to enjoy a sexual encounter without the corresponding counterbalance of potential procreation. This isn't to say that every time a man and woman have sex there will be—or should be—a resulting pregnancy, but we cannot forget that sex holds the potential for new life. This is the miracle of children, and Scriptures tell us that each new life is a blessing.

In Deuteronomy 28, there is a large list of blessings that God promised to give to His people if they would honour Him and keep His commandments. These promised blessings included physical health and strength, fruitful harvests in the land, multiplying assets, and . . . children. In today's culture, a lot of people would stand in line for every blessing except for children. Increasingly, modern thought is that having kids should be avoided for as long as possible, added sparingly, and in some cases, survived resentfully.

I remember when I realized that my idea of "blessing" was different from God's idea. What I had in mind was actually something more like narcissism, where I could sit back, put my feet up, and live the 'all-inclusive resort' life. God's idea of blessing certainly includes rest (Hebrews 4:1-11), but it is also about finding fulfillment as we live with purpose, cultivating the people and the world around us. In many Western nations, children are considered a nuisance and a burden, not only on a personal level but on society as well. It is a grievous thing when the nations of the earth begin to call a 'curse' what God has deemed a 'blessing'.

In the Gospels of Matthew, Mark, and Luke, we read that some parents were trying to bring their children to Jesus in order to receive a blessing from Him. The disciples, playing the role of bodyguards and seeking to protect Jesus from the crowds, tried to send those families away. Jesus' response was profound: "Don't stop them from coming. The kingdom of heaven belongs to them." (Matthew 19:14). He knew that they were the loud ones, the messy ones, the needy ones with undeveloped potential. But He also knew that often it is the grown-ups who have forgotten how to play, forgotten how to ask for help, and forgotten how to dream. It is the adults who have forgotten how to ask curious questions and how to put Band-Aids on their scraped knees, get up, and try again. Jesus was inviting all the 'mature' grown-ups to look at the children and take notes. When we welcome children into our world the way Jesus did, we are welcoming the ways of His kingdom. Psalm 127:3-5 reminds us,

> "Behold, children are a gift of the Lord. The fruit of the womb is a reward. Like arrows in the hand of a warrior, so are the children of one's youth. How blessed is the man whose quiver is full of them."

In the original language that this psalm was written in, the Hebrew word *nahala,* translated 'gift', includes the meaning of 'an inheritance, estate, or portion'. The Hebrew word *'sakar'*, translated 'reward', also means 'wages, compensation, or benefits'.

Because we have a larger-than-average family, I've heard more than my fair share of comments about how expensive, destructive, and exhausting children are. Unfortunately, this is the culture that our children have to grow up in. It is a culture that is driven by productivity, perfectionism, and performance. Children *are* often messy, loud and unpredictable, and unfortunately, there are few adults who really make space for the young. Sure, parents are taking them to basketball practice and buying them cell phones. Children may have organic diapers, college funds and dentist appointments, but at a deeper level, do we know how to give them the simple invitation to exist in our presence the way Jesus did? Are we willing to slow it down in order to listen to their drawn-out, rambling story? Are we able to put our devices down long enough to give them a high five? Can we get out of our own thoughts, so that we can ask them about theirs?

Remember, the kingdom of heaven belongs to them.

Don't get me wrong on this—I'm just like you at the end of a long, tiring, *no-one-is-listening, everything-feels-impossible, leave-me-alone, I'm-trying-to-make-dinner* kind of day. I've made my share of mistakes in this, using a tone that likely makes my kids feel like a nuisance rather than a delight. I've groaned, sighed, rolled my eyes, raised my voice, and begged for a moment of silence. On occasion, I've also shut myself in my room and cried with my face to the carpet.

But at the core of who I am, oh, I truly do believe what is written in Scripture—that my children are a blessing and a treasure (Psalm 127). When I can humble myself and apologize to my kids for my selfish attitude, I am able to come back to a place more resembling the philosophy of the kingdom—that children are welcome and honoured . . . and genuinely enjoyed!

I've been a mother since 2008, and I can honestly say that this assignment of parenthood has utterly transformed me. Sometimes in our day-to-day experiences, we forget to look at the big picture and to recognize the significance of our lives in the big scheme of things. We forget the role we play, being salt and light in a society that generally dismisses children.

"Where Is My Mother? Where Is My Father?"

From a baby's first cry, there is a demand for someone to take responsibility for it. The baby's presence asks, "Who brought me into this world? Where is my mother? Where is my father? Who will care for me?"

Of all creatures, human beings take the longest to reach maturity. *Someone* will need to feed, clothe, and raise that defenceless little one and help him or her find their way. The infancy and toddler stages are demanding—and as I've now discovered, the teenage years are difficult in a whole new way!

When a baby is born—and in every stage that follows—a mother and father have the opportunity to take one another's hand, lean on their marriage vows, and face the new challenge together. The challenge of bringing a baby into the world is far greater when a woman finds herself alone for whatever reason. Knowing that would be the reality, God deeply desires that every woman would be supported through the vulnerable years of motherhood, that every father would share the load of responsibility, so that every child can be nurtured.

Given the gravity of raising children, I've realized why many men and women just want the pleasure of sex, untethered from any resulting responsibility. But what happens if a pregnancy does occur? Will the mother and father step up and take responsibility, or will they try to find a way to remain free of that weight?

THE REALITY FOR WOMEN

Some people may think about abortion as a relatively new concept, a right that has needed to be 'fought for' in modern times. But history shows us that for millennia, women have found ways to get rid of unwanted pregnancies and babies. The first written reference to abortion is in an ancient Egyptian document, *The Ebers Papyrus*, a medical text from around 1550 BC that describes a dietary compound that would induce abortion. There are also artifacts from ancient Greece and Rome depicting botanical substances used to terminate pregnancies. In the biblical text, we read of ritualistic sex as a form of worship, and the offering of the resulting infants to the Canaanite gods Baal and Molech (Leviticus 18:21; Deuteronomy 18:10; Jeremiah 19:5).

In medieval times, many cultures saw abortion as taboo, not necessarily because of the value or rights of the infant, but because abortion could hide a pregnancy that came as a result of a woman's sexual infidelity. In the mid 1800s, many nations made abortion illegal after the point when a mother felt the 'quickening' of the baby within her womb. At that time there were no home pregnancy tests; the quickening was the first evidence of new life within her.

In our modern era, most Western nations have now legalized abortion even into the third trimester (and beyond), claiming that it is a woman's right and arguing that legalized abortion is needed to prevent inevitable 'back-alley abortions' or medical complications. Others assert that the fetus is not human, but merely a clump of cells until viability—in which case, abortion for the sake of convenience is justifiable. Some go so far as to describe the embryo or fetus as a parasite sucking the life from its host, almost as if the procedure is designed to improve a woman's quality of life.

We need to acknowledge that there are varying scenarios in which a pregnancy occurs. In some cultures, a husband's demand for sex is non-negotiable—the woman isn't given the luxury of 'mutual consent'. When she finds herself pregnant, she is often left wondering how the family will feed and support another child. Contrast her with the college girl who really hasn't given it much thought at all. She hooks up with a different guy every weekend, but isn't concerned because she has easy access to the morning-after pill. Of course, there is also the rape victim who is trying to heal from the trauma, and then is mortified when her period is late. Increasingly, there is also the extreme feminist who intentionally gets pregnant just so that she can 'exercise her right' to clear out the contents of her womb—boldly proclaiming, "My body, my choice!"

Given the spectrum of circumstances these and other women are in, no wonder there are so many emotions connected with abortion. More than ever before, we need a wider conversation that inspires us to be full of both compassion and conviction.

The reality is that throughout history, wherever the true church has spread, the status and treatment of both women and children have been elevated. It was the early Christians who brought about something of a sexual revolution to the Roman Empire. In his book *The Air We Breathe*, Glen Scrivener writes,

"Nineteen centuries before 'the summer of love', another revolution in sexual values and practices was unleashed on the world—and its impact was even more transformative. The first century sexual revolution has given the world certain understandings of sex, love, freedom, choice, the body, the family, gender and equality which remain operative today, even among those who consider themselves free from the church's strictures." [30]

One of the ideas that the early church advocated for was mutual sexual consent in marriage. These believers spread and popularized Jesus' teachings about sexual restrictions for men—absolute faithfulness within marriage or chastity in singleness[31]—ensuring that a virile man wouldn't leave a trail of impregnated, vulnerable women behind him. (Considering that today, nine out of ten abortions are accessed by unmarried women,[32] we can see that this ethic has huge implications.

And it was the church that introduced the radical concept of human rights for all, regardless of their sex, economic status, or race. This wasn't just lip service; the Christians provided food, healthcare and education to the poor, the sick and the outcast, out of their own pocket. Human dignity wasn't just outsourced to government programmes—Christians followed the example of Jesus who, during His time on earth, modelled what it looked like to serve people who could do nothing for Him in return.

At the Last Supper, mere hours before He would be arrested, beaten and crucified, Jesus shared with His disciples about the new covenant that He was making with humanity. He took bread in His hands, broke it and declared, "This is *my* body. This is *my* choice." This is the way of Jesus—*to love* and *to sacrifice* so that others may live (2 Corinthians 4:12; Luke 22:19).

In this conversation about abortion, we are not just trying to win a debate and prove a point. We are looking for a heart-level transformation within the peoples of the earth so that we will partner with God—not only for life, but also for human flourishing.

---

30 Glen Scrivener, *The Air We Breathe: How We All Came to Believe in Freedom, Kindness, Progress, and Equality.* The Good Book Company, 2022.

31 See Matthew 19:4-11

32 Claire Cain Miller and Margot Sanger-Katz, "Who Gets Abortions in America?," *The New York Times, December 14, 2021,* https://www.nytimes.com/interactive/2021/12/14/upshot/who-gets-abortions-in-america.html.

Talking to Kids about Abortion

I was a church kid raised in the nineties in Canada, at a time when it was still quite acceptable and even common to talk in church about the sanctity of life in church and how our faith informed our view on abortion. When I was just a girl, I remember one man in our church encouraging the congregation to raise funds for our local pregnancy centre. He always wore this little pin on the lapel of his jacket—it was the shape and size of the feet of a ten-week-old preborn baby. Throughout my childhood, I saw the pamphlets with sonogram images of babies at different stages of development in the womb. I learned that the heart begins to beat only twenty-two days after conception. The brain, kidneys and liver are developing by ten weeks, and babies begin sucking their thumbs by fourteen weeks. It was incredible! Informed by scientific data, I understood that each baby was its own person with his or her unique DNA from the moment of conception.

I was grieved when I learned about the brutal ways that babies were being aborted—chemical baths, starvation, dismemberment, and forced premature labour—many at a point in their development when the pain was excruciating for them. To this day, there is no legislation in Canada limiting or stopping women from aborting a child even up to full-term and partial-birth. Roughly one in five pregnancies end in abortion here in Canada, with over three million lives now terminated since it was made legal in 1988.

Later, as young adult woman, I volunteered at the local pregnancy centre and gathered weekly with a handful of others to pray about this issue within the churches and our nation. I was a youth leader in my local church at the time, and ended up having the opportunity to walk alongside a teen girl who had just started attending church and was facing an unexpected pregnancy.

One summer evening at youth group, she pulled me aside to tell me about it. She was fourteen—barely past the age of consent in Canada at the time. The father of the baby, an adult man many years her senior, had disappeared and the school counsellor was recommending abortion. We sat together on that ratty old couch, and I put my arm around her hunched shoulders. I happened to have a brochure on hand and was able to show her what the baby looked like at that point in its development. She wasn't convinced that evening, but within days she made the choice to carry that baby to term, with the intention of releasing him to be adopted. I had the privilege of visiting her in the hospital soon after she gave birth to that baby boy, and every year on his birthday, October 10th, I think of her courageous choice and pray for her son (who was adopted by a family from our church).

Even after all of this, I wasn't emotionally prepared for what it would be like to tell our own children about abortion. My sons stared at me in disbelief. I remember a sense of betrayal in their eyes, and questions poured out: "Why would a mom not want her child? How could someone hurt a baby?" It was like they were experiencing the jolting realization that the world wasn't as good and safe as they had believed only moments prior.

All of my sons have reacted with strong emotion. Some have pounded the table in anger and tried to devise ways to make it stop. Other times we've sat in silence, no words at all—just tears streaming down our faces and an ache in our chests.

Talking to our kids about abortion has always been difficult because the goal is multifaceted. We do not want to villanize anyone, but we also want them to recognize the gravity and injustice of the situation. Joanna Hyatt, author of *A New Position on Sex,* spent years as a spokesperson and resource creator for Live Action, a pro-life advocacy organization. As a mother of five, she understands the difficulty of talking about abortion with kids. Joanna shares,

"Ask any child what is in a woman when she's pregnant, and they will say, 'A baby!' It won't be difficult for them to understand that abortion is wrong because it intentionally destroys that life. It's only as we get older that we make up fancy and complicated arguments to try and convince each other of what we know at a gut level is wrong.
Never forget to weave grace into every conversation about abortion. Chances are good that you or someone you know has had an abortion. We are not aiming to raise kids who are legalistically righteous. We're raising kids who understand this world is broken, who are grieved by the things that grieve the heart of God, and who are seeking to bring the love and grace of Christ into their corner of the world, that people

might be transformed and renewed. Truth wrapped in grace will keep our children tender as they rebel against an upside down world."

We want our kids to think compassionately about the infants, mothers, and fathers involved, while pointing to God's design for sexuality so that every child is treasured, every mother is supported, and every father is a protector.

Here are a few keys to remember in these conversations about abortion:

1. **A baby does not gain its value or human rights at birth or viability.** The child's value is intrinsically connected to the fact that it is *human*, made in the image of God, granted its own DNA at the moment of fertilization. We do not have the right to kill other humans because the circumstances of their conception are less-than-ideal, or because their future may contain struggle. The argument that a pre-born baby is a parasite, sucking life from its host is not scientifically accurate. By definition, a parasite is a different species from the host, meaning the host's body would naturally fight against the presence of that parasite. Instead, the mother's body instinctively nourishes the fertilized egg, and is designed to deliver a healthy baby (of the same species) at full term if the process is not hindered.

2. **Advocating for a change in legislation is a great step to take.** Policies matter because people matter, and policies affect people. However, if the only thing in our society that keeps us from killing babies is a law, there is still a problem in our hearts. It is the intrinsic belief in the value of every human life that makes all the difference. Those of us who have experienced the self-sacrificial love of Jesus Christ carry a unique responsibility to stand up for the vulnerable—at a grassroots and a governmental level.

3. **Abortion doctors, pimps who pose as caring boyfriends, and extreme modern feminists who flaunt abortion are *not* our enemy.** We do not wrestle with flesh and blood but with principalities and powers that are eager to destroy a young generation (Ephesians 6:12). We can raise our voices against the wicked things that people do and the damaging philosophies

that people believe, but we can't allow anger and hatred to turn us against the very ones whom Jesus gave His life for. In the conversation about abortion, we can't stand up for one person's dignity while degrading another.

4. **Those little ones who have been aborted are in the loving care of God and will be safe for all of eternity.** The killing of innocent children is part of the enemy's scheme, but our kids need to know that God is a God of redemption. Aborted babies are not ultimately lost. They are not in pain anymore. They are already experiencing the peace and presence of God (Revelation 20:4).

5. **Throughout history, the people of God have played a key role in rescuing and protecting the vulnerable.** For instance, in the Roman Empire, it was common practice for unwanted infants to be abandoned outside the city walls, but it was the Christians who became notorious for sneaking out after nightfall to rescue those babies and adopt them as their own! These kinds of efforts have been a mark of the church ever since. Christians continue to show up in a beautifully disproportionate way in the world of adoption and fostering. It is a natural expression that comes from the hearts of those who have experienced 'spiritual adoption' and who also understand the profound value that God places on every child.

From our experiences with these weighty conversations, I'd like to also offer a few recommendations:

1. **Be cautious with how many details you give kids about abortion procedures.** They may ask for more information than they can handle. Depending on their age and sensitivity, you may need to withhold details about the violence involved.

2. **Be sensitive about the time of day that you share abortion-related information.** When our boys were young, if one of them asked a question about abortion too close to bedtime, I would usually postpone the conversation and tell them that we would talk about it in the morning. We want our kids to bring their

questions to us, but we also don't want to leave them alone with those heavy thoughts in the dark.

3. **Try to direct any conversation about abortion or child abandonment towards a proactive stance.** As a family, we don't want to avoid the discomfort of grief, but as the conversation moves on, we can brainstorm ways to practically help children or single mothers. Perhaps you could sponsor a child, donate items to be distributed to moms in need, or volunteer at the local pregnancy centre. You could also look at fostering or take a step in the direction of adopting—either internationally or locally.

Topics like abortion can often leave people feeling overwhelmed or helpless, but if we are willing to pray and respond to the nudges of God's Spirit, we can each play a role in a pro-life movement, not just a pro-*birth* stance.

CLOSING THE DOOR TO DEATH

Not long ago I attended a church leadership conference in eastern Canada. As the morning session was closing, the service host invited people to come forward if they would like some prayer. I was standing beside a young woman who knelt down and raised her hand, indicating that she was in need. I knelt beside her, placed my hand on her shoulder and asked,

"What can I pray with you for?"

"I struggle with mental health."

I felt the Lord nudge me to ask some follow-up questions.

"How long has this been going on?"

"Four years."

"Can you tell me what was going on four years ago?"

"I was in a really toxic relationship."

I paused and again felt the Lord bring another question to mind.

"Was there an abortion?"

"No," she answered quickly.

"Was there a morning-after pill?" I gently asked.

At this point, the young woman literally folded over in half and began to weep. I sat grieving with her, praying grace over this dear woman, then asked if her mental health included a sense of despair—a temptation to end her own life. She nodded, head still bowed low. Even though she didn't know for sure if she had ended the life of her child, and despite the fact that it had all happened at a time of her life when she wasn't following Jesus, she had been carrying great sorrow and regret ever since.

I sat with her and we prayed together. She was aware that she had violated her own maternal design, but in prayer she began to see that in taking the morning-after pill—essentially a "tool of death"—she had unknowingly opened a door for the enemy, whose only objective is to steal, kill and destroy. Suicidal ideation, confusion and despair had crept in through that door. She repented for the part she had played, and through the power of the blood of Jesus and in His name, we closed the door to the demonic torment she was experiencing. As I slowly lifted her head, cradled her face in my hands, and asked our heavenly Father to bring His healing touch to her mind and body, her tears of sorrow changed to become tears of joy. She smiled in relief and told me that she could tangibly feel the love of God being poured into her.

This is the heart of God: to bind up the broken-hearted and to end the injustices—even the self-inflicted ones—that have caused death and sorrow in so many lives. With thousands of unborn babies losing their lives every day across the nations of the earth, and thousands of mothers living with the weight of regret from abortion, we cannot remain silent on this matter.

Abortion is an issue that deeply affects individuals and families, but it also affects regions and nations. Remember, the collapse of every great empire or society on earth had two predictors in common. It is not a coincidence that these factors keep showing up; it's as if the enemy has come up with a scheme to ensure the downfall of the human race: the distortion of sexuality and the devaluing of human life. In the case of abortion, the second naturally follows the first, because the temptation is to eliminate responsibility and be able to have "no strings attached" sexual experiences.

If the enemy can get us to see children as a burden and not a blessing, if moms and dads will abandon their assignment, if babies are killed in the womb, then there will inevitably be destruction in homes and in nations. In contrast, if we can welcome a child into our lives, bless the kids in our homes, our neighbourhoods and our church communities—then we become a defence against the enemy's ploys. This is the power of every loving family, every foster and adoptive parent, and every committed youth leader or legacy-minded grandparent. As Mother Teresa once said, "If you want to change the world, go home and love your family." Let's speak life and encouragement over our children with *that* in mind.

Defending the Rights of the Afflicted

There is a tragic story about Adam and Eve's children found in the early pages of Genesis that gives us insight into God's heart for the innocent. Adam and Eve had two sons, Cain and Abel. The narrative explains that as grown men, the older brother Cain, became so jealous of his younger brother, Abel, that he plotted his death:

> *One day Cain suggested to his brother, "Let's go out into the fields." And while they were in the field, Cain attacked his brother, Abel, and killed him. Afterward the Lord asked Cain, "Where is your brother? Where is Abel?" "I don't know," Cain responded. "Am I my brother's guardian?" But the Lord said, "What have you done? Listen! Your brother's blood cries out to me from the ground! Now you are cursed and banished from the ground which has swallowed your brothers' blood."*
> **Genesis 4:8-11 NLT**

Here we see a principle introduced—that whenever innocent blood is spilled, though the living person is no more—it's like their blood in the ground is crying out for justice. We see the concept repeated throughout the Scriptures where God warned His people about the travesty and national consequences if innocent blood was shed in the land without reparation.[33]

When speaking about God, the Bible explains,

> *"Righteousness and justice are the foundation of your throne; love and faithfulness go before you."*
> **Psalm 89:14 NIV**

---

33 Numbers 35:6-34; Deut. 19:1-13; Deut. 21:8-9; Deut 27:25; 1 Samuel 19:5; 2 Kings 21:16; 2 Kings 24:4; Psalm 106:38; Proverbs 6:17; Isaiah 59:7; Jeremiah 7:6; Jeremiah 22:3, 17; Jeremiah 26:15; Matthew 27:4; Acts 18:6

Notice the connection between justice and love; it is God's love that compels Him to defend the innocent. For those who have endured injustice, it is comforting to know that God does not turn a blind eye to these acts. He is a righteous King who sees and hears it all. If in that story of Cain and Abel, God could "hear the cries" of one man's blood, do we not also think that He can hear the cries of the blood from millions of aborted babies? And would He not also stir His people to respond and advocate for them?

Hebrews 12:23-24 (NIV) says,

> *"You have come to God, the Judge of all . . . to Jesus the mediator of a new covenant, and to the sprinkled blood that speaks a better word than the blood of Abel."*

The innocent blood of Abel cried out for justice—for someone to avenge his death. But the innocent blood of Jesus that He willingly poured out for us, speaks a *better* word. It proclaims, "Justice has been satisfied; now mercy is available for all."

To the mother who is weighed down with regret for past decisions: *there is mercy available.*

To the father who once coerced someone to get an abortion: *there is mercy available.*

To the doctors and nurses involved in procedures that brought death, or pro-choice lobbyists who ushered people through this doorway: *there is mercy available.*

If you are reading this today and abortion is a part of your story, I want you to rest assured that God's forgiveness and healing are available for you. Hebrews 10:22 says,

> *". . . our guilty consciences have been sprinkled with Christ's blood to make us clean, and our bodies have been washed with pure water."*

You are not disqualified as a mother or father; your past need not dictate your future! Jesus wants you to be released from all guilt, to be free to receive and give love. Don't walk alone—I implore you—let someone you trust into this part of your story.

REFLECTION QUESTIONS

1. When you were a child, were there any people in your life who clearly believed in the value of children and cared for you? Do you have memories of people who treated you as a nuisance or burden?
2. When you think about the biblical estimation of children as a blessing and a reward, how do you see this contrasted with Western culture? Are there any adjustments that you want to make when you consider the value of children?
3. Is there an aspect of the pro-life/pro-choice debate that you want to research further so that you can feel more confident in your beliefs?

17

A CONVERSATION ABOUT MARRIAGE AND MAKING LOVE

"I'm going to marry you, Mommy."

Over the years, I've been proposed to (or more accurately, claimed) by every one of our six sons. And each time, my heart melted into an absolute puddle. They were so little, and this was the most obvious way they knew how to express their commitment to love me forever. I can recall one of them bent over a grilled cheese sandwich, and in between bites, making the declaration to his brothers, "I'm going to marry mommy when I'm a man."

At that stage in their development, being only three or four years old, they couldn't fathom the idea of loving anyone more than they loved me. I was truly honoured. When I broke it to each of them that I was already married to Daddy and couldn't marry someone else, they were slightly heartbroken. And maybe a little jealous of Daddy.

Their confession of commitment was just a natural response to their love for me. In all relationships—familial, platonic, or romantic—the deeper the connection we make with someone, the more prone we are to desire exclusivity and loyalty, and we feel anxious at the idea of losing that connection.

God designed marriage to be the place of deepest commitment and intimacy. Marriage is not a social contract or a government-issued piece of paper. It is a covenant. A covenant is the deepest promise someone can make. It is a key relationship on earth that reflects Christ's love and commitment to His people, the church. And it is within this covenant that God wholeheartedly encourages sexual intimacy and pleasure between husband and wife. Marriage is also the context where God places the sacred responsibility of raising the next generation.

And in case you are wondering, when one of my sons would tell me of their plan to marry me, I would guide them to find new vocabulary for their affections, "Are you telling me that you are going to love me forever? Because, I promise you that I will love you forever too."

The Forgotten Significance of Covenant

Before Bryan and I had begun dating, we were a part of a discipleship school where we learned about the significance and power of covenant. A woman from our church taught a class every week, opening the Scriptures to highlight the way God loves us—with covenantal love. She spoke with passion in her voice and a spark in her eye! She knew that if we could grasp the concept of covenant, our faith would grow. I remember nodding along, taking notes, trying to wrap my head around God's love in that new way.

It makes me think of Ephesians 3:14-19 where the apostle Paul wrote,

> *"For this reason I kneel before the Father, from whom every family*
> *in heaven and on earth derives its name... I pray that you, being*
> *rooted and established in love, may have power, together with all the*
> *Lord's holy people, to grasp how wide and long and high and deep is*
> *the love of Christ, and to know this love that surpasses knowledge—*
> *that you may be filled to the measure of all the fullness of God." (NIV)*

Paul wanted the early church to understand the love of God that surpasses cognitive acknowledgement. God doesn't just *feel* His love for us. His choice to love us is fixed. God in heaven has made a covenant with us mere mortals here on earth.

Covenant may sound like an old-fashioned religious word, but the concept was common before it was ever recorded in the Scriptures. Covenant was used for the joining together of nations, of tribes, of families, or of individuals. These covenants were strategic vows, where both parties would benefit. For instance, a tribe with notoriously strong warriors might join with a tribe that was rich in natural resources. Or one individual who had abundant land might form a covenant with someone who had strategic alliances. Whatever the case, each party was committing to offer its strength to offset the weakness of the other.

In the ancient Middle East, when such covenants were made, it was called "cutting a covenant". And it was a messy process.[34] First, the two parties involved would determine the conditions, then a day would be set when they would meet to express their commitment clearly before witnesses. There would also be animal sacrifice, where multiple animals (sheep, cows, goats, etc) would be lined up, slaughtered, cut in half, and dragged apart—resulting in an aisleway of blood. The two parties, or a representative from each party, would walk together side-by-side down that aisle, making a solemn commitment, "I will offer my strengths for your sake. And may it be done to me, as was done to these animals, if I break this covenant."

Essentially they were saying, "until death do us part."

The individuals would also mark their body—the resulting scar or piercing was a permanent reminder and an indication to the world, that they were in covenant. When these ceremonies were complete, a giant celebration would break out, with dancing and feasting to commemorate the occasion. The two had become one.

In our Western culture today, marriage is the last vestige of this ancient practice. When a wedding invitation arrives, we generally know what to expect—of course, there is the question of what colour the bridesmaid dresses will be, and if there will be a funny emcee at the reception. But we all know that the ceremony will include walking down the aisle, witnesses on either side, with verbal commitments made and rings exchanged. And we know there will be a party—covenant is worth celebrating.

Throughout the Scriptures, covenant language is used to describe the relationship between God and humanity.[35] In fact, the words "Old Testament" literally mean the "old covenant", and the New Testament is the record of the "new covenant" that was made available through Jesus.

---

34 David Noel Friedman, ed., *The Anchor Bible Dictionary.* New York: Doubleday, 1992. s.v. "covenant."

35 For an example of a biblically-recorded covenant, see Genesis 15:1-10.

In the hours before Jesus faced crucifixion, He sat down with His disciples for a Passover feast, a tradition that Jewish people celebrated annually. But this night was different than all the others—Jesus told them about the new covenant:

> *And when He had taken some bread and given thanks, He broke it and gave it to them, saying, "This is My body which is given for you; do this in remembrance of Me." And in the same way He took the cup after they had eaten, saying, "This cup which is poured out for you is the new covenant in My blood."*
> **Luke 22:19-20**

The very next day, Jesus himself became the covenant sacrifice—the "lamb", wounded and bloody, walked down an aisleway towards the hill of Golgotha with the crowds serving as witness. As He carried the cross, Jesus fully represented both parties—mankind and God. He was crucified that day, innocent, yet slain. Three days later, when He was raised from the dead, He chose to keep the scars on His resurrected body—an eternal indication of the covenant He has made with humanity. He gave His strength to cover our weakness, His life to overcome death for us.

The Bible begins with a marriage—between Adam and Eve. Did you realize that the Bible also concludes with a wedding? In the book of Revelation, the apostle John paints a beautiful picture of how at the end of this age, all that was broken will be made new because of the victory of the Lamb who was slain:

> *And I heard a loud voice from the throne saying, "Behold, the tabernacle (dwelling place) of God is among men, and He will dwell among them, and they shall be His people, and God himself will be among them, and He will wipe away every tear from their eyes; and there will no longer be any death; there will no longer be any mourning, or crying or pain; the first things have passed away."*
> **Revelation 21:3-4 (parentheses added)**

Then an angel shows up and says to John, "Come here, I will show you the bride, the wife of the Lamb" (Revelation 21:9).

This is all symbolic language; Jesus is not waiting in heaven as a literal lamb with hooves and wool, and the church—the people of God—are not a literal bride with a white gown and veil. But together they portray a picture of the covenantal love that God has shown to humanity. He has initiated the relationship, He has "proposed" to us, and He has vowed His utmost faithfulness. This marriage is just as real—in fact, even *more* real—than the marriages we commit to in our comparatively short lives. Yet, our marriages here on earth catch the light of that heavenly reality and point to something greater, something beyond the material realm.

THE MYSTERY OF MARRIAGE

Years ago a friend paid Bryan and I a great compliment. At the time, she was not a Jesus-follower and wasn't sure what she thought about God in general. But one day she commented, "When I see the way you two love each other, it makes me think that there really may be a God."

In Ephesians 5, the apostle Paul lays out both the responsibilities of the husband and wife, but also the significance and sanctity of marriage.

> *"Wives, be subject to your own husbands, as to the Lord. For the husband is the head of the wife, as Christ also is the head of the church, He Himself being the Savior of the body. But as the church is subject to Christ, so also the wives ought to be to their husbands in everything. Husbands, love your wives, just as Christ also loved the church and gave Himself up for her...for no one ever hated his own flesh, but nourishes and cherishes it, just as Christ also does the church, because we are members of His body. For this reason a man shall leave his father and mother and shall be joined to his wife, and the two shall become one flesh.* **This mystery is great; but I am speaking with reference to Christ and the church."**
> Ephesians 5:22-25, 29-32

"This mystery is great; but I am speaking with reference to Christ and the church." The significance of marriage goes beyond human companionship, partnership, and intimacy. Somehow, mysteriously, marriage is the shadow cast into this earthly realm from the transcending reality of the covenant that God made with humanity. This is why we, the church, are called the Bride of Christ. God says, "You are mine and I am Yours. The two have become one."

Then He commissions us, men and women in all our frailty and brokenness, to do our best to represent that covenantal loyalty within our marriages. I don't know about you, but when I consider this God-ordained commission, I am inspired—and challenged—to continue offering my strengths for the sake of my spouse.

When Marriages Don't Make It

I remember my gut response as a kid when I first heard the words of Malachi 2:16, "For I hate divorce!" says the Lord, the God of Israel.

"Yikes!" I thought, *"God hates divorce?! That sounds pretty harsh."*

Later in my teen years, I remember prayerfully reflecting on that verse. I sensed the Lord whisper to my heart, "I hate it for all the same reasons that people do."

Divorce is rooted in heartache, and it causes heartache. It creates tension among families and friends, and it leads to instability for children. It's simply not the happily-ever-after that most people are aiming for. Yet divorce is a reality for many people today.

Regardless of the events that led to someone's divorce, it can be a tricky thing to talk about with your kids. A good friend of mine, Ruth Erickson, author of *(Un)faithful: finding healing after your husband's affair (whether your marriage survives or not)*, shared some thoughts with me about how she helped her kids navigate divorce:

> "I never imagined my children would walk through the trauma, pain and loss of a divorce, and when it became reality after my ex-husband's unrepentant affair, the effect on my sons was one of the hardest griefs I faced. I could not shield them from all the pain, but I determined to do what I could to absorb as much of it as possible and protect them from further damage.
>
> Many parents in my situation are tempted to react to such deep agony with retaliation toward their ex, but a child's attachment and self-concept are tightly knit with both parents, regardless of the quality of their character. It was important in those early days to realize that my sons' attachment to their dad is important to their mental and emotional health. Since learning that, I have done everything I can to be positive

and encouraging of that attachment. The price for the broken marriage is not something I want my children to pay. If co-parenting has to be hard, and it often is, I want it to be hard for me, not them.

Unavoidably, there is still heartache for my sons that I cannot eliminate, and I have done my best to give them the tools they need for healing. God's love is ultimately what they need most, and I have made it a priority for them to learn about and experience His presence and goodness. I have also learned to be emotionally attuned to them, so they are safe to process all their feelings without worrying about my reaction. I encourage relationship with other healthy adults in our church community, and I have had them in professional counselling during different stages of their grieving process.

Ultimately, being the most whole version of myself that I can, offering them a faithful witness to my own connection with God, prioritizing their needs over my own emotions, and contending for them in prayer have guided me as I have led them on this painful path."

If you have gone through a painful divorce, I encourage you to take steps like this mom has done. Process your own pain, and make space for conversations with your kids so that they can process too. Stay connected with community, and seek professional counsel when needed. Divorce isn't the end of your story, or your child's story.

We don't point at the Scriptural ideal of a faithful, godly marriage to rub salt in anyone's wounds, but to provide a lighthouse that can give guidance in the fogginess of our culture. We want our children's future relationships to be healthy and joyful, so in spite of the prevalence of divorce in our culture, we need to keep pointing to what helps marriages stay strong.

GOD'S GOOD DESIGN FOR SEX

There is an entire book of the Bible called *The Song of Songs*, dedicated to celebrating the pleasures of marital sex. I'm so grateful that God deemed the topic necessary to be included in Scripture. In the midst of discussion about those things more traditionally considered 'holy', like prayer, faith and forgiveness, God is unafraid to announce, "Sex is *good*. Enjoy! Explore! Rejoice! Embrace and savour your spouse—body and soul!"

In *The Song of Songs,* the writer says that sexual love is a powerful force, like a burning fire or a rushing river. Fire brings warmth and energy, and water sustains life all along that riverbank in a steady, refreshing way. However, without a firepit to contain those flames, without riverbanks to hold back the rushing water, there is risk of great destruction. Fires and floods cause damage if they are not held within their proper place. God's boundaries around sexual experience serve to preserve that life-giving power. That boundary is emphasized within the Bible—one man and one woman, together in marriage covenant.

In recent decades there has been a lot of focus in the church on the ways that sex can go wrong. Perhaps well-meaning leaders were trying to prevent people from experiencing the physical and relational harm that comes from sexual immorality. The problem is that this tone cultivated a degree of intimidation around the idea of sex. The message in the church was often communicated something like, "sex outside of marriage is bad", but in many minds that sentiment was reduced to, "sex is bad".

I've heard from many people who are facing frustration and loneliness within their marriage because they can't seem to find freedom or intimacy with their spouse in the bedroom. Because of faulty messaging in the church, perversions within culture, or personal experiences that have caused deep shame, they find it hard to believe that God's design for sex is good.

The truth is, in its God-given context, sex is beneficial, even just at a physical level. Positive sexual experiences release endorphins into our bodies which are natural pain-killers, mood boosters, and stress relievers. These endorphins stimulate cells in our immune system that fight disease and protect against infections. Women who have sex regularly will also benefit from the increased production of estrogen in their system, which helps prevent conditions like heart disease, osteoporosis and Alzheimer's. Men who have sex regularly also tend to have less heart disease, lower stress levels and better sleep quality.

Of course, sex is not just about our bodies. As my one friend explains to her kids, "Sex knits our hearts together."

THE HORMONES OF CONNECTION

Sexual experiences, inside or outside of the marriage covenant, are embodied experiences, impacting us—body, soul and spirit. Jesus taught His followers,

> *"Have you not read that He who created them from the*
> *beginning made them male and female, and said, 'For this*
> *reason a man shall leave his father and mother and be joined to*
> *his wife, and the two shall become one flesh'?"*
> **Matthew 19:4-5**

Modern science has proven these words of Jesus to be true—sex binds people together. Intercourse and orgasm release dopamine and oxytocin—hormones which knit people together at a psychological level, stimulate connection, trust and relaxation, and can linger for up to forty-eight hours after a sexual encounter. Men in particular also experience an increase in vasopressin, a hormone that binds him with his partner and stirs up a protective instinct over his partner. Within marriage, these "binding hormones" help individuals remember all the things they love about their spouse, even in the midst of life's inevitable challenges.

Young children will not be ready to understand all of these elements, but as they get older, we as parents can share with them about the benefits of God's design for sex.

The "marriage bed" is meant to be a place of complete intimacy, with nothing coming between husband and wife. It is meant to be a place of vulnerability, safe from the risk of rejection. When we as parents grow to understand sexual intimacy, we can pass on hopeful expectations to our children of the joy that can be theirs in a marriage of their own one day.

INVESTING IN YOUR MARRIAGE

As a guest at wedding ceremonies, I've often heard the phrase, "What God has joined together, let no one separate."

Yes, that's a good sentiment. I always nod in agreement. But can we also agree that it's one thing to give mental assent; it's a whole other matter to intentionally resist "marital drift", especially when kids are added to the mix. We can be having key conversations with our kids about what makes a healthy marriage, but perhaps more importantly, we want to *model* a healthy marriage. Here are a handful of ideas to consider:

1. **Prioritize quality time with your spouse.** Life is full—sometimes it can feel like a runaway train! It takes intentionality to 'pump the brakes' long enough to go for a walk, a coffee date, or an overnight anniversary away from the kids. Bryan and I have often said that we don't want to end up as strangers who just stare blankly at each other once all our kids have left the nest. Your dates don't have to be fancy, but be sure to show your kids that this primary relationship still matters to you.

2. **Schedule your values.** And in this case, by "values" I actually mean "sex". As parents, we are in the midst of a season that is productive and fulfilling, but also extremely tiring. I know it doesn't sound romantic, but trust me, *scheduled sex* is far superior to *no sex*. So strategize the best time of day and optimal days of the week, and lock your door. Your kids will never know the steps you took to invest in physical intimacy, but the resulting release of oxytocin in your relationship will benefit the whole family.

3. **Thoughtfully establish boundaries together that will protect your marriage.** Within Christian circles, a lot of emphasis can be placed on boundaries *before* marriage—what appropriate emotional intimacy and physical affection looks like—but I don't hear as much about the boundaries necessary to protect your relationship *within* marriage. Historically, covenant partners wore a symbol or marked their body to indicate to everyone around, "I belong to someone else!" Wedding rings provide that sign for most couples today, but what other behaviours could a husband or wife choose that would declare this message and prevent relational drift? I encourage you to discuss with your spouse about online and in-person discretion—and the safeguards that can prevent secrets from accumulating. You might choose to share your phone or email passwords with one another, discuss what types of affection you feel comfortable showing to members

of the opposite sex, or what situations you will choose to actively avoid. We protect that which matters most to us, so let's never feel embarrassed about the need for boundaries in our marriage.

4. **Be transparent about conflict.** It is impossible for two people to live in close proximity without disagreement. On the occasions that you and your spouse have tension or a conflict and you know your kids have overheard or picked up on it, I recommend talking it through with them once there has been resolution. Don't give them all the details, but let them know that it's very normal for people to dispute and need reconciliation—even when those people love each other.

5. **Maintain a unified front.** You and your spouse are teammates; our kids need to know that we have each other's backs. In our home, this means that if one parent makes a decision that the kids don't like (ie. "no screen tonight" or "you have to finish your chores before playing"), they cannot undermine authority by trying to get a different answer from the other parent. Bryan and I also try really hard not to correct or confront one another in front of the kids. We want to give security to our children by developing an atmosphere that states, "Mom and Dad are a team."

When I consider the distractions and difficulties that Bryan and I have faced in our marriage—sickness, mental health challenges, miscarriage, financial pressure, workplace stress, friendship loss—the instruction of Scripture becomes something of a prayer: "What God has joined together, let no one separate. *Lord, not even us.*"

LEAVING A LEGACY

I know that these conversations about marriage can be a source of deep pain for many people. You may not have witnessed a healthy marriage between your parents, or any relatives, for that matter. Or perhaps you've experienced the pain of unfaithfulness in marriage through adultery or an emotional affair. You may struggle with flashbacks of previous partners or pornographic content while you are having sex with your spouse. Possibly, old relational wounds have left you struggling to be vulnerable or build intimacy.

If that is your situation, you are not alone. What God asks of us is to come out of hiding—to let some light in. Don't be afraid of being real about what you are going through, to ask for help, and to learn from the wisdom of others. Even on our best day, none of us will achieve a marriage that is beyond the need of God's grace. And even on our worst day, we are not disqualified from receiving that grace. His covenant of love remains. He offers His strength as a covering for our weaknesses. In the midst of our unsteadiness, difficulties and fears, He remains faithful.

Reflection Questions

1. How have you viewed sex, and how has your journey of faith impacted that view?

2. What did you learn about covenant that will impact how you treat your spouse? How will it change the way you talk about or view marriage in general?

3. If you've experienced divorce, are there any follow-up conversations that you now realize you need to have with your child?

18

A CONVERSATION ABOUT DATING AND SINGLENESS

One of our sons once informed us that he doesn't think he'd like to get married. He says that he would like to be a dad, but he doesn't like the idea of kissing a girl on the lips. So, he's considering adopting. An older, wiser brother advised him that since kids would probably want to have a mom too, this may not be a good idea. Maybe he could find a wife who didn't want to kiss either? I smiled knowingly, "Sure, bud. That might be a good option."

We have had so many funny conversations over the years as our sons have talked through their views on romance and marriage. Kids are watching and wondering what their future marriage could look like, based on what they observe in us—their parents—but also in the relationships of their friends' parents, their grandparents, and their wider community.

Though the idea of "one man, one woman, till death do us part" has been distorted and belittled over the years, when asked, the majority of young people still disclose that they would like to get married and have a family one day. In 2024, a room full of *OnlyFans* social media influencers who specialized in porn production were asked whether they'd prefer "a successful career, or a happy marriage and family". Every one of them vulnerably admitted that their primary desire was for the latter. [36]

There is a flame of romance still burning in the hearts of people—the idea of being chosen and treasured by someone is appealing to most. In

---

36 Brian Atlas, host. *The Whatever Podcast*, Episode 172. Released June 24, 2024.

fact, a 2025 *Times* article shared that members of Gen Z (born 1997-2010) are roughly twice as likely to think that marriage is important and relevant compared with Millennials (born 1981-1996).[37]

Though the majority of young people see marriage as a desirable thing, the average marrying age is on the rise in most Western nations. People are also older than in previous generations when they date for the first time.[38] As the *American Institute for Boys and Men* explains,

> "Until very recently, American culture has operated on the flawed notion that teenage dating and sex required little encouragement. Teenage romance was once seen as a natural part of American adolescence. This, it turns out, is completely wrong. Teenage dating is not inevitable, and it's a rapidly disappearing part of the American teenage experience."[39]

The next generation is timid when it comes to approaching the opposite sex, and they are also more hesitant to commit. The question is, why is this happening?

There are many contributing factors to this shifting social landscape, one of the most impactful being the advent of widespread online content in the 2010s, which still today is keeping teens isolated and distracted.[40] Instead of heading to the mall after school or to the beach on the weekend, this generation is more likely to connect in a digital space, meaning fewer face-to-face, real-life chances to communicate and relate. Not only is this factor negatively impacting their mental health, teens are also getting less practice in the "courting rituals" (a.k.a. flirting) that indicate interest in a relationship.

Add to this the fear of vulnerability or heartbreak, a lack of positive marriage role models, hesitation to commit, fear of marriage failure, and

---

37 "Gen Z, Marriage, Sex, and Relationships Survey," *The Times*, accessed October 11, 2025, https://www.thetimes.com/uk/society/article/gen-z-marriage-sex-relationships-survey-The-Times-Generation Z study,be married before having children.

38 "Marriage: 'I Do'? More Like 'I Don't,'" *Statistics Canada*, accessed October 11, 2025, https://www.statcan.gc.ca/o1/en/plus/2507-marriage-i-do-more-i-dont.

39 Daniel A. Cox, "Gen Z's Romance Gap: Why Nearly Half of Young Men Aren't Dating," *American Institute for Boys and Men*, February 8, 2024, accessed October 14, 2025, https://aibm.org/commentary/gen-zs-romance-gap-why-nearly-half-of-young-men-arent-dating/.

40 Haidt, *The Anxious Generation*.

widespread economic challenges that prevent young people from feeling "ready", and we can understand why dating and marrying rates are at a historic low, with an average of only four marriages annually per every thousand people in most Western Nations.[41] [42]

Whereas parents of a previous generation were primarily concerned about their teenager dating too young or jumping into a relationship too quickly, parents today may have to approach things a little differently, nudging our sons or daughters out the door, supporting them as they make friends with members of the opposite sex, and yes, even encouraging them to find ways to express interest when the time is right.

As parents we need to think through three key questions: What should our role as parents be in a teen's "love life"? What is the primary goal of dating? And what does a healthy, God-honouring dating relationship look like?

THE ROLE OF PARENTS: MATCHMAKER OR SPECTATOR?

Growing up, my older sister and I watched the film *Fiddler on the Roof* regularly—so often, in fact, that we knew most of the song lyrics by heart and would turn our mandated, post-dinner dishwashing sessions into theatrical performances of *If I Were a Rich Man* and *Miracle of Miracles*. The story is set in a Jewish community of Ukraine in the early 1900s when time-worn traditions were being challenged. The main character, the father Tevye, along with his wife and five daughters, must navigate the shifting political and social perspectives.

As a pre-teen, I was amused—and even appalled—by the role of the village matchmaker, Yente. This comical, invasive old woman lived her life trying to arrange future marriages between the neighbourhood boys and girls and showed up regularly at Tevye's home with suggestions of matches for his daughters. This ended up being one of the most controversial themes

---

41 *Statistics Canada*. "Marriage and Family Statistics." Accessed October 14, 2025. https://www150.statcan.gc.ca/n1/daily-quotidien/221114/cg-b003-eng.htm.

42 *The Marriage Foundation*. "The Collapse of Marriage Among Men Z." December 2024. https://marriagefoundation.org.uk/wp-content/uploads/2024/12/MF-briefing-note-Collapse-of-marriage-among-Gen-Z.pdf.

of the film. *Should it be the matchmaker and parents who are primarily responsible for finding an eligible spouse? Or should the younger generation be released to make that decision on their own?*

For most of human history, the pressure of choosing a suitable life partner was deemed too great to place squarely on the shoulders of young people, who inevitably had less life experience. There is evidence of matchmaking rituals in the ancient Aztec civilization, as well as in ancient China and Greece, Japan, India and Israel—most often the matches were based on social standing, beauty, wealth or skill sets. At times when communities and people groups were isolated from one another, matchmakers were commissioned to venture into other regions with the hopes of finding good prospects.

As a teen, I would have considered matchmaking archaic and laughable. The idea of parents or a community being actively involved in the process of 'finding love' felt stifling. Little did I know that our *modern* idea of dating was the actual social experiment, and that it wasn't guaranteed to get us the results we were aiming for. Most men and women, even those who are now in a happy marriage, carry some form of regret from their dating experiences ranging from gnawing memories of embarrassment to significant emotional or sexual trauma. Traditional intermediaries are rarely used in the West anymore but a growing percentage of single people have turned to another form of matchmaker—the algorithms of dating apps—in the hopes of finding love. Yet success rates remain low, and frustration levels are at a record high. Monthly subscription fees, ghosting, catfishing, and experiencing deplorable treatment on first dates are among the pitfalls. I believe that we as parents can help the next generation keep their eye out for a potential life partner, and that by asking good questions and having rich conversations, we can help guide both the timing and the goal of a healthy dating relationship.

Parents are called to be more than spectators in this season of life. We can learn to support our growing children—without becoming that intrusive 'Yente' busybody everyone is trying to avoid.

THE PURPOSE OF DATING

The ministry that Bryan and I co-founded—The Union Movement—is all about supporting local churches to have gospel-centred conversations about sexuality. We have been invited to participate in a considerable number of young adult gatherings with Q&A panels, where people can anonymously text in their questions about all things related to sex, identity, or relationships. We have found that a good percentage of the questions coming in are about what healthy dating looks like. Young people are wondering how they can honour their faith in Jesus *and* find Mr. or Mrs. Right.

I find joy when I read the letter from the apostle Paul to the church of Corinth—a city that would have dealt with a lot of the social issues that we do today. 1 Corinthians 7 begins, "Now concerning the things about which you wrote..." Paul then proceeds to give lengthy descriptions about singleness and marriage. It turns out Jesus-followers have been sending in their relationship questions for centuries!

As parents, we can have conversations with our children—even from a young age—about what the deeper purpose of dating is. Dating is not a recreational sport to help people avoid loneliness on a Friday night, but it is also not something that inevitably leads to marriage. Dating—or courting, if you'd prefer to call it such—is the process by which two people can determine if they are compatible or not.

Especially within Christian culture, we need to remember that a successful relationship does not necessarily lead to marriage. Many young people get paralyzed by that kind of pressure, and won't even go out for coffee with someone unless they are sure he or she is "the one". A dating relationship can be a successful thing, whether it ends in a respectful break-up or progresses towards marriage, because so long as honour was maintained throughout the process, the goal of discovering compatibility was fulfilled.

Paul gave one key word of advice to the Corinthian church on this topic of compatibility within relationships:

> *"Do not be unequally yoked with unbelievers. For what partnership has righteousness with lawlessness? Or what fellowship has light with darkness?"*

2 Corinthians 6:14 ESV

Even though our family lives near farmland, I don't think our boys have ever seen a yoke in their lives! But Paul is using an excellent analogy here; a yoke was a wooden device placed across the shoulders and necks of two oxen, holding them together as they carried a load assigned to them by their master. That master knew how important it was to team animals together that were similar in both their capacity and willingness to follow his directions—otherwise it would lead to the frustration or even harm of the oxen. This analogy of being equally yoked is to encourage believers to marry someone who shares a commitment to Christ, but compatibility includes other factors too.

In the search for a life partner, young people will naturally look for someone they are physically attracted to (attraction certainly isn't *everything*, but it is *something!*), someone they can laugh with, and even someone to share hobbies or interests with, but we can also remind our kids to ask the more practical questions, such as, "Does it look like this person is heading a similar direction as me? At a comparable pace? With similar values?"

Inside Pretty and Outside Pretty

When I was in my early twenties, serving as a youth leader in our local church, I was talking with some teen girls who were probably about fifteen years of age. They were gushing and giggling about a famous young musician, showing me pictures of him on their phone.

"What do you like about him?" I asked with genuine curiosity.

"Oh, he is just *so* funny and has such good hair!" one girl responded enthusiastically.

I had a strong enough level of relationship with these girls to speak candidly, "No offence, but good hair is a dime a dozen."

They both looked up from their phones, mouths gaping, shocked by my opinion. The conversation has stuck with me, because I realize that so much of our consumer-driven culture is pushing us to evaluate one another's worth primarily on external features rather than on one's character and personhood.

Years ago while driving home in our minivan, I overheard our sons talking about cartoon characters. Though they would be mortified to acknowledge it now—I am a witness—they were each commenting on which Disney princess they thought was the prettiest. There was nothing inappropriate about the conversation; most kids have a natural awareness of feminine beauty. I joined in, and we discussed Cinderella with her lovely singing voice and kindness towards animals. We talked about Belle's bravery and desire to read and learn. We talked about Snow White's bright smile and willingness to help. I asked them, *"What if Cinderella had pretty eyes but was mean? What if Belle had pretty hair but was foolish? What if Snow White had a pretty smile but was lazy?"*

We agreed that true beauty is about more than what we see with our eyes. Some people are 'outside pretty', but not necessarily 'inside pretty'. The idea is expressed in Proverbs 31:30, "Charm is deceitful, and beauty is fleeting, but a woman who fears the Lord is to be praised."

In my own paraphrase, this could read,

> "A woman's appearance may be pleasing, but it can also make you overlook character issues. Youthful beauty inevitably fades over the years, but the woman who honours the Lord should be honoured in return."

Of course, this type of evaluation easily applies to the guys as well. We encourage and affirm our sons whenever they work out, when they practice good hygiene or style their hair, but we also are coaching them—discipling them—towards greater character. Because, like I commented to those youth girls, "Good hair is a dime a dozen." The flower of youthful beauty and strength eventually fades. Attraction alone cannot sustain an intimate relationship.

Our children are growing up surrounded by altered images of unrealistic, unsustainable beauty and strength. If they aren't alert to it, these delusions can shape their ideals of the type of person they want to date. We can remind the next generation to look beneath the skin, beyond the shape of someone's body, to the substance of their heart. As parents we more accurately understand that in the joys and crises of life, having a virtuous spouse who will stand by your side is far more valuable than having someone around who is just nice to look at.

MARRIAGE MATERIAL

There is a classic story of romance recorded in Genesis 24—the love story of Isaac and Rebekah. The chapter begins with a statement about Abraham, Isaac's father: "Now Abraham was old..."

Abraham was getting close to the end of his life, and looking around, he noted that there weren't any eligible wives in the area. At this point, Isaac was already forty years old, wealthy, established, and charactered...but also *lonely*. So Abraham commissioned a trusted servant to go out on a mission, in search of a young woman who would be a good life partner. The servant loaded up ten camels' worth of supplies and headed to Mesopotamia, to the city of Nahor.

> *He (the servant) made the camels kneel down outside the city by the well of water at evening time, the time when women go out to draw water. He said, "O Lord, the God of my master Abraham, please grant me success today, and show lovingkindness to my master Abraham. Behold, I am standing by the spring, and the daughters of the men of the city are coming out to draw water; now may it be that the girl to whom I say, 'Please let down your jar so that I may drink,' and who answers, 'Drink, and I will water your camels also'— may she be the one whom You have appointed for Your servant Isaac..."*
> **Genesis 24:11-14 (parentheses added)**

As the story goes, a beautiful single woman named Rebekah soon approached. When the servant requested some water to drink, she did exactly as he had prayed and offered to draw water for all the camels as well. The servant was in awe at the 'coincidence' of her offer, and in short order, he met with her family and explained the purpose of his journey. He then showered the family with gifts, demonstrating the security that Isaac could provide. Rebekah confidently accepted the marriage proposal, packed her bags, enlisted a female servant to come with her, and journeyed with this stranger to meet her fiancée.

Watering camels may have seemed like a strange initiation for the servant to use, but when we consider the magnitude of the feat, we gain some insight into what the servant was aiming at. Because those camels had journeyed a great distance, they were thirsty; to satisfy one of them would have required forty gallons of water—which weighs about three hundred pounds. To satisfy all ten of the camels required Rebekah to draw over three thousand pounds of water! Rebekah knew what she was offering, and she completed the task without complaint.

When Rebekah approached the well, the servant could instantly see her external beauty, but in the time it took to water those camels, he also found out that she was hospitable, generous, strong and persistent. He saw that she was more than a pretty face—she was marriage material.

In Genesis 24 we read about the moment when the servant and Rebekah approached the land of Canaan, where Isaac lived, and the young couple first saw each other:

> "Isaac went out to meditate in the field toward evening; and
> he lifted up his eyes and looked, and behold, camels were
> coming. Rebekah lifted up her eyes, and when she saw Isaac, she
> dismounted from the camel. She said to the servant, 'Who is that
> man walking in the field to meet us?' And the servant said, 'That
> is my master.' Then she took her veil and covered herself . . . and
> Isaac took Rebekah, and she became his wife, and he loved her."
> **Genesis 24:63-65, 67**

"He loved her." What a sweet conclusion to the story. Though their marriage would have had its share of struggles, here were two people who had the compatibility and character needed to build a life and family together.

As parents, Bryan and I don't expect our sons to have an overflowing bank account or be fully established in a career before they get involved in a serious relationship, but we want them to be rich in 'marriage material'— integrity, self-restraint, good communication skills, and a strong work ethic—among other characteristics needed to sustain a healthy relationship.

The Right Thing at The Right Time

One day, as I was driving with my teenage sons (so many conversations happen while driving, don't they?), they wanted to play a song for me that they had recently heard. I knew the chorus and began singing along, which surprised the boys. As the song ended, I commented, "That song has a covenant message. Could you hear it? He was singing all about faithfulness and building a life together and choosing one another over and over again. That is beautiful."

The force of romantic love *is* a beautiful thing, and it is worth writing songs about! I definitely prefer songs like this to the ones about infatuation or animalistic lust. It is certainly better than the relationship songs that are all about isolation or revenge.

We were almost home, so I quickly added, "The thing is, you will probably be tempted to say those kinds of words to someone before it's actually the time to say them. But trust me, it'll be better to wait until you are entering into covenant with someone before you make big promises like this."

Song of Songs 8:1 (NIV) implores us, "Do not arouse or awaken love until it so desires."

In a generation that simultaneously resists commitment and yet endorses sexual encounters or relational flings, it is a unique challenge to support our son or daughter as they express a desire for marriage, while encouraging them to not fantasize or obsess about the future.

For most young people, a desire for a special relationship—and the corresponding physical affection—will come years before they are ready for the weight of that responsibility, often around the onset of puberty. As moms and dads, we can actively coach our teens to use this time wisely in a few different ways:

1. **Encourage friendships with the opposite sex.** When I was young, my parents set me up for success and confidence in a very simple way. They spoke repeatedly about the value of having friends of the opposite sex and how their friendship with one another was the foundation for their marriage. They welcomed my sister and me to have boys as friends—and they didn't flinch when we took

them up on it! In my teen years, my parents happily opened our home to group hang-outs that included both guy and girl friends. They kept the pantry stocked with food, and didn't complain about our volume—not very often, at least. Our home had some basic boundaries—for instance, no boys in bedrooms—and my parents were almost always present. Though I didn't have any biological brothers, my parents created a space where I could grow in my ability to relate to and communicate with guys around me. Bryan and I got to know each other in a setting like this, where we were able to discover some key aspects of compatibility before we even started to date.

2. **Ask them questions about qualities to look for in a future spouse.** From my own experience as a kid, and from what I've observed now as a parent, from a young age, kids will ask each other, "Who do you like?" We want them to be asking an alternative question: "What do I like *about* them?" I explained it to one of my sons this way: "You know that you won't be able to drive a car until you are at least sixteen. You know that you likely won't be able to purchase your dream car until you are much older than that. But, when nice cars drive by, it is natural to notice them. Ask yourself, 'What do I like about that car?' Though you may never drive that particular vehicle, you can begin to recognize what type of car you'd like to be *committed to* one day." Obviously, this analogy is a simplistic one, but it helps them admire a person's qualities, without feeling the need to 'claim' them as their own.

3. **Guard against unrealistic romanticism.** Both boys and girls can be susceptible to unrealistic expectations when it comes to romance. In movies, music and literature, there is often messaging about finding a 'soul mate' or your 'other half', and it carries the idea that a young person's life will be incomplete or unfulfilling without a significant other. Fictitious characters and story lines romanticize dating so much that when young people start dating and discover that not every day is rainbows and fireworks—or when their boyfriend or girlfriend can't read their mind—they think something must be wrong with them and

that it's time to break up. As parents, we need to be involved with both the *filtering* of what kind of content gets consumed, but also the *processing* of messaging that is around us as a family. This is a great example of how being involved in a larger community can help. When our children hear true stories of life and love—with all the bumps people face along the way—they are more likely to bring realistic expectations to their dating relationships.

4. **Initiate conversations about what healthy relationships look like.** It's valuable to communicate with our teens about the deeper purpose of dating—building friendship and determining compatibility. Although every couple's story will be unique to them, we want to lay out some basic principles that healthy, God-honouring relationships have in common: honour, communication, purity, and community. *Honour* ensures that the young man and woman treat one another with mutual respect, placing God as Lord over their relationship as they prayerfully follow Him. Prioritizing clear and forthright *communication* in the relationship enables the individuals to get to know one another without pretence. We can help them develop the skill of asking good questions and giving thoughtful responses. Making decisions that guard sexual *purity* (1 Timothy 5:2, Hebrews 13:4) helps the relationship stay true to the objective of dating, without pumping it full of the hormones that physiologically bind a couple together prematurely, before they've entered into covenant with one another. And finally, keeping *community* as a high priority allows the couple to stay connected to the other valuable relationships in their world—especially those from older generations like parents, pastors and mentors—people who can offer wise counsel and support along the way.

THE LESSON OF SINGLENESS

In time, you may find yourself the parent of a son or daughter who, for any number of reasons, is wrestling with their singleness. There are plenty of friendly, attractive, and inspiring men and women who have never dated or been in a serious relationship before—I've talked with many over the years. At one time or another, they almost all deal with the nagging question, "Is God keeping me single to teach me a lesson?"

First of all, God doesn't keep people single because of their imperfections—that would suggest that all the married people figured out the secret to life and were perfect when they stood there at the altar on their wedding day. And we know *that* can't be true. But is there a lesson to be learned in the waiting? Of course.

Bryan and I met the summer after we had graduated. I had been the homeschooled church-kid in the 90s, complete with a *VeggieTales* themed birthday party, *DC Talk* cassette tapes in my Walkman, and summer youth camp. When we met at age seventeen, Bryan had only recently begun coming to church and figuring out what it meant to be a Jesus-follower. Prior to a radical encounter with the presence of God, his high-school experience had been full of pornography, drugs, sports, alcohol, parties... and deep depression that he kept hidden from everyone.

Though our teen years had been so vastly different, when we met, we hit it off immediately and became friends. Bryan made me feel like I could really be myself, and he made me laugh whenever we spent time together. It wasn't long before our feelings for one another grew, and we spent months in a strange "we're not technically dating, but everyone knows we like each other" season. We'd save seats for one another at church, and drive together to meet friends at the Chinese restaurant after the service. We bought little gifts for one another, went to movies together, and watched sunsets at the beach—you know, because 'just friends' do that.

"I think I'm falling in love with you," I vulnerably scribed in a note to him one fateful day. Bryan recounts that when he read those words at home later, he jumped up and threw a giant fist pump in the air. Yet, the Spirit of God led us on an unexpected road. It would be two more years before we ended up together. In those two years, we both had some learning to do.

Now looking back, we can see that the biggest lesson of all was the one that we all need to learn at some point: *There are some needs in my life that only God can fulfill.*

If we had jumped into a relationship or marriage before grasping that lesson—as best as twenty-year-olds can—we would have suffocated one another under the weight of our expectations. In those years of official singleness, I learned to trust God in a new way. I began to experience His love, His conviction, and His affirmation of me as a daughter. Bryan found freedom from the shame and addictions of his past and was established in his new identity as a son of God—a man of honour—who protected women instead of preying on them.

Through those two years, we maintained something of an awkward, distanced friendship. There were times when I feared losing Bryan, and I ached to run back to the rich conversations we had enjoyed. In that season of waiting, I came across the words of Jim Elliot, who had written about a similar scenario that he had been in with a young woman named Elisabeth. Even though they were compatible, God had made it clear to them that they were to take a step back and wait before proceeding into marriage. Elliot wrote in his journal, "Let not our longing slay the appetite of our living."

When we learn the lesson of singleness—there are some needs in my life that only God can satisfy, and that He alone can carry the full weight of the human heart—we find our appetite for living is renewed.

SOME THINGS TAKE TIME

As parents of single teens and young adults, we need to recognize how vulnerable they may be feeling. They likely have a timeline in their mind of when they thought they would be married—but these timelines do not always match reality, and usually, they are outside of our control.

Our kids will inevitably go through seasons when they don't get what they desire as quickly as they had hoped. In many ways, this is a testing time for young people. As parents, it's helpful to remember that the Biblical idea of "testing" is not like sitting down at a desk in front of a written-form test—some multiple choice, others in essay form—where our kids are trying not to fail. Rather, the picture of "testing" in Scripture is one of metal being heated in order to be forged and shaped for a purpose. The testing our kids are facing in singleness is about establishing them for what is ahead. So then, the single man or woman does not need to assume they are 'getting it wrong', but that there is life beyond the struggle of today.

As parents, we can pray that God would use the circumstances of their lives, as uncomfortable as they may be, to draw our kids closer to Him. In the waiting, we can encourage them to live with intentionality, surround themselves with life-giving community, grow as an individual, and lift their eyes beyond themselves, serving the world around them with abandon.

Some things just take time, not because there is something wrong, but because good things require patience. Consider the seed planted in the dark soil. Though we may eagerly wait for the plant to spring up and have great desire to taste the fruit, we aren't surprised that this process takes time. We know that digging up the seed to check on its progress won't help at all. Why do some plants germinate after one or two weeks, and others after eight weeks? It is all a part of God's sovereign plan. Like the baby in the womb, development isn't something to be rushed along. No matter how uncomfortable the pregnant mother gets, we know that the process is both necessary and worth the wait. Premature birth only brings complications. Unripened fruit is not as sweet. Some things just take time.

If you are the parent of a single son or daughter who is growing older and is wondering if God has a covenant partner for them in the future, your words of blessing and encouragement are so important. You can bring them comfort, reassurance, and perspective. They need to know that we are their biggest fans. Have your heart soft and sensitive to what they might be needing. We can provide a place of companionship and belonging as they may be facing the challenge of loneliness. Be generous with your affirmation, and say it out loud: "You're beautiful", "You're incredible," "We know the treasure of who you are", "There's nothing wrong with you."

Whatever their relationship status is, God has kind intentions towards our kids. They have a bright future ahead—and we will be there to champion them along the way.

REFLECTION QUESTIONS

1. What conversations can you initiate with your child(ren) about healthy dating relationships and expectations?
2. Is there anything you need to do to find closure from negative dating relationships that you've experienced in the past?
3. Take a little time to consider (and discuss with your spouse if possible) what you believe your role as parents should be in supporting your kids' dating relationships.

19

A CONVERSATION ABOUT WHEN THINGS GO WRONG

I once thought that if I was diligent enough, I could protect my kids from all kinds of brokenness, even that of their own making. Theologically, I knew it wasn't possible—all of humanity falls short of the glory of God . . . but somewhere deep inside of me, I believed that if I prayed enough, cared enough, and prepared them well enough, I would be able to save them from the schemes of the enemy, from sexual perversion and pain. I would do it right. I would stay alert. And my kids would adore me for it and never cease to follow my advice.

I suppose my good intentions were rooted in love. They are likely similar to the good intentions that led you to pick up this book in the first place and have carried you this far through the pages. But it wasn't just love. I was also terrified of the pain I would experience if I had to watch them suffer. As a young adult leader, I watched the effects that would happen when someone stepped outside of God's design for sexuality—I saw the sorrow on the faces of their parents and their family. I wanted so badly to honour the position of motherhood that God had set me into, and in my naivete, I thought my diligence would guarantee the outcome.

My husband and I make no claim on perfect parenting—far from it! Lord, have mercy!—but we can honestly say that we have been intentional. We've prioritized heart connection, read the Scriptures as a family, and talked openly about these awkward topics. We've had strict boundaries about screens in bedrooms and tried to filter what type of content is coming into our home. We've modelled what it is to live in community, confide in those we trust, and seek counsel from those wiser than us.

Yet . . . yet . . . yet . . . in spite of all our efforts, we have raised kids who trip over their feet and stumble sometimes—or even, at times, deliberately disregard what we have taught them. When I find out about it, my stomach drops, I get a lump in my throat . . . and I am reminded that, just like me, our children are in desperate need of the Saviour named Jesus. Because it is Jesus alone who can touch our stubborn, unyielding hearts and cause them to be soft and responsive again. It is Jesus alone who can change our innermost desires so that the sexual distortions we once relished become repulsive to us.

It is Jesus alone who can redeem the most broken of circumstances. He has a beautiful way of turning what the enemy meant for evil into an opportunity for glory. I've finally come to grips with the reality that we will never be a 'perfect family'—but I've also finally found rest in knowing that Jesus loves my kids even more than I do. He doesn't get tired. He never needs a day off. He is committed to them, and He will walk this road with us, whatever we may face.

CLEANING UP MESSES

When our boys were little, we helped them sop up the spilled apple juice or wash glue and finger paints off the kitchen table. I remember many times sitting with young ones on the floor in front of a big, dumped-out pile of blocks. It was time to clean up, but they were intimidated by the task. Every time they made an effort and tossed a block into the bin, I would match their effort and toss one or two in too. It always seemed to me like a picture of the grace of God—sitting with me in my mess, urging me on, and helping me accomplish what I couldn't do on my own.

In our home, we've often said, "Everyone makes messes. It's what we do with them that really matters."

As our kids grow older, their messes can feel more complicated, with more embarrassment and heartache connected to them. Whether accidental or intentional, it is good for our kids to know that we will be there for them, to guide them in that cleaning-up process.

Right from the beginning of time, God has been a Father who helps His children clean up the mess that they make. We see it in the way He drew near to Adam and Eve, pursuing them, inviting confession, and offering forgiveness. We can learn a lot from Him.

THE WHISPERS OF SHAME

If you are a student of the personality and tendencies of your child, you will likely be able to pick up when they are acting abnormally. I've lost track of the number of times my husband or I have been talking about one of our kids and commented curiously, *"He's just not himself right now. Something's up."* We have spent countless hours interacting with our sons, in play, in rest, and in work. We can recognize their 'normal', and we can tell when something funky is going on in their hearts. We don't always know what it is right away, but we become prayerful detectives, asking the Holy Spirit for clues and insight so that we can have purposeful conversations with them.

Our children need us to remember who they *really* are, even when they have temporarily forgotten. No matter how they are behaving, we get to call them back to their place of identity and connection. Every child makes mistakes, but as parents, our priority is maintaining relational connection. When a child resists relationship or seems to be hiding their heart from us, we need to ask, "Why?"

We may have unknowingly hurt their feelings, they may be feeling afraid of something, or there may be a tough situation with a friend that they don't know how to navigate. But we have found over the years that another common culprit is that they are carrying feelings of shame.

Shame is a heavy emotion that, if left unchecked, can become a barricade between people who were once in a close relationship. In some ways, shame is a natural internal response that we feel when we have violated God's boundaries, broken trust, or gone against our own design. Remember, shame is like a check engine light that shows up on the dashboard of our soul, begging for our attention so that things can be made right and we can go back to living peacefully in relationship with those we love. Because our sexuality is such a deep part of our being, the shame or brokenness that we can feel—especially if we have a soft conscience—is particularly potent.

Our enemy will always attempt to amplify the presence of reasonable guilt and turn it into a looming mountain of shame. The Bible tells us that Satan is an "accuser of our brothers and sisters" who "accuses night and day" (Revelation 12:10). His voice will attempt to distort how someone sees themself, how they see God, how they think others see them, and how they perceive God feels about them.

It is helpful to recognize the accusations of the enemy. He says things like:

"If anyone finds out what you've done, they will not love you anymore."

"You're dirty. You contaminate whatever you touch."

"You've ruined everything."

"God is disgusted with you."

"Don't bother crawling back to God now. You've messed up too many times."

"You're the only one."

"You're a monster."

God never speaks this way. Jesus promised us that when He returned to heaven, He would send us His Holy Spirit to help, comfort, and convict us. This is how we can discern between the whisper of God and the whisper of darkness. God's voice will always offer dignity. Even when He points out an area of weakness in our life, His voice inspires hope and often gives specific details to enable us to change. In contrast, when the enemy speaks his words of accusation, it will feel vague and despairing, trying to make us believe that we are alone and that there is no hope for us.

This is the difference between the kind conviction of the Holy Spirit and the condemnation that the enemy throws on people. Even when we have legitimately "messed up", Romans 8:1-2 (NIV) contains a beautiful promise for every child of God:

> "Therefore, there is now no condemnation for those who are in
> Christ Jesus, because through Christ Jesus the law of the Spirit who
> gives life has set you free from the law of sin and death."

By regularly talking about the Gospel—this good news of 'no condemnation' because of Jesus—in our homes, we establish an atmosphere of hope and our kids are more easily able to identify the lies of shame.

In the last few years, we've made it a practice in our home to take communion together—we pass a plate of crackers and a big cup of juice around the dining room table, we give a prayer of thanks for Jesus' sacrifice, and we remember the freedom He has granted us. Bryan and I have also discovered the power of sharing our testimonies with our boys—using discretion around the details depending on their age. We want them to know that we, too, have experienced the redeeming work and healing touch of Jesus.

Over the years, we have told our sons over and over (and over and over) again, on the good days and the bad days, "There is nothing you can do that can make me stop loving you." Sometimes they roll their eyes, groan, and with a little grin exclaim, "I know, Mom!"

When they were young, they may have imagined that we were saying, "I'll love you, even if you sneak cookies." Or, "I'll love you even if you push your brother." But as they grew older, they realized we weren't giving them an invitation for selfish behaviour. Instead, we were laying a foundation for all the extra challenges we knew they would face as adolescents learning to govern their thoughts and decisions in a sex-saturated culture. Nowadays, when they overcome the shame and share with us about something going on, we still wrap our arms around their broadening shoulders and whisper into their ear, "There's nothing you can do to make me stop loving you. Not even this."

WRONGLY PLACED SHAME

The reality is that many people, children included, are dealing with a significant level of shame because of sexual content they were exposed to or from a sexual encounter that was forced on them. On the occasion that a child is touched in the wrong way, either by an adult with full knowledge or by another child who didn't understand what they were doing, it is valuable for us to understand how shame shows up in complicated ways.

Many people are living with a mashup of two kinds of shame—one kind that came into their life because of their own choices, and another kind of shame from the things that other people have done or said. It is essential to be able to identify the particularly cruel and confusing voice of shame that barrages abused individuals with accusations such as:

"You wanted it to happen."

"You liked the attention."

"Your body is the problem."

"Something is wrong with you."

The truth is that this was *not* their fault. Even if they went along with it, they did nothing to deserve that abuse, they never would have chosen it, and God does not expect the abused to repent for what happened to them. Rather He wants them to find healing in His presence and comfort in connection with safe people who love them.

If your child has been violated in any way, I'm so sorry. I know that your heart must be broken right now. I want to remind you that God is close to the brokenhearted and aches with you. His arms are open to you, to draw you and your child close to His heart, speaking truth over you by His Spirit, and eliminating that voice of shame from your lives. Though you may feel shaken, you can partner with Him by speaking the following kinds of statements over your child:

"You never wanted this to happen."

"You are a pure child of God."

"There is nothing wrong with you."

"What happened to you is bad, but your body is good."

"God is making all things new. He is your Healer."

"We are so glad you are our child, right now, in the middle of this."

The Lord is a steady source of love and care for all His children. Just as He sought out Adam and Eve, we are called to seek connection with our kids when they are hiding in shame. Our friend and mentor Jim Anderson often says, "Shame will always try to keep you from the place where it can be broken." So then, how can shame be broken? By talking about it. This is the principle and power of confession.

THE POWER OF CONFESSION

Back in the Garden, after Adam and Eve disobeyed and had isolated themselves from the presence of God, He called out to them and asked them, "Where are you?" "What have you done?" As an all-knowing God, He wasn't looking for new information—rather, He was giving Adam and Eve a chance to be real and acknowledge what had happened. Secrets weigh heavily on us all. Research shows that shame is directly linked to increased anxiety, depression, symptoms of poor health, and even the more rapid progression of disease.[43] God didn't want Adam and Eve to carry the heaviness of secret sin, or to allow what they had done to further distort their relationship. He welcomed their 'confession' as a way to relieve them of their burden.

In the New Testament, we find two kinds of confession. There is a confession between us and God. This is explained in 1 John 1:9 (NIV),

"If we confess our sins, He is faithful and just and will forgive us our sins and purify us from all unrighteousness."

This confession is an admission to God about the ways that we have chosen sin—or even the ways that sin has affected us. Sexual sin, especially, can leave people feeling degraded or dirty. I heard of one young woman who, after getting home from a one-night stand, spent an hour in a hot shower, scouring her body, scrubbing away at her skin until it was raw, trying to feel clean again. God's promise to her—and to us—is, "Be honest with Me about what has happened, and I will forgive and purify you."

The confession that takes place *between* people is equally necessary. James 5:16 (ESV) says,

"Confess your sins to one another and pray for one another, that you may be healed."

Sometimes people avoid this kind of confession, reasoning that God knows all their secrets and all has been forgiven. It is terrifying to share 'the worst' about yourself with another human. We fear the disgust or rejection that we may see in their faces. For this reason, so many people—inside and outside of the church—live with the burden of secrets and shame.

---

43 Why the Secrets You Keep are Hurting You, https://www.scientificamerican.com/article/why-the-secrets-you-keep-are-hurting-you

The promise of Scripture is that this kind of confession from one person to another brings a level of freedom and healing that cannot be experienced any other way.

When my husband became a Christian, he was quickly released from many destructive, sinful habits. He stopped drinking, swearing and smoking almost immediately after encountering the love and conviction of God! But, as he often shares, his struggle with pornography did not wither up so easily. He had first been exposed as a five-year-old and had been regularly consuming it through his teen years, but now he was actively trying to give it up! Bryan says how he managed to string together some good days, but then would inevitably slip back, access the explicit content, then be left to deal with suffocating self-hatred and shame afterward.

One Sunday morning while at a church service, he felt ready to give up on faith altogether. He determined that after the sermon, he was going to walk to the front of the church and confess his "gross sin" to someone on the prayer team. But it wasn't really prayer he was looking for; he wanted someone to punish him. To tell him that he was an apostate. To kick him out of the church. He looked at the various members of the prayer team and chose the most intimidating-looking man among them. He was an elder of the church, a broad-shouldered, solemn-faced individual, well-known for his fiery sermons about 'end times'. Bryan faced up to this man, told him about the pornography, and braced for a rebuke.

The elder placed his hand firmly on Bryan's young shoulder. "Well, Bryan . . . He loves you."

Bryan still chokes up today when he recounts this life-altering moment. Where he had expected judgment, he met mercy. And it was mercy that gave him the strength to get back up again.

Today, Bryan freely shares the details of his story that once caused him so much grief because he wants people to realize that freedom—from porn, self-hatred, and shame—is available. But first, we must make ourselves vulnerable. Healing is found on the other side of confession.

REAL-LIFE CONVERSATIONS

The conversations we have with our kids will be diverse. There are countless scenarios that will need to be talked through, but if we can remember to speak tenderly, invite confession, partner with God to eradicate shame, and reestablish relational connection—we'll be in a good place.

Not long ago, I had a conversation like this with one of our younger boys:

"What's going on, buddy? You don't seem like yourself today. You're getting into trouble a lot today, hey?"

(He paused, struggling to lift his head or make eye contact)

"Yeah. I had a bad dream last night. But it's too embarrassing; I don't want to tell you about it."

"Oh, sweetie. That is no fun. I hate when I have bad dreams like that. But remember, it's good to tell us those things and get the heaviness out of your heart, right? We are here for you."

"Yeah. I just don't want to say the words."

"Do you want to try whispering it in my ear? Would that be better?"

He leaned in, whispered a few details of a dream that he knew was sexually inappropriate. In this case, it wasn't extreme at all, but to his sensitive heart, even a hint was too much for him to contain.

I responded, "Thank you for telling me that. Remember that you can tell me anything. Is there anything else you remember from your dream that made you feel embarrassed?"

"No. That's all I remember."

"Okay, can I give you a hug, buddy? And can I pray with you? God knows how to wash away all of the dirt that gets onto our hearts from stuff like this."

"Yeah, sure."

"Lord, thank You that You see us right now, and that You love us. You don't want our hearts to feel heavy because of this kind of stuff, so God, we ask that by Your Holy Spirit, You would wash his heart so that it feels clean again. Would You also dig up any weed that the dream tried to plant into his life? We know that he is called to be a joyful boy, full of life. Thank you that he told me about this so that he didn't have to be alone in it. In Jesus' name we pray, amen."

THE SAFEST PLACE FOR YOUR CHILD

Sometimes the sexual issue that our child is facing is short-lived—yes, a boundary is crossed, but confession comes easily, forgiveness is released, and relationship is restored. Everything goes back to normal by dinner. But sometimes—and oh, how our heart aches in these times—our child hardens their heart to us and it takes more than a couple of conversations to draw them back.

As our children grow older, we come to realize all the more that we cannot control them. We can continue discipling, praying, making space for relationship with them, keeping standards in the home, and laying out consequences, but . . . we cannot control them. In this world of conflicting philosophies and overt sexualized pressures, this can be terrifying.

I was recently reflecting on the story of Moses as recorded in the book of Exodus. At the time of his birth, the Israelites were enslaved in Egypt, and the Pharaoh was becoming increasingly intimidated by the sheer number of them. He had a sense that if they continued multiplying, they would revolt, so he decreed that all infant Hebrew boys under the age of two were to be killed.

Moses' mom, Jochabed, could see that her baby was special—something most mothers can relate to. This mother disobeyed the cruel order and risked her life to keep her son hidden for three months. Exodus 2:3 tells us,

> *"When she could hide him no longer, she got him a wicker basket*
> *and covered it over with tar and pitch. Then she put the child into*
> *it and set it among the reeds by the bank of the Nile."*

What courage it would have taken for her to weave that basket, to hold her baby close and press her cheek against his one final time, then gently place him into the river! What faith it would have taken to surrender this son to the Lord! She was desperate. Yet she must have known that the safest place for her son was in the hands of God. I'm sure she prayed fervently, likely with tears streaming down her face. The Lord did indeed watch over Moses. Of all the unexpected outcomes, He directed the daughter of Pharaoh to rescue the baby from the river and take responsibility for his welfare. Moses, the son of a slave, grew up in Pharaoh's courts!

Later in his life, at age forty, Moses witnessed a fellow Israelite being abused by an Egyptian. He jumped to action, murdered that Egyptian, and was forced to flee as a fugitive into the nearby wilderness.

It would be another forty years before Moses encountered God at the renowned 'burning bush' and was commissioned to return to Egypt as a deliverer. He came back, confronted the evils of Egypt, performed mighty miracles, and ultimately led the Israelites across the Red Sea into freedom. All's well that ends well.

But the question in my mind is, "Did Moses' mother, Jochabed, live to see him return as a deliverer for the Israelite people? Or was her last memory of him as a murderer, in exile?"

She likely never saw with her own eyes the fulfillment of destiny that she had once hoped for her son Moses when she held him as a baby. Yet, of this I am confident: God heard every whispered prayer that rose up from her burdened heart. That first act of trust—when she stood on the Nile River bank and placed him into a woven basket—she must have repeated countless times throughout the years while her son was a fugitive shepherd out in the wilderness. I can imagine Jochabed as an aging woman, whispering the prayers of a desperate mother, still believing that the safest place for her child was in the hands of God.

No one gets through this life unscathed. Some of you reading this today are living with chronic heartache, wondering when, if ever, your child will come 'home from the wilderness' of pornography addiction, or transgender ideology, or a toxic relationship that has deluded them. You might be puzzled or shocked, wondering where things went wrong. "They know better!" you try to console yourself. Perhaps you have realized the ways in which your home was infiltrated by the lies of worldly philosophies. And some of you may even be repenting, with a pit in your stomach because you know that you contributed to the dysfunction. The shame of the past has cast a shadow, and now you are left wondering if you'll get another chance at relationship with your son or daughter.

I want you to hear me clearly now: The story is not over.

The story is not over.

Just as God heard Jochabed's prayers, He also hears the prayers of fathers and mothers today. These prayers are powerful and effective, availing much in the lives of the next generation. No matter how deep into the wilderness a child may have wandered—or how long they have been there—we serve a God who knows how to show up in a burning bush. He does it for the sake of a 'Moses', but also for the sake of a generation who is enslaved in 'Egypt', crying out for deliverance.

Hold steady, dear friend. Do not allow the whispers of shame to force you from your God-given position. Remember that there is no condemnation for those who are in Christ Jesus.

REFLECTION QUESTIONS

1. How have you experienced shame in your life or observed its effect on your spouse or children? How has the content of this chapter helped you understand God's heart for restoration?
2. Who do you have in your life with whom you feel safe to confess temptation or sins? Prayerfully consider: Is there anything that the Spirit of God is bringing to your mind that would be good to share with them about?
3. Do you struggle with relinquishing control of your child or their future? What is God teaching you about this matter from the life of Jochabed?

20

A CONVERSATION ABOUT THE DIFFERENCE ONE PERSON CAN MAKE

I hope you are now convinced that God's design for sexuality and humanity has always been good. Each one of us has been granted *imago dei* —the image of God—and has thus been given unparalleled dignity and worth among all of creation. I hope that you can also recognize our common enemy—the one who has targeted us from the beginning, scheming to debase God's children, establishing strongholds that lead to sexual perversion and the devaluing of human life. Examine the annals of history through this lens and you'll see evidence of an epic spiritual war that is being played out on the battlefield of Earth.

When we consider that the Lord has commissioned His people to be actively engaged in the preservation and flourishing of civilization, it can be an intimidating thought: *What difference can I possibly make?*

How could we ever bring down the billion-dollar porn industry or halt the horrors of sex trafficking? How can we push back the tide of gender ideologies that endorse the sterilization of minors? Or undo the tragedy of millions of unborn children losing their chance for life? How can we restore the sacred relationship of marriage as something intended to be between one man and one woman?

In some ways, I can understand why many Christians just avoid the conversations altogether and try to mind their own business. They honour God, love their neighbour, are faithful to their spouse, and work to provide security for their kids. It's a good life. A respectable one. No one dares say otherwise.

The only problem is, it leaves the enemy's strongholds unconfronted.

THE DIFFERENCE BETWEEN A GOOD LEADER AND A GREAT ONE

In the Old Testament, after the people of Israel had been set free from slavery in Egypt, after they had wandered in the wilderness for forty years with Moses, after they had occupied their Promised Land under Joshua, and having been under the leadership of a dozen judges, they began to be ruled by kings. The first three are the most well-known—Saul, David and Solomon—but after that, in the books of 1 and 2 Kings, we find the accounts of another thirty-nine kings that ruled over the nations of Israel and Judah over a span of four hundred and fifty years.

The description of each kings' term in office includes their achievements, struggles, and family relations. And then there is an overall evaluation of their leadership; were they righteous kings, or were they wicked?

Of the thirty-nine kings, thirty-one are described as evil because of the way they established or endorsed the worship of false gods within the land. Many of these wicked kings built 'high places' as dedicated gathering spaces for sexual debauchery and child sacrifice—some of them even offering their own children—all in the name of worship to the Canaanite deities. Though expressly prohibited by God (Deuteronomy 16:21) they also erected Asherah poles—sacred trees or poles carved with pornographic imagery in honour of the Canaanite goddess named Asherah. For instance:

> *"Manasseh was twelve years old when he became king, and he reigned in Jerusalem fifty-five years. His mother's name was Hephzibah. He did evil in the eyes of the Lord, following the detestable practices of the nations the Lord had driven out before the Israelites. He rebuilt the high places . . . he also erected altars to Baal and made an Asherah pole."*
>
> **2 Kings 21:1-3**

During that four hundred and fifty year span, there were only six kings who did "what was right in the eyes of the Lord." Scripture honours these

kings for resisting immense national and international pressure in order
to worship God faithfully, and for personally holding to their convictions
regarding sexual morality and the value of children. Jotham was one such
king:

> "...Jotham son of Uzziah king of Judah began to reign. He was twenty-five
> years old when he became king, and he reigned in Jerusalem sixteen years.
> His mother's name was Jerusha daughter of Zadok. He did what was
> right in the eyes of the Lord, just as his father Uzziah had done."
> **2 Kings 15:32-33**

But every record of these six good kings—Asa, Jehoshaphat, Amaziah,
Joash, Azariah, and Jotham—includes a note about their reign: "The high
places, however, were not removed."[44] Though the good kings didn't visit
the high places, by leaving them unconfronted, they allowed those bastions
of idolatrous worship to stand as a mockery to the true God, an obscenity
that publicized shame, and a stumbling block for future generations.

Over that period, there were also two *great* kings: Hezekiah and Josiah.
Though they were not perfect leaders, they are esteemed within Scripture
for their private lives, and also for the way that they pushed against the
perversions of their day. For instance, the record about Hezekiah goes like
this:

> "He did what was right in the sight of the Lord, in accordance with
> everything that his father David had done. He removed the high places and
> smashed the memorial stones to pieces, and cut down the Asherah ... He
> trusted in the Lord, the God of Israel; and after him there was no one like
> him among all the kings of Judah, nor among those who came before him."
> **2 Kings 18:3-5**

In 2 Kings 22 and 23 we read about King Josiah. During the early years
of his reign, the High Priest Hilkiah recovered the Book of the Law and
brought the scrolls to Josiah. After reading them, though he was a young
king, Josiah was gripped by the way the nation of Judah had become
unfaithful in their worship of God. He began a national campaign to tear

---

44 1 Kings 15:14, 1 Kings 22:43, 2 Kings 12:3, 2 Kings 14:4, 2 Kings 15:4, 2 Kings 15:35

down high places and the 'Asherah', eradicate cult prostitution, and break the altars to Baal and Molech throughout the land (Judges 6:25-26).

In 1 Kings 23:25, we read this glowing estimation of Josiah's courageous leadership:

> *"Before him there was no king like him who turned to the Lord with*
> *all his heart, all his soul, and all his might, in conformity to all the*
> *Law of Moses; nor did any like him arise after him."*

This Old Testament narrative shows us that the key difference between a *good leader* and a *great one* is the difference between those who had a *personal, private conviction* regarding sexual holiness and those who had *a burden to enact change* in their generation. The same is true for us today—in whatever sphere of influence God grants us.

Raising Up Reformers

You might be thinking, "Be reasonable, Bonnie. We're not kings and queens. We're the educational assistants, the dental hygienists, the janitors and the graphic designers. We're the soccer team coach and the Sunday school teacher. We as parents will never have the ability to influence a nation in the way that Hezekiah and Josiah did."

You are right. Most of us will never rise to a place of influence that directly impacts the destiny of entire nations. And most likely, our children will not either.

But what if they do?

What if God has entrusted key leaders for the next generation into your care because He knows that you will guide them to walk in honour and sexual integrity, preparing them for their future purpose and assignment? The reality is that God hasn't placed the burden of societal healing and reformation onto the shoulders of just one of us. He is calling all of us—young and old—to take our place.

Some of our sons and daughters will grow up to take a seat in the halls of government or courtrooms, using their voice to stand up for justice and righteousness. Some will be elected to school boards, where they can influence the policies and curriculum that affect elementary-aged children. Others will step into the arts and use their gifting to tell stories of redemption or sing songs of heaven's freedom. Still more will become the social workers, counsellors, and youth pastors of the future—helping the traumatized find their way again. And every one of them will have the opportunity to sit beside a broken-hearted loved one and offer hope in the midst of despair.

Daniel 12:3 says it this way,

> *"Those who are wise will shine as bright as the sky, and those who lead*
> *many to righteousness will shine like the stars forever." (NLT)*

Our family lives in a rural area; when we step outside on a clear night, it is awesome to see the expanse of stars. We always pause to look up, take a deep breath, and savour the beauty. But stars aren't just pretty to look at. Historically, before the days of GPS, satellites or compasses, stars were for navigation. The constellations served those who were trying to find their way.

A growing number of people in this generation are searching for guidance. They are hungry for spiritual truth and are increasingly open to learning about Jesus.[45] And like all of us, they want to be free from sexual shame and settled in life-giving relationships. If the people of God will follow His design for sexuality, identity and relationships, and confidently share about what God has done in their own lives, it will certainly catch their attention.

But one star cannot fulfill that navigational purpose on its own. We each need to take our place, shining our light in whatever square inch of space the Lord has assigned to us.

In Isaiah 60:1-3, we find a beautiful declaration of this very thought:

> *"Arise, shine, for your light has come, and the glory of*
> *the Lord rises upon you. See, darkness covers the earth and thick*
> *darkness is over the peoples, but the Lord rises upon you and*
> *his glory appears over you. Nations will come to your light, and*
> *kings to the brightness of your dawn." (NIV)*

---

45 The Open Generation Barna Study https://www.barna.com/the-open-generation/

We are not called to be those who shrink back from a sexually deviant culture, minding our own business while the enemy wreaks havoc around us. God has called us—and our children—to take our place as reformers and restorers. He has called us to radiate love and revolutionize broken systems, and He has given us His Spirit to empower us to this end.

The great kings of Israel were able to bring down physical high places in their culture. Ephesians 5 tells us how we can be a part of a reforming work today:

> *"But among you there must not be even a hint of sexual immorality, or of any kind of impurity, or of greed, because these are improper for God's holy people...For you were once darkness, but now you are light in the Lord. Live as children of light...and find out what pleases the Lord. Have nothing to do with the fruitless deeds of darkness, but rather expose them."*
> **Ephesians 5:3, 8-11 NIV**

Tearing down the strongholds of the enemy begins by exposing the way that darkness operates. If we will simply *talk about* the things that are going on, we have already become a part of the solution.

So, dear parents, let's step past the whispering threats and boldly tell our stories of redemption. Let's give ourselves diligently to praying for sexual restoration in the lives of those around us. Jesus continues to reign—and He will do so until all his enemies are placed under His feet (1 Corinthians 15:24-25). Let's stand with Him, forcing darkness to retreat as we invest ourselves in the lives of our sons and daughters . . .

. . . one awkward conversation at a time.

REFLECTION QUESTIONS

1. What is something that God has impressed on your heart throughout the chapters of this book?
2. What topic related to sexuality, identity or relationships would you like to continue learning about?

PRAYERS

- For the One With Regrets -
A prayer for forgiveness

"As far as the east is from the west, so far has He
removed our transgressions from us."
Psalm 103:12

Oh Father, You know all and see all. Nothing in my entire life has been hidden from Your sight. I am done hiding from You. I recognize my sin and am bringing You the weight of my shame and regret.

I need You to wash me. I need You to cover me.

I need your mercy and forgiveness, so that I can have a fresh start.

I am so weary of the memories that play over in my head. By the authority of the blood of Jesus and the power of Your Holy Spirit, would you renew my mind?

In Jesus' name, I am believing that You make all things new.

That you take what the enemy meant for evil, and you turn it for good.

I've heard that You are a Good Shepherd, that You know how to lead me to rest and fulfillment. I yield my heart to You today. I entrust my life into Your hands. Would You please convince me of Your love?

I have done nothing to deserve this gift, but I will gratefully receive the mercy that comes from Your kind heart and Your willing hand.

- FOR THE BROKEN ONE -
A prayer for healing

"The Spirit of the Lord God is upon me, because the Lord has anointed me to bring good news to the poor; He has sent me to bind up the brokenhearted, to proclaim liberty to the captives, and the opening of the prison to those who are bound."
Isaiah 61:1

Jesus, I am learning to trust that it is Your kind intention to heal my broken heart. I am bringing You my small faith, to ask that You heal me and set me free from the prison of my past. Some of the pain is from my own decisions. Some of the pain came from the choices of others, but regardless, Lord, I believe that You long to restore me.

To give me a crown of honour where I have felt rejected and ashamed.

You are teaching me the way of the overcomer. I believe that You are here with me, and that You will never leave me or forsake me, but will walk with me, restoring my soul.

I have done nothing to deserve this gift, but I will gratefully receive the healing that comes from Your kind heart and Your willing hand.

- FOR THE WOUNDED SON OR DAUGHTER -
A prayer of release

"Forgive us our debts, as we also have forgiven our debtors."
Matthew 6:12

*"So you are no longer a slave, but God's child; and since you
are His child, God has made you also an heir."*
Galatians 4:7 NIV

*Lord God, You know the ways my earthly mother and father let me down.
The ways they abdicated their responsibility.*
The ways they failed me and did not—or could not—give me what I needed.
*Their own brokenness spread into my life, and I now carry wounds that I
don't know what to do with.*
*Father in heaven, I am starting to see the significance of the invitation You
have offered me—to be adopted as Your child. Though my parents wounded
me, Heavenly Father, I see that You can heal and restore me. With that in
mind, in the name of Jesus' I choose to release my parents from their failures.
I see their humanity—that they are made of the same material I am. Even
as You have forgiven me, Lord, I choose to forgive them. And as memories
resurface in the coming days and years, would You give me the grace to
continue releasing them, so that I can remain free. Would You now take me
by the hand, and walk me along a new path of righteousness and peace?*
*I have done nothing to deserve this gift, but I will gratefully receive this
inheritance that comes from Your kind heart and Your willing hand.*

- FOR THE ONE WHO IS BOUND BY SIN -
A prayer for deliverance

"If we say that we have no sin, we are deceiving ourselves and the truth is not in us. If we confess our sins, He is faithful and just to forgive us our sins and to cleanse us from all unrighteousness."
1 John 1:8-9

Lord God, the truth is that I have been living in compromise. There is a door to darkness that is open in my life, but I want to be free—nothing missing, nothing broken. My heart is stirred to surrender all to You; I need to be rescued, from the enemy of my soul and from the way I am prone to wander. When I consider the story of the Israelites being released from slavery in Egypt, I remember that it was the blood of the sacrificed lamb that provided protection from death. Right now, I submit myself under the covering of the slain Lamb, Jesus the son of God, and am determined to follow Your guidance out of my own slavery, into a wide, spacious land that You will show me. I have done nothing to deserve this gift, but I will gratefully receive this freedom that comes from Your kind heart and Your willing hand.

- FOR THE FEARFUL PARENT -
A prayer for courage

"Do not fear, for I am with you; do not anxiously look about you,
for I am your God. I will strengthen you, surely I will help you.
Surely I will uphold you with my righteous right hand."

Isaiah 41:10

Dear Father, I need to acknowledge that fear has been talking to me, trying to guide my decisions, trying to reach into my relationships. I do not want to be afraid any longer. I remember that Your Word says that You have not given me a spirit of fear, but of love, of power and of a sound mind.
In Jesus' name, I submit myself to God, resisting the enemy, knowing that he will have to flee. I thank You, Lord, that You know how to quiet me with your love.
If I face persecution or rejection because of my convictions, and if I must endure suffering because of the name of Christ, I know that You will be with me. You will uphold me. You will guide me and comfort me. You will be my exceedingly great reward.
And so I need not fear.
I have done nothing to deserve this gift, but I will gratefully receive this comfort that comes from Your kind heart and Your willing hand.

- FOR THE ONE UNSURE OF WHAT TO DO -
A prayer for wisdom

"But if any of you lacks wisdom, let him ask God, who gives to all generously and without reproach, and it will be given to him."
James 1:5

Lord, when I consider the issue in front of me, it is easy to get flustered, to complain and flail around within my mind. But in this moment, I choose to silence myself, to humbly approach Your throne of grace, turn my face towards Yours, and to present an honest request:

Please. Grant me wisdom that is beyond me.

I don't know what to do. I don't know how to think about this from a different perspective.

Please. Grant me wisdom that is beyond me.

I believe that You will give me an idea. A step to take. A key that will unlock the door that seems impassable.

I'm taking a deep breath now. I'm quieting my anxious mind.

I have done nothing to deserve this gift, but I will gratefully receive the wisdom that comes from Your kind heart and Your willing hand.

- For the One Whose Child is Wandering -
A prayer of intercession

"All your children will be taught by the Lord, and great will be their peace."
Isaiah 54:13

*"And He (the Holy Spirit), when He comes, will convict the
world concerning sin, righteousness and judgment."*
John 16:8

*Father, when I don't know what to pray, I know that You can translate the
ache in my heart and the tears that I cry into prayer. A prayer for restoration.
A prayer for the eyes of our child to be opened to the truth, and for their heart
to be softened by the warmth of Your love.*

*I thank You, Holy Spirit, that You are relentless. You can reach into the human
heart, and for centuries, You have been regenerating the ones who are dead
in their trespasses.*

Help me to remember that it is not up to me to bring about change.

You speak from the burning bush.

You send dreams and prophets.

You orchestrate circumstances.

*I am asking, on behalf of my child, that You show mercy, and that You release
the resources of heaven into their life.*

*My prayer is that they would be ruined for any life other than the abundant
one found in Christ. In the mighty name of Jesus, I ask these things.*

*My child has done nothing to deserve this gift, but we will rejoice when we
see them gratefully receive the salvation that comes from Your kind heart
and Your willing hand.*

- For the Young Generation -
A prayer of dedication

*"I have also dedicated him to the Lord; as long
as he lives, he is dedicated to the Lord."*
1 Samuel 1:28

*"Then our sons in their youth will be like well-nurtured plants, and
our daughters will be like pillars carved to adorn a palace."*
Psalm 144:12 NIV

*Thank You, Father, that You are not surprised by the challenges that we face
in this era of history. This darkness is no match for the light of Your presence,
and You are eager to redeem and establish the young generation as a
beacon of hope.*

*In Jesus' name, I am acknowledging the sins of our nation. Lord, we repent
and ask that You have mercy. Forgive us for the way we have participated in
idolatry and immorality, for the way we have worshipped the created rather
than the Creator, and for the way we have thrown off the boundaries You
gave to us for our good.*

*As we repent and turn from our wicked ways, I remember Your promise that
You will hear from heaven, that You will forgive us our sins, and heal our land.
I will look for the indications that this healing is on its way, and determine to
keep my heart open to the young generation.*

Let revival come.

What other hope do we have, but You?

*We have done nothing to deserve this gift, but we will gratefully receive the
healing of our land that comes from Your kind heart and Your willing hand.*

RECOMMENDED RESOURCES

General

Divine Romance by Gene Edwards
Live No Lies by John Marc Comer
Our Bodies Tell God's Story by Christopher West
Strange New World by Professor Carl Truman
The Air We Breathe by Glen Scrivener
Total Truth by Nancy Pearcey
Unmasked by Jim Anderson

Parenting

Age of Opportunity: A Biblical Guide to Parenting Teens
        by Paul David Tripp
Hold On to Your Kids by Dr. Gordon Neufeld and Dr. Gabor Mate
Raising Boys Who Respect Girls by Dave Willis
The Story of the Family by Dale Ahlquist

Marriage and Divorce

Empowered to Love by Tara Lalonde and Robert S. Paul
*(Un)faithful: Finding healing after your husband's affair (whether your
        marriage survives or not)* by Ruth Erickson

Dating and Relationships

Breaking up with Babel by Nikki Dent
Loveology by John Marc Comer
Outdated: Find Love That Lasts When Dating Has Changed
        by Jonathan "JP" Pokluda (with Kevin McConaghy)

Men and Women

Captivating by John and Stasi Eldridge
The Men We Need by Brant Hanson
Toxic War on Masculinity by Nancy Pearcey
Wild at Heart by John Eldridge

Understanding Pornographic Culture

The Last Relapse by Sathiya Sam
Wired for Intimacy by William M. Struthers

Understanding LGBTQ+

Five Lies of Our Anti-Christian Age by Rosaria Butterfield
Holy Sexuality by Dr. Christopher Yuan
Irreversible Damage by Abigail Shrier
Is God Anti-Gay by Sam Allberry
Love Thy Body by Nancy Pearcey
The Body God Gives by Robert S. Smith
The Secret Thoughts of an Unlikely Convert by Rosaria Butterfield
Transformed by Kyla Gillespie

Childhood Education

God Made All of Me: A Book to Help Children Protect Their Bodies
    by Justin and Lindsey Holcomb
Good Pictures, Bad Pictures: Porn-Proofing Today's Young Kids,
    by Kristen Jensen
Signal Hill, free school-aged curriculum on matters of identity, health
    and self-image. https://thesignalhill.com/
The Prevention Project, free video curriculum for kids, focused on
    online etiquette, boundaries and trafficking prevention.
    https://www.thepreventionproject.ca/
The Ultimate Girl's Body Book
    by Dr. Walt Larimore & Dr. Amaryllis Sanchez Wohlever
The Ultimate Guy's Body Book by Dr. Walt Larimore
What Am I? by Andy Stieger
What Am I Worth? by Andy Stieger

GLOSSARY OF TERMS

We would be wise to understand the language and serve as an interpreter for our kids so that we can be ready for conversations about all the letters and colours that are flagrantly flown in our paths every day. Language around the topic continues to morph, but as of the time of the publication of this book, here is a list of phrases and widely understood definitions from the acronym 2SLGBTQI+ along with a few key terms that are helpful to know:[46]

2S: An English term used to broadly capture concepts traditional to many Indigenous cultures. It is a culturally-specific identity used by some Indigenous people to indicate a person whose gender identity, spiritual identity and/or sexual orientation comprises both male and female spirits.

L: Lesbian. Typically a woman who is sexually and/or romantically attracted to other women.

G: Gay. A person who is sexually and/or romantically attracted to people of their same sex or gender identity.

B: Bisexual. A person who is sexually and/or romantically attracted to two or more genders.

T: Transgender (also 'trans'). A person whose gender identity differs from what is typically associated with the sex they were assigned at birth.

Q: Queer. Historically a derogatory term used as a slur against 2SLGBTQI+ people, this term has been reclaimed by many 2SLGBTQI+ people as a positive way to describe themselves, and

46 https://women-gender-equality.canada.ca/en/free-to-be-me/2slgbtqi-plus-glossary.html

as a way to include the many diverse identities not covered by common 2SLGBTQI+ acronym.

I: Intersex. An umbrella term to capture various types of biological sex differentiation. Intersex people have variations in their sex characteristics, such as sex chromosomes, internal reproductive organs, genitalia, and/or secondary sex characteristics (e.g. muscle mass, breasts) that fall outside of what is typically categorized as male or female.

+: This is included in the list to include anyone who doesn't identify in any one of the other listed categories.

Cis-gendered: A person who identifies with the gender they were assigned at birth.

Gender fluid: A person whose gender identity varies over time and may include male, female and non-binary gender identities.

Non-binary (also 'genderqueer'): Referring to a person whose gender identity does not align with a binary understanding of gender such as man or woman. It is a gender identity which may include man and woman, androgynous, fluid, multiple, no gender, or a different gender outside of the "woman—man" spectrum.

Pan-Sexual: A person whose choice of sexual or romantic partner is not limited by the other person's sex, gender identity or gender expression.

Gender Dysphoria: A medical diagnosis that can be understood as discomfort or distress experienced by a person who feels their sense of their gender identity differs from their body, based on societal expectations.

MAPs: A "minor attracted person" who is sexually attracted to those under the age of 18, including children. This name has been introduced in an attempt to remove the stigma attached to pedophilia.

THANKS

My husband, Bryan—I could never have gotten this far without you. Thank you for all the laughter ever since the summer of 2003, for knowing when I need to be held, and for believing in the words I write. (And yes, I would go with you.)

My sons—thank you for the sacrifices you've made. I believe in every one of you and the call of God on your lives.

> Samuel, you are a catalyst.
> Micah, you are an anchor.
> Hadden, you are a man of mercy.
> Charles, you are a reformer.
> Kaleb, you are a galvanizer.
> Theodore, you are the warmth of sunshine.

How am I so blessed that I get to have you all?

My parents, Rod and Doris. Dad, thank you for yielding to the Holy Spirit time and time again and modelling for me what it looks like to keep learning. Mom, thank you for teaching us to serve, to forgive, to be friendly and to honour. And for forcing me to journal every day in my grade 8 year. That was pivotal. And thank you for never speaking doubt or fear over me when I step out to obey the Lord.

My in-laws, Dave and Terry. It was really nice of you to retire shortly before we had kids. I am a blessed woman indeed to have in-laws as supportive as you.

Church family—I would not be who I am without you. I know that I am a mere cell in the greater, expanding body of Christ. Indisputably, I have received so much more than I have ever offered.

Jim Anderson—for going through what you had to go through and becoming who you needed to be in order to faithfully bring a message of redemption to this generation. When I was nineteen years old and heard you preach in that Chilliwack classroom, my heart was simultaneously burdened and filled with hope. And I've never recovered.

Lisa Anderson—for showing me the power and beauty of a mother's apron.

Christy, Jaclyn, Jennel, Jenny, Stephanie, and Tiffany—for being the encouraging voices in my head that helped me fight off my internal critic as I sat down to write.

Anya McKee—I didn't realize that I was an unconventional speller until you worked through the manuscript with me. Thanks for letting me keep the distinct voice of a Canadian who has been steadily influenced by American content. But really, thank you for labouring with me. You saw what I was trying to do with this manuscript, and helped me find the words to say what I really meant.

Our ministry supporters—thank you for seeing the need for these conversations, and for investing for the sake of a young generation. Every gift has enabled us to keep doing what we are doing. In particular, LifeSpring Church, Riverside Calvary Chapel, Russ and Jenn Williamson, and Darryl and Lavonna Shaw, your generosity has made this book possible.

ABOUT THE AUTHOR

Bonnie was the homeschooled, church girl who lost count of the number of times she "asked Jesus into her heart". All seemed to be going smoothly until at age 15 she learned about the sexual sin of a leader in her local church. Bonnie was devastated; in the coming years her eyes were opened to the widespread heartache and distress that comes when God's boundaries for sexual expression are violated.

After graduation, while attending a discipleship school, she began to see in Scripture about God's desire to heal men and women from their sexual pain and shame. She soon realized that this was a key to unlock revival in the nations. Over time, she was stirred to use her voice and prophetic gifting to bring messages of hope and healing.

Bonnie married Bryan in 2007, with a desire to start a family right away. In 2008, Bonnie gave birth to identical twin boys, and her calling as a stay-at-home mom began, and in the coming years more boys were added to the family. Together, Bryan and Bonnie are now doing their best to raise up these six sons, in all of their unique strengths and challenges.

Bonnie finds great joy in mothering and homeschooling, with an awareness that the years are fleeting. Bonnie also dedicates time and space for writing, serving at their home church, and developing the ministry of The Union Movement.

She loves being active out in nature whenever possible, but she can also regularly be found with a book, a journal, and a cup of tea in hand.

THE UNION MOVEMENT

The Union Movement exists to help people find wholeness by presenting a gospel-centred, holistic approach to the topics of identity, sexuality, and relationships. We develop resources, speak at events, support local churches, and strengthen leaders who desire to cultivate healthy cultures.

We are gospel-centred.

This means that in a world of judgment and despair, we bring a compassionate message focused on the redeeming work of Jesus Christ. Through Him, all are welcome and restoration is possible.

We are holistically-minded.

This means we share insight about human sexuality—with all its wonder and struggle—by bringing together Biblical, historical, and cultural perspectives. The messages are designed to bring personal freedom, untangle confusion, and address sensitive topics (family of origin, past sexual experiences, self-perception, etc.) so that people will find freedom, families can be made whole, and Christ will be glorified.

You can learn more about the work we do and access free resources by visiting our website:

www.theunionmovement.com

FB | IG: @theunionmovement

Subscribe to The Union Podcast:
www.theunionmovement.com/podcast

AWKWARD VIDEO SERIES

You've read the book now—that's great! You can take your learning a little further with the six-part Awkward Video Series. This free resource will help you dig deeper into what you've learned in this book with your spouse, friends, family members or small group.

Each video is about fifteen minutes long and comes with a viewer's guide to aid discussion and reflection.

Check it out here:

www.theunionmovement.com/video-resources

www.ingramcontent.com/pod-product-compliance
Lightning Source LLC
Chambersburg PA
CBHW030916120626
46554CB00001B/167